OXFORD WORLD'S CLASSICS

THE OXFORD SHAKESPEARE

General Editor · Stanley Wells

The Oxford Shakespeare offers new and authoritative editions of Shakespeare's plays in which the early printings have been scrupulously re-examined and interpreted. An introductory essay provides all relevant background information together with an appraisal of critical views and of the play's effects in performance. The detailed commentaries pay particular attention to language and staging. Reprints of sources, music for songs, genealogical tables, maps, etc. are included where necessary; many of the volumes are illustrated, and all contain an index.

SUSAN SNYDER, the editor of *All's Well that Ends Well* in the Oxford Shakespeare, is Emeritus Professor of English at Swarthmore College, Pennsylvania.

Currently available in paperback

All's Well that Ends Well

Anthony and Cleopatra

As You Like It

The Comedy of Errors

The Complete Sonnets
  and Poems

Coriolanus

Cymbeline

Hamlet

Henry V

Henry IV, Part 1

Henry IV, Part 2

Henry VI, Part One

Henry VI, Part Two

Henry VI, Part Three

Julius Caesar

King Henry VIII

King John

King Lear

Love's Labour's Lost

Macbeth

Measure for Measure

The Merchant of Venice

The Merry Wives of Windsor

A Midsummer Night's Dream

Much Ado About Nothing

Richard III

Pericles

Romeo and Juliet

The Taming of the Shrew

The Tempest

Timon of Athens

Titus Andronicus

Troilus and Cressida

Twelfth Night

The Two Noble Kinsmen

The Winter's Tale

The rest of the plays are forthcoming.

OXFORD WORLD'S CLASSICS

WILLIAM SHAKESPEARE

All's Well that Ends Well

Edited by
SUSAN SNYDER

OXFORD
UNIVERSITY PRESS

OXFORD
UNIVERSITY PRESS

Great Clarendon Street, Oxford OX2 6DP

Oxford University Press is a department of the University of Oxford.
It furthers the University's objective of excellence in research, scholarship,
and education by publishing worldwide in

Oxford New York

Athens Auckland Bangkok Bogotá Buenos Aires Calcutta
Cape Town Chennai Dar es Salaam Delhi Florence Hong Kong Istanbul
Karachi Kuala Lumpur Madrid Melbourne Mexico City Mumbai
Nairobi Paris São Paulo Shanghai Singapore Taipei Tokyo Toronto Warsaw

with associated companies in Berlin Ibadan

Oxford is a registered trade mark of Oxford University Press
in the UK and in certain other countries

First published by the Clarendon Press 1993
First published as a World's Classics paperback 1994
Reissued as an Oxford World's Classics paperback 1998
Reissued 2008

British Library Cataloguing in Publication Data

Data available

Library of Congress Cataloging in Publication Data

Shakespeare, William, 1564–1616.
All's well that ends well / edited by Susan Snyder.
(Oxford World's Classics)
I. Snyder, Susan. II. Title. III. Series.
PR2801.A2S66 1994 822.3'3—dc20 93-32341

ISBN 978-0-19-953712-9

3

Printed in Great Britain by
Clays Ltd, St Ives plc

PREFACE

I AM fortunate to have first encountered *All's Well that Ends Well* not as a 'problem' text to be puzzled over in a classroom, but as compelling stage drama. Noël Willman's 1955 production, which I saw twice as a student in Stratford, involved me thoroughly as an enactment of clashing human desires. This initial impression has remained the primary context for my later more scholarly explorations into this play, and I am grateful for the illumination provided by that production and later those of John Houseman (1959) and Elijah Moshinsky (1980). Most recently, the Royal Shakespeare Company's nuanced, haunting *All's Well* directed by Trevor Nunn (1981–2) was for me a magical theatrical event in both London and New York. For my understanding of the play's stage fortunes beyond my own experience, I owe a great deal to the studies of Joseph Price and J. L. Styan.

My debt to previous editors is equally important in a different way. I have been guided and enlightened in my own work by many predecessors, especially G. K. Hunter. His learned and elegantly sensible edition of *All's Well* in the new Arden series (1959) is a hard act to follow.

I did most of the work for this edition at the Folger Shakespeare Library in Washington, DC, and the Furness Shakespeare Library at the University of Pennsylvania in Philadelphia. I am grateful to both institutions, and to individuals in them who provided thoughtful assistance at every turn: at the Folger Nati Krivatsy, Betsy Walsh, and the Reading Room staff, and at the Furness curator Georgianna Ziegler, who is a staff all by herself. For my term appointment as Eugene M. Lang Research Professor, which facilitated research at a crucial period, I am happy to record my gratitude to Swarthmore College, which awarded the chair, and to its donor Gene Lang.

Friends and colleagues at the Folger, Swarthmore, and Penn, as well as others buttonholed at meetings of the North American and International Shakespeare associations, have been generous with encouragement and advice on everything from fistulas to speech prefixes. In particular, I appreciate Gary Taylor's sharing with me his own reasonings in the process of editing *All's Well* for the Oxford 1986 *Complete Works*. In their separate capacities, general editor Stanley Wells and copy editor Christine Buckley have been models of judgement and tact. If Heminge, Condell, Jaggard, and those alphabetical compositors had had such assistance, Shakespeare editors would long since have had to look elsewhere for employment. Christine also scouted illustrations from the Nunn production, which I hope was more fun for her than copy-editing.

Lastly, I thank Leighton Whitaker for helping me through the times when all was cheerless, dark, and deadly.

SUSAN SNYDER

CONTENTS

List of Illustrations   ix

Introduction

From Boccaccio to Shakespeare   I

The Mingled Yarn   8

'All's Well that Ends Well' as a 'Problem Play'   16

Dating: The Jacobean Shakespeare and 'All's Well that Ends Well'   20

'Is not this Helen?': The Fortunes of an Unorthodox Heroine   25

Seeking the Generic Fix   40

Anatomy of Desire: (I) 'All's Well' and the Sonnets   44
(II) All's (?) Well (?) that Ends (?) Well (?)   49

The Text and its Evolution   52

Editorial Procedures   68

Abbreviations and References   70

ALL'S WELL THAT ENDS WELL   75

APPENDIX A
1.1.60: *'How understand we that?'*   217

APPENDIX B
2.1.168–72: *Helen's Gamble*   218

APPENDIX C
Speech Prefixes: Variations   220

APPENDIX D
Alterations to Lineation   223

APPENDIX E
Giletta of Narbonne   225

APPENDIX F
Erasmus' 'Colloquies'   233

Index   241

LIST OF ILLUSTRATIONS

1. The Countess and the Clown, Stratford-upon-Avon, 1981   4
   (Shakespeare Centre Library; photograph by Joe Cocks)

2. Paroles and his interrogators, Stratford, Ontario, 1953   4
   (Stratford Festival, Peter Smith photograph)

3. Paroles, Stratford-upon-Avon, 1955   25
   (Harvard Theatre Collection; photograph by Angus McBean)

4. Bertram arrives at court, Stratford-upon-Avon, 1981   28
   (Shakespeare Centre Library; photograph by Joe Cocks)

5. Helen chooses Bertram, Stratford-upon-Avon, 1959   28
   (Harvard Theatre Collection; photograph by Angus McBean)

6. Bertram kneels to Helen, Stratford-upon-Avon, 1959   29
   (Harvard Theatre Collection; photograph by Angus McBean)

7. Helen and the Countess, Stratford, Ontario, 1977   37
   (Stratford Festival, Robert Ragsdale photograph)

8. Helen, Old Vic, 1953   46
   (Harvard Theatre Collection; photograph by Angus McBean)

   From Whitney's *Emblems* (by permission of the Folger
   Shakespeare Library):

9. Bees returning to the hive   66

10. Leaking sieve   66

11. The fox and the grapes   67

12. Occasion   67

INTRODUCTION

From Boccaccio to Shakespeare

SCHOLARS generally agree that Shakespeare's ultimate source for the situation and plot of *All's Well that Ends Well* was the ninth story of the Third Day of Boccaccio's *Decameron*. He probably knew it through the translation of William Painter, which appeared in *The Palace of Pleasure* (1566, 1569, 1575) as the thirty-eighth novel.[1]

Painter summarizes the story as follows:

Giletta, a physician's daughter of Narbonne, healed the French king of a fistula, for reward whereof she demanded Beltramo, Count of Roussillon, to husband. The Count, being married against his will, for despite fled to Florence, and loved another. Giletta, his wife, by policy found means to lie with her husband in place of his lover, and was begotten with child of two sons; which known to her husband, he received her again, and afterwards he lived in great honour and felicity.[2]

The tale proceeds in similarly brisk and straightforward fashion. Howard C. Cole has discerned a satiric subtext in Boccaccio's Third Day, based on characters in several tales who use religious practice as a means of achieving their sexual desires and present their clever contrivances as acts of

---

[1] H. G. Wright ('How Did Shakespeare Come to Know the "Decameron"?' *MLR*, 50 (1955), 45–8) argues that Shakespeare may have used a French translation by Antoine le Maçon (Paris, 1545, with seventeen subsequent printings). His term 'Senoys' for the Sienese (Boccaccio's *Sanesi*) points to a French intermediary, as perhaps do his forms 'Bertram' and 'Gerard de Narbon'. On the other hand, Painter also has 'Senois', and while he gives the Italian forms 'Beltramo' for the hero and 'Gerardo of Narbona' for Helen's father, Shakespeare might easily have Frenchified the names himself. Wright's case is not strong enough to hold against the probability that Shakespeare would use a popular English version rather than a less widely available one in French. As G. K. Hunter observes, he may have used both. Since Wright has also shown ('The Indebtedness of Painter's Translations from Boccaccio in *The Palace of Pleasure* to the French Version of Le Maçon', *MLR*, 46 (1951), 431–5) that Painter used le Maçon's *Decameron* when making his version, and since no one has advanced any detailed influence of one or the other text on *All's Well*, the question is not central.

[2] See Appendix E.

divine intervention.[1] But neither phenomenon is so wide-spread as to characterize the Third Day as a whole and thus to tarnish by association, as Cole wishes, Giletta's 'miraculous' cure of the King and her wearing of pilgrim's garb in pursuing Beltramo to Florence. One suspects that Cole would not have detected such a preponderance of religious hypocrisy in Boccaccio if he had not started by trying to resolve the tangles of Shakespeare's much more problematic text.

By decree of the day's queen, Neifile, the tales of the Third Day concern human initiative: they focus on people who through their own efforts obtained something they desired very much, or got back something they had lost. If there is a common theme in this section of the *Decameron* more specific than the announced one, it is the narrowing of 'efforts' to 'stratagems', the focus on how the protagonists win out *through their ingenuity* against their adversaries' stupidity, self-preoccupation, and conventional expectations. The ninth story is propelled by Giletta's clever devices in overcoming external obstacles to marriage with Beltramo. When the King awards him to her in recompense for his cure, Beltramo's vehement objection is conceived equally externally, based entirely on her inferior social position. Giletta thus sets out to prove herself worthy of him, first by efficiently running his estates and winning the affection of his subjects, and then by inventing a ruse to obtain his ancestral ring and become pregnant by him. When she returns with the ring, and with twin sons who look just like their father, the effect is of a second job interview in which the rejected applicant has come back with stronger credentials. Giletta has demonstrated her success in the chief functions of a countess, keeping the estates in order and bearing male heirs. Accepting her as his wife will please Beltramo's subjects as well as honour his promise. In addition, there is gratification for his ego in Giletta's persistent pursuit, as well as in the replication of himself in their two sons, chips off the old block. It follows naturally in such a context that when this excellent bargain is offered to him again he takes it up, impressed by his wife's

---

[1] Cole, *The 'All's Well' Story from Boccaccio to Shakespeare* (Urbana, Ill., 1981), ch. 2.

'constant mind and good wit' (Appendix E, p. 232). Boccaccio goes below the plot surface just enough to ground Beltramo's change of heart believably in egotism, political expedience, and appreciation of a clever helpmeet. In his treatment the story prompts no deeper questions.

But in Shakespeare's dramatization, the same actions are handled so as to break down Boccaccio's neat closure and at several points to generate uneasy questioning. The straightforward story of a clever woman who surmounts obstacles to get what she wants is complicated by admixtures of social realism, by disquieting inversions of the fairy-tale pattern, and by a more intimate view of the emotions and reactions of both Helen[1] as pursuing maiden and Bertram as reluctant bridegroom. Shakespeare added to the main action, the heroine's achieving of her husband, a sub-plot involving another character without rank, Paroles. The elaborate pretensions of this talkative poseur, observed with biting mockery by Lafeu, and the equally elaborate hoax by which he is finally shown up provide most of the play's comic appeal; on-stage they are genuinely funny, especially the comeuppance scene with its menacing nonsense-language. By introducing Paroles into the main action Shakespeare sets against Helen's efforts to win and hold Bertram a strong counter-force luring him toward male bonding and military adventure. But posing this fraudulent figure in structural parallel to the heroine, as another middle-class character aspiring to intimacy with the noble Bertram, may also open the way to interpretation of Helen as another kind of unscrupulous social climber.

Shakespeare inserted several older characters into the action whose principal function seems to be to dispose the audience in Helen's favour by their unanimous approval of her, and thus to defuse any negative reactions when she transgresses class and gender conventions. The Countess of Roussillon and Lafeu are his creations (as is the Clown, whose association with Bertram's father links him with the older generation); the King, and to a lesser degree the Widow of Florence, are expanded and particularized from their prototypes in

---

[1] For the form of Helen's name, see general note to The Persons of the Play.

1. Two older characters added by Shakespeare to his source story: after sharing some foolery, the Countess (Peggy Ashcroft) in Trevor Nunn's 1981 production sends a message to Helen by the Clown (Geoffrey Hutchings).

2. A captive Paroles (Douglas Campbell) and his interrogators (Eric House, Peter Mews, Robert Goodier), in World War II gear: production directed by Tyrone Guthrie, Stratford, Ontario, 1953.

Boccaccio's story; even the dead fathers, the old Count of Roussillon and the fabled physician Gérard de Narbonne, are present by frequent recollection in Shakespeare's play as they are not in the source. The sanction of the Countess and the King is especially important in promoting Helen's worthiness in the eyes of the audience; yet when the elder authority-figures who appear in the play vote for merit over rank and support rather than thwart the young heroine's wishes in marriage, they subvert the familiar fairy-tale formula that is the backbone of the play, by failing to play their traditional roles as blocking parents. More than that, their prominence in the script makes for more complexity in general, as they meditate on their own youth and on the difficulties of ageing, of 'holding on and letting go'.[1] However focused they are on the doings of the young, they nevertheless go considerably beyond functional demands to project a composite sense of a whole generation in passage: their backward orientation to long-ago love, achievement, and status, in counterpoint with the impatient forward thrust of the young, informs the strains of intergenerational relations in the play.

Shakespeare also added to Boccaccio's archetypal story-line elements that, in Bullough's fastidious formulation, 'bring the whole thing into close contact with the seamier side of Tudor life':[2] among characters, not only Paroles the posturing pseudo-courtier but the 'foul-mouthed and calumnious' Clown (1.3.56–7). Bertram is portrayed more harshly than his prototype Beltramo: as a callow snob with Helen, as an eager but crass seducer with Diana, as a dupe lacking even ordinary discernment with the tinsel Paroles whom everyone else quickly sees through. There is no counterpart in Boccaccio for Bertram's repellent lies and cowardly evasions in the play's last scene.

In the larger milieu, unromantic social realities of Early Modern Europe jostle against the fairy-tale elements: a

---

[1] Ruth Nevo, 'Motive and Meaning in *All's Well that Ends Well*', in *'Fanned and Winnowed Opinions': Shakespearean Essays Presented to Harold Jenkins*, ed. John W. Mahon and Thomas A. Pendleton (London and New York, 1987), 26–51; p. 30.

[2] Geoffrey Bullough, *Narrative and Dramatic Sources of Shakespeare*, vol. ii (London and New York, 1958), p. 380.

remarkably unheroic petty war, an ugly exposure of class prejudice in marriage, a side glance at the abuses of royal wardship, even unexpected invocations of an exchange system based not on moral absolutes—inner worth or the pledged word commanding loyalty—but on money. Paroles advises Helen to make the most of her virginity while it is still 'vendible' (1.1.157) and tells Diana to insist on payment in advance for her sexual favours; Helen herself when engineering the bed-substitution wins the Widow's necessary co-operation not through the power of virtue alone but with gold.[1]

In dramatizing the tale of the clever wench, then, Shakespeare also deconstructs it. He brings to the surface its latent tensions by getting inside awkward moments rather than simply gliding over them (how would a nobleman react when handed over in marriage to a commoner woman? how would it feel to receive the lovemaking your husband means for another woman?), and also by subjecting some of the plot-mechanisms to scrutiny (wouldn't a large bribe make it more probable that the Widow would help a strange woman in a sexual deception?). In his hands Boccaccio's more or less homogeneous story-line thus becomes a weave of disparate threads. Like the 'web of our life' in a line from the text which critics delight in applying to the play as a whole, it is 'a mingled yarn' (4.3.71). But before we turn away from the question of source material to examine those threads more closely, two other probable influences on *All's Well that Ends Well* deserve mention. One is the unhappy experience of inequalities in love, apparently Shakespeare's own, set forth in the Sonnets. I discuss this theory and its implications in a separate section below. The other is Erasmus' colloquy titled 'Proci et puellae', a lively dialogue between a girl and her suitor. As the *Colloquia* was a standard school text, the Latin original may well have been familiar to Shakespeare, but it was also available in the English translation of Nicholas Leigh

---

[1] The offer of payment for the Florentine gentlewoman's help occurs in Painter's story of Giletta, but it is de-emphasized there by stress on her 'noble heart' and by her later assertion that she gave her assistance 'not for hope of reward but because it appertained to her by well doing so to do' (Appendix E, pp. 230, 231). Shakespeare omits these ennobling details.

(*A Modest Mean to Marriage*, 1568), of which excerpts appear in this volume as Appendix F.

An accumulation of echoes and common contexts in *All's Well*, especially its first act, suggests that this dialogue was fresh in Shakespeare's mind when he was writing his play. G. K. Hunter, glossing the first scene in the Arden edition, notes that the opening exchange between Paroles and Helen— 'Save you, fair queen. | And you, monarch' (1.1.108–9)— may recall 'I shall be to you a king, and you shall be to me a queen' (Appendix F, p. 236), and that Paroles (1.1.128 ff.) and Erasmus' Pamphilus (p. 235) use the same argument, that virginity must be lost to produce virgins. Peggy M. Simonds[1] adds more parallels. The 'withered pear' featured in Paroles' case against virginity (1.1.163–5) seems to draw on 'old wrinkled maid' in the parallel passage from Erasmus (p. 235), which also occurs in a context of lost fruit. His paradox that virgins like men who do not like virginity (1.1.154–5) recalls the remark of Erasmus' Maria that 'Virginity would seem always to be taken with violence—yea, though sometime we love the party most earnestly' (p. 238).[2] In its play with the idea that Maria can raise Pamphilus from the dead (p. 233), by means medicinal ('the herb *Panaces*') or sexual ('a light thing'), the dialogue anticipates Shakespeare's treatment of Helen's cure of the King of France, which gathers in both notions. Maria's reminder to Pamphilus that his suit is in its early days—'Your harvest is as yet but in the green blade' (p. 239)—also finds an echo in *All's Well*, when the Countess tries to excuse Bertram's sins on grounds of his youth: 'I beseech your majesty to make it | Natural rebellion done i'th' blade of youth' (5.3.5–6).

Given the connection thus strongly indicated by close parallels, I think it likely that other features of the dialogue were suggestive for Shakespeare as well. It invokes Mars in the early exchanges, and later Venus, presenting the goddess as herself a powerful warrior. Shakespeare structures Bertram's

---

[1] 'Sacred and Sexual Motifs in *All's Well that Ends Well*', *Renaissance Quarterly*, 42 (1989), 33–59.

[2] Hunter perhaps has this passage in mind when in glossing Paroles' paradox he refers to a parallel in Erasmus, though he quotes the less relevant '*violanda virginitas, ut discatur*'.

choice, to run away from the marriage bed and fight in the wars, in terms of the traditional opposition between Mars and Venus.[1] His Helen, following the less familiar paradox also sketched by Erasmus, invokes the powerful warrior-Venus when she complains of being suddenly taken captive by love, 'surprised without rescue in the first assault or ransom afterward' (1.3.115–16). The elements of her grievance against Cupid, who seems to observe class distinctions by wounding her but not her high-born beloved (1.3.113–14), are also anticipated in the same Erasmus passage, when Pamphilus warns Maria that a rebuffed Cupid may make her fall in love with someone beneath her and then fail to make the loved one reciprocate (p. 234). Later in the same scene of *All's Well,* when Helen describes her ever-hopeless, ever-desiring state in terms of a sieve perpetually taking in water and losing it, her image calls up the contrasting figure of the Vestal Virgin Tuccia, who proved her chastity when it was challenged by carrying water in a sieve; this allusion too was perhaps suggested by the Erasmian dialogue, especially if Shakespeare was remembering the Latin original in which Maria refers to a vestal virgin in the context of forbidden love.[2]

The Mingled Yarn

Whether prompted by Erasmus or not, the archetypes of myth and legend provide further dimensions to *All's Well,* already an unstable collocation of different discourses. Perhaps the most dramatic clash between romantic wish-fulfilment and brutal social fact comes in Act 2 Scene 3, when the King rewards Helen for curing his near-fatal illness by allowing her to choose a husband from among his wards, and Bertram angrily rejects both the low-born bride and the high-handed gesture of giving him away. He violently disrupts the whole familiar scenario in which humble merit wins its heart's desire.

---

[1] See 2.3.280–4, 3.2.36–42, and especially 3.3.8–11. I explore this opposition in my article 'Naming Names in *All's Well that Ends Well*', *SQ*, 43 (1992), 265–79.

[2] 'Quid si iuvenis amet inconcessam, hoc est, uxorem alienam aut virginem Vestalem?', *Opera omnia* (Amsterdam, 1972), i. 3. 280; the *Modest Mean* translates '*virginem Vestalem*' as 'a virgin which hath professed continual chastity'.

> My wife, my liege! I shall beseech your highness
> In such a business give me leave to use
> The help of mine own eyes. . . .
> A poor physician's daughter my wife!
>
> (2.3.107–16)

As Alexander Leggatt says, 'We come back to earth with a bump. It is as though Portia had said to Bassanio, "You may be good at riddles, but who ever said this was a sound basis for marriage?"' [1] Bertram's speech is disobliging not only in content but in form: as Leggatt observes (p. 30), his refusal, in blank verse with run-on lines, contradicts through sound and rhythm the formal couplets that Helen and the King have been using in this scene of ritual reward. Story-book romance is attacked by the very mundane realities that it must exclude in order to work.

This episode is singular only in its dramatic emphasis. The clash of discourses is not unique but typical of the play as a whole. On the one hand is the folk-tale plot which W. W. Lawrence taught us to see informing *All's Well*: the Clever Wench fulfils the Impossible Tasks, and All is finally Well. It is not only a familiar story, but THE story: the hero's quest, his testing, his exploits, and finally his completion of the difficult mission, upon which the grateful King gives him the Princess as his reward.[2] But even in this rehearsal of archetypal sequence, complication arises, for in *All's Well* the woman is not the prize but the active, desiring quester; and it is the King's (foster) *son* that she wins. This is not a simple reversal. Given the asymmetries of gender ideology, it defamiliarizes and destabilizes the whole action. This change alone, the replacement of the conventional risk-taking, conniving hero by a risk-taking, conniving heroine, is enough to call into question Lawrence's conclusions that the play calls only for a primitive, fairy-tale response and that a marriage brought about against the wishes of the bridegroom, consummated by trickery, and lacking personal as

---

[1] '*All's Well that Ends Well*: The Testing of Romance', *Modern Language Quarterly*, 32 (1971), 21–41; p. 29.

[2] The paradigm is set out by Vladimir Propp in *The Morphology of the Folktale*, trans. Laurence Scott, 2nd edn., Publications of the American Folklore Society, Bibliographical and Special Series, 9 (Austin, Tex., 1968).

well as class compatibility, need arouse no embarrassing questions.[1]

But even apart from the problems inherent in reversing the genders of lover and love-object, the play keeps giving voice to other aspects of life about which fairy-tale and folk-tale traditionally have nothing to say. Sexuality itself is not just an unexamined ground of action, operating on the schematic level but never explored or even directly represented. On the contrary, the maiden Helen's desire for Bertram is clearly physical; as a bride, her one step out of submissive passivity is to beg him for a physical token of love, a kiss; and after they have actually made love she muses not only on the strangeness of being embraced as another woman but on the pleasures of Bertram's 'sweet use' and 'play' in bed.[2] It is because of the presentation of the 'bed-trick' not just as device but as dramatic experience that this episode in *All's Well* has generated a degree of critical unease not evoked by similar ones in contemporary drama—including the carefully elided sexual encounter between Angelo and Mariana in Shakespeare's own *Measure for Measure*—or in classical myth and the Bible.[3] The sanctifiers of Helen (see below) perform their

[1] W. W. Lawrence, *Shakespeare's Problem Comedies* (New York, 1931), pp. 32–77. Northrop Frye seems to assume a similar response when he views the bed-trick unproblematically as a variation on the disguise motif characteristic of the middle of comedy (*A Natural Perspective* (New York and London, 1965), p. 76) or finds in Helen's rise in social station an echo of the Magnificat: 'He has put down the mighty from their seats, and exalted them of low degree' (*The Myth of Deliverance: Reflections on Shakespeare's Problem Comedies* (Toronto, Buffalo, and London, 1983), p. 55).

[2] Helen's desire at first comes through indirectly in physical metaphors: she laments that 'wishing well had not a body in't | Which might be felt, that we... | Might ... follow our friends, | And show what we alone must think' (1.1.183–7); when contemplating union with Bertram, she talks in abstractions but her figures of speech again physicalize the process—'*feed* mine eye ... *join* like likes, and *kiss* like native things' (1.1.223–5, italics added). For the more overt articulations, see 2.5.80–8 and 4.4.22.

[3] William R. Bowden's survey—'The Bed-Trick, 1603–1642: Its Mechanics, Ethics, and Effects', *Shakespeare Studies*, 5 (1969), 112–23—lists six instances of bed-substitution in plays between 1601 and 1605. Zeus' impersonation of Amphytrion in Alcmena's bed was dramatized in Heywood's *Silver Age*, 1611. For Biblical bed-tricks (Lot's daughters, Jacob and Leah, Tamar and Judah), see Zvi Jagendorf, ' "In the morning, behold, it was Leah": Genesis and the Reversal of Sexual Knowledge', in *Biblical Patterns in Modern Literature*, ed. David H. Hirsch and Nehama Aschkenasy, Brown Judaic Studies, 77 (1984), pp. 51–60.

own elision on her reaction, suppressing her hints of pleasure to concentrate on how she saves her husband from adultery through her submission to 'degradation'. (It is sometimes unclear whether this degradation is caused by her being taken for another woman or by her engaging in sexual activity at all.)

Another line of criticism takes the very improbability of the bed-trick as meaningful in this context, seeing in Bertram's failure to tell Helen from Diana an unromantic view of sexual desire as blind, indiscriminate appetite—whether as typical of all 'lust in action'[1] or as peculiar to the inexperienced Bertram. In any case, the young man's own sexuality is certainly seen in an unromantic light when he pleads with Diana to satisfy his 'sick desires' (4.2.35). Equally alien to romance is the less confident side to Bertram's sexuality which Richard P. Wheeler has convincingly read in his earlier panicked refusal of marriage: the immature youth's fear that 'standing to't' in the marital bed will overwhelm his fragile virility.[2]

It is the Clown who actually gives voice to this fear (3.2.41–2). Nor is this the only time that this character contributes to the sexualizing of Helen and Bertram by saying directly what social convention or *amour propre* forbids them to articulate themselves. When in a single scene he proclaims that he is driven by fleshly desire, and then a few lines later anticipates such sexual weariness that he will welcome being cuckolded (1.3.28–55), his views are so discontinuous that they sound less like his own convictions than indirect comments on the young hero and heroine, who after all are the play's centres of sexual interest. In voicing on the one hand all-powerful desire and on the other hand weary inability to satisfy the inexhaustible appetite he fears in his wife, the Clown speaks to the conditions of both Helen and Bertram.

Conventional romances glide from heroic exploit to matrimonial reward without ever coming down to earth in realities

---

[1] 'The incredible fact that a man can mistake in bed the woman he detests for the woman he desires is not the difficulty but the point of the bed trick, a commentary on the reductiveness of lust in action': Howard Felperin, *Shakespearean Romance* (Princeton, 1972), p. 93.

[2] *Shakespeare's Development and the Problem Comedies: Turn and Counter-Turn* (Berkeley, Los Angeles, and London, 1981), pp. 35–45; see also William Babula, 'The Character and the Conclusion: Bertram and the Ending of *All's Well that Ends Well*', *South Atlantic Bulletin*, 42 (1977), 94–100; p. 95.

of war and marriage. But in *All's Well* actual social practices frequently intrude on the fairy-tale action. The King is enabled to give Helen the husband she desires not by the absolute royal power of story-books but by the legal arrangement that makes the monarch guardian to young noblemen who are left fatherless as minors. Indeed, Bertram's dismay at being married to a physician's daughter has prompted some to see the King as abusing the wardship system in the manner of the actual Elizabethans documented by Joel Hurstfield—the Queen and her nobles choosing for their own advantage marriage partners for wealthy minors in their charge.[1] According to Cole, by insisting that the Count of Roussillon marry a bourgeoise the King violates one of the few limits placed on this corrupt prerogative, the stipulation that such a marriage imposed by the guardian should not disparage the ward's rank. It is not easy to see what kind of reaction the play calls for on this point: Bertram's outrage is easily interpreted as a response to such disparagement, but the King's assertion that virtue is the true nobility is equally easy to accept according to the values dominant in another generic milieu. Bertram's class scruples get no support from other representatives of the nobility—even his mother and the family friend Lafeu, who might be expected to care about the degradation of the Roussillon blood if that were truly an issue. The King's other wards raise no objections to marriage with Helen; and yet, here again Shakespeare creates uncertainty, for while the script assigns them speeches welcoming her suit, Lafeu in looking on at the choosing scene (presumably out of earshot) reads in their actions rejection of the offered bride. The King is certainly not reaping a profit from this marriage; nevertheless, he is using it as a way of paying his own debt to Helen. Perhaps the point is that the script is open to such question, even if it cannot be resolved. No such social concerns arise in a more homogeneous romance like *Pericles*, where King Simonides sanctions his daughter's marriage to a stranger knight on the basis of his courage and prowess, with no worries about disparaging his own line; even with everyone

[1] Cole, pp. 95–100; Hurstfield, *The Queen's Wards: Wardship and Marriage under Elizabeth I* (1958).

on-stage ignorant of Pericles' true rank, objections on the basis of rank seem irrelevant, and none are advanced. It is also typical of romance that Pericles is really a prince. The marriage promoted and apparently approved in *All's Well* is untypical of Shakespeare's drama in its crossing of social barriers that were formidably real and important in his time.[1]

Class differences colour other dramatic attitudes in the romance plot: Helen's servant-like subservience to her husband after the marriage, Bertram's overbearing manner in wooing Diana and then in disowning his vows when she brings a breach-of-promise action against him. In the words of that acute social observer Paroles, 'He did love her, sir, as a gentleman loves a woman. . . . He loved her, sir, and loved her not' (5.3.245–8); that is, in the usual manner of the well-born male with the base-born female (*woman*, not *lady*) he eagerly sought her sexual favours but wouldn't dream of marrying her. Nevertheless, the bargaining between Bertram and Diana in Act 4 Scene 2 refers fairly clearly to the sexual economy underlying Elizabethan marriage deals. She barters her honour for his, her chastity—the unviolated anatomical 'ring' that was the bride's contribution to the marriage exchange—for his family ring, which symbolizes the giving of name and rank, the endowment of the woman as vehicle for the male succession, that is the bridegroom's side of the bargain. This particular deal is invalid, of course, because neither party means to adhere to what is promised. Diana does not intend to go to Bertram's bed, and Bertram does not intend to marry her when he is free. But the bargain itself resonates with contemporary social practice. Less certainly, the licence with which Paroles baits Helen about her virginity and offers to 'naturalize' her as a woman may be his imitation of the nobility's freer, less respectful manners with lower-class girls.

[1] 'In none of his other comedies do we find a marriage that attempts to cross such wide social boundaries, and those characters who dream of such things, such as Malvolio, are rudely put in their place': Christopher Roark, 'Lavatch and Service in *All's Well that Ends Well*', *Studies in English Literature*, 28 (1988), 241–58; p. 243. In this interclass marriage, as John D. Cox says, Shake-speare is 'defying received social opinion more clearly than he does in any other marital relationship he dramatizes': *Shakespeare and the Dramaturgy of Power* (Princeton, 1989), p. 128.

Bertram at first refuses to give away his family ring, reluctant to part with this ancestral 'honour 'longing to our house'. But, with only a superficial understanding of his noble inheritance, he has no defence against Diana's logical rebuttal that this 'honour' of his should pay for the loss of hers. The play keeps generating conflicting notions of honour, and this scene focuses some of the conflicts: between gendered conceptions, between honour as intrinsic and as ornamental. Another site on which the contention over the meaning of honour is played out is the war. War is traditionally the arena in which male honour is tested and validated, and Bertram succeeds on the battlefield. Yet both his mother and his peers put less value on the honour thus conventionally won than on the counterweighing shame incurred by his treatment of his wife (3.2.93–4; 4.3.68–70).

Indeed, the whole presentation of the war prevents our taking it unproblematically as a stage for heroic achievement. Shakespeare takes over the conflict from his source. He may conceivably have known that Florence and France were allies in the late fifteenth and early sixteenth centuries, and used that knowledge in inventing the letter from Florence requesting the French King's assistance; but he does not appear to be referring to any particular hostilities between Florence and Siena. The grounds of this war seem of no importance when the King offhandedly introduces it ('The Florentines and Senois are by th'ears', 1.2.1); he takes no side himself and allows his young lords to use service in either army as an opportunity for the 'breathing and exploit' their restless youth makes desirable. In this situation, apparently the means justifies the end: any armed hostilities will do as the scene for martial bravery, and the political issues are irrelevant. Yet in Act 3 Scene 1, the Duke of Florence concludes an exposition of these issues for the French lords and presses them not only for approval of his cause but for an explanation of why France is not giving official support. When the First Lord assures the Duke, 'Holy seems the quarrel | Upon your grace's part, black and fearful | On the opposer' (3.1.4–6), he is presumably being tactful rather than sincere; certainly his disclaimer of knowledge about the French King's decision not to support

Florence is a diplomatic lie, as he was on hand in Act 1 Scene 2, when the King acceded to Austria's request not to intervene. But to raise moral/political issues at all gives more substance to this war than it seems to require for its comic-opera function. Yet we hear no more about the holy cause, and in the next act the hostilities are abruptly ended by a casually mentioned 'peace concluded' (4.3.40). We never find out who wins, if anyone does. Even the French lords' conversation with the Duke undercuts the just-cause notion almost as soon as it is enunciated, for the First Lord smooths over his king's lack of co-operation by saying that young Frenchmen will no doubt be quick to follow the colours, not because of the rightness of the cause but for 'physic' against too much ease. We are back to 'breathing and exploit'. But to bring up and then suppress the causes of the hostilities creates a different effect from just omitting them. The effect is to expose the fictional basis of the war, pointing not to the playwright's plot device but beyond dramaturgy to the public relations fictions of actual Renaissance princes in justifying armed action, fictions which have to be advanced and ritually assented to but have no compelling reality.[1] If this Florence–Siena war is to be seen as a typically tawdry bit of military adventurism, it is no wonder that the one battle action we hear about is a muddle in which the Florentine cavalry destroyed some of their own soldiers by mistake: friendly fire, in our modern oxymoron (3.6.48–50). Furthermore, the comment of the First Lord that the cavalry's mistake in charging its own army's wing was not bad generalship but 'a disaster of war that Caesar himself could not have prevented' (3.6.52–3) suggests that the lethal muddle is endemic to the enterprise. That's war for you. In the army camp as in the court and the bedroom, *All's Well* is poised uneasily between the high endeavours of honour, the world of miracle and chivalric romance, and the 'modern and familiar' world of Shakespeare's own time when miracles were past (2.3.1–3) and human motives often less than idealistic.

[1] Cox sees 'Renaissance political reality' reflected also in the French King's duplicity when he meets Austria's request by denying official aid to Florence but allows his nobles to fight on the Florentine side (pp. 133–4).

'All's Well that Ends Well' as a 'Problem Play'

The hard look at war and its heroics in *All's Well* resonates with a similar cynical scrutiny in *Troilus and Cressida*. And in *All's Well*, as in *Troilus*, an international army generalizes the deflation of martial glamour: besides the French youth fighting on both sides, Paroles' list of commanders (4.3.163–7) suggests a mixture of nationalities fighting for Florence, while there are Muscovites on the Sienese side. In *Troilus and Cressida* combatants on both sides doubt the worthiness of their cause and do more posturing than fighting. War—as a preoccupation if not an activity—is more successful in displacing love than in *All's Well*, but the battle lines are similarly drawn between romance and seamy realism.

This unglamorous vision of war, matched in spirit by a fleeting reference in *Measure for Measure* to soldiers' impatience with peace as an impediment to their livelihood (1.2.1–16), is one instance of the dark mood that links the so-called 'problem plays'. Since so much critical thinking about *All's Well* has taken place in the context of this category, it deserves some examination here. The label was proposed in 1896 by F. S. Boas for *Troilus and Cressida*, *All's Well that Ends Well*, *Measure for Measure*, and *Hamlet* as well, as plays of social and psychological malaise that seemed to him to need a separate generic designation because they fit neither the comic nor the tragic mould. They pose intricate ethical issues which require unorthodox solutions, and their resolutions fail to satisfy completely.[1] But in the previous decade Dowden had already grouped all of these plays except *Hamlet* as Shakespearian comedies written against the grain, at a time when his creative bent had turned toward tragedy.[2] Since Dowden and Boas, critical history has produced variations on the paradigm they created between them, often questioning the label 'problem play' and disputing the inclusion of *Hamlet*, but nevertheless finding the basic grouping too useful to abandon in approaching the untraditional, disturbing nature of these plays.

[1] Boas, *Shakspere and his Predecessors* (1896), p. 345.
[2] Edward Dowden, *Shakspere Primer* (New York, 1887, reprint of 1877 edn.), p. 53.

For many, the defining note of the group is just the counter-point—or clash—between romance and prosaic reality that I have been exploring in *All's Well*. It is helpful to contrast a romance like *The Winter's Tale*, which also contains both aspects: its story-book events are infused with some raw, ugly emotion, and the comic–regenerative outcome is overseen by a scolding, strong-minded woman. But these elements are notably better adjusted in the later play. For one thing, the characters, including Paulina herself, are all co-operating with the fairy-tale course of action. In the more wayward and disparate mode of *All's Well* this practical woman, apparently widowed and in complete ascendance over the repentant Leontes, might well decide to give up on the slim hope posed by the oracle and abandon the cloistered Hermione in order to seek her own advantage and become queen herself. For another thing, the oracle with the surrounding apparatus of the god Apollo, the seasonal patterning, and the thematizing of Time as a purposeful power all work to situate the entire action in a larger providential movement that is beyond even Paulina's control. Everything evolves by necessity toward the linked miracles of Leontes' redemption, Perdita's restoration, and Hermione's resurrection. *All's Well*, on the contrary, presents its providential event much earlier, and more ambiguously: is the King's cure a miracle, or simply the result of good medicine? (or sexual arousal?) In any event, for the achievement of the impossible that brings about her full heart's desire, Helen must be her own providence. Where it is easy to accept Paulina's deception and manipulation of Leontes in the service of his evolution towards a more generous love, Helen has caused considerable discomfort to her public (see below, pp. 30–40) by being at once lover and contriver.

Others seeking the key to the 'problem' category focus on the difficult, unsatisfying endings. In this light, the plays in question take on a self-reflexive quality, thematizing the inadequacies of conventional artistic formulas by displaying the happy ending as forcibly imposed on intractable human nature (*All's Well, Measure for Measure*) or by denying formal closure entirely (*Troilus and Cressida*). When Helen in the last scene confronts Bertram with her fulfilment of his impossible tasks—'Look you, here's your letter. . . . This is done'

(5.3.311–13)—she has indeed carried out the letter of his stipulations, but ignored the spirit in which they were made: he meant not conditions to be met but total dismissal.[1] As the whole elaborate dénouement resembles that of *Measure for Measure*, so Helen herself here comes uncomfortably close to the high-handed Duke as he consigns some to penance and some to marriage without regard for their actual dispositions or desires.[2]

Many attempts to define the 'problem plays' seem to originate in generic anomaly: in *Troilus* potential tragedy is increasingly compromised by anti-heroic satire and indecisive events, while the elaborately comic shaping of *Measure for Measure* and *All's Well* cannot comfortably accommodate the direct address to pain and desire and the perceived deep-seated pessimism about human worth and power.

To some degree, *All's Well* certainly participates in this pessimism about faulty humanity left to its own devices. Like Angelo and Lucio in *Measure for Measure*, the erring Bertram and Paroles seem totally incapable of discovering and developing any better natures in themselves. Both are dragged into redemption, such as it is, quite against their wills, and the hero does not even arrive at the self-knowledge that similar shameful exposure generates in the parasite. The lack in these plays, noted by Howard Felperin, of any 'fully realized second world where the romantic imagination has room to maneuver, is free to create constructs that rival and rehabilitate the first',[3] is the structural expression of this bleak view of a hard-core depravity that resists the easy transformations of earlier comedies. *All's Well* also shares the accompanying tendency toward abstract moral commentary: the Clown, the

[1] See note on 3.2.61.

[2] In the most acute analysis of the 'problem' category, Peter Ure lists as one shared feature 'an art whose apparent contempt and carelessness about ... the machinery for achieving consistency and smooth running mediate the reach and pressure of a mind profoundly aware that energy and meaning in the theatre may spring from the attempt to embody in its forms the very resistance which life offers to being translated into the expressive modes of art': *William Shakespeare: The Problem Plays* (1961), p. 7. See also Felperin, p. 96; Anne Barton, Introduction to *Measure for Measure*, Riverside; and David Scott Kastan, 'All's Well that Ends Well and the Limits of Comedy', *ELH*, 52 (1985), 575–89.

[3] Felperin, p. 82.

King, and even the French lords have this penchant in common with Ulysses and Thersites in *Troilus and Cressida*, Duke Vincentio and almost everyone else in *Measure for Measure*. But Tillyard's conclusion that the problem plays show Shakespeare in the mood for abstract philosophical speculation, while it has some validity for *Troilus and Cressida* and *Hamlet*, seems unwarranted for the two dark comedies.[1]

More suggestive is Tillyard's observation that the three traditional problem plays and *Hamlet* have a common focus on the maturing of the (male) adolescent through harsh experience.[2] Although Tillyard does not dwell on it, the nature of these shocks that precipitate growth tends to be sexual: Claudio's impending fatherhood and arrest for fornication, Hamlet's disgust at his mother's adultery and incest, Troilus' separation from and betrayal by Cressida, Bertram's enforced marriage and final exposure as an unprincipled seducer. The theme of young men in crisis, then, leads into another marked feature of the problem plays (including *Hamlet*): their obsession with desire in the raw, with sexuality as tormented and tormenting. Noting one manifestation shared by *All's Well* and *Measure for Measure*, the young man's reluctance to marry and paradoxical concomitant wish to deflower a virgin, Alexander Welsh reads an interesting subtext founded on unconscious male reasoning. In that reasoning, cohabiting with one's wife to beget a child, a replacement of oneself, is assenting to the passage of one's own generation; young men, in denial of their own mortality, wish rather to seduce a virgin in a one-time, challenging enterprise that requires no continuing commitment.[3] Welsh's notion gains support from *All's Well*'s preoccupation with inheritance and with the passing of power from one generation to the next. Like Hamlet, though more covertly and less gallantly, Bertram in his play must face death.

---

[1] E. M. W. Tillyard, *Shakespeare's Problem Plays* (1950); the illustrative examples he provides, pp. 3–4, are more indicative of a sharp awareness of human frailty than a bent for abstract speculation.

[2] Tillyard, pp. 6–8.

[3] Alexander Welsh, 'The Loss of Men and Getting of Children', *MLR*, 73 (1978), 17–28.

Dating: The Jacobean Shakespeare and 'All's Well that Ends Well'

Considerations of *All's Well* in the 'problem play' group tend
to assume that these three or four plays are close to each
other in time of composition. In some analyses, they are
thought to reflect external pressures of changing theatrical
taste or, in the older formulation now questioned, dispiriting
events on the national scene, in Shakespeare's own life, or
both. Dowden's periodization, with *All's Well* assigned to the
Third Period of Shakespeare's development, 'In the Depths',
had great influence, and it took several generations to dispel
by careful historical scrutiny the link between the unfestive
problem plays and a supposed melancholy phase—uncertain
in its personal causes, but for English society in general
supposed a result of the failed Essex rebellion, the decline and
death of the old Queen, and concomitant fears for the succession and the new reign. R. W. Chambers argued against
this tissue of suppositions in his 1937 British Academy lecture, the title of which my section heading is designed to
recall.[1] He was certainly right in criticizing the facile corres-
pondences between the supposed mood of England or Shakespeare and the temper of the plays, though in my view on
shaky ground in refusing to admit any cynicism in *Measure
for Measure*. By borrowing his phrase I mean to assert, first,
that the play *is* Jacobean and not late Elizabethan, and second,
to re-emphasize Shakespeare as at this time, quite apart from
his mythical sorrows or the national state of mind, a playwright
well launched on a series of dramas about serious issues, most
of them tragic and none of them lightheartedly comic.

The features shared by the problem plays do not in themselves make nearness in time a certainty, but in fact internal
echoes and results of language and metre tests do support a
proximity in time. In the summary of Gary Taylor,

In rare vocabulary, *All's Well* is linked most closely (in descending
order) to *Measure, Troilus, Othello,* and *Coriolanus* (see Slater, 1977).
The colloquialism-in-verse test puts it after *Measure* and *Othello,* and
Oras's pause tests locate it between *Macbeth* and *Antony.* Its metrical
figure places it after *Othello* and before *Lear*; a more detailed analysis
of the metrical characteristics of the text by Lowes puts the play

[1] *The Jacobean Shakespeare and 'Measure for Measure'* (1938).

in the period 1606–8. Brainerd's statistical test (1980) would also place the play in that period (p. 229). Fitch's more reliable redaction of the 'sense-pause' test puts *All's Well* somewhere between *Measure for Measure* and *Lear* (p. 300).[1]

To this collection of near relations we may add the echoes of *Hamlet* in the play's opening scene (see note on 1.1.0.1–3). In the absence of any external indications of date, the accumulated internal evidence points to the first few years of the seventeenth century, and toward the later rather than the earlier end of that span.

It was once thought that there *was* an external indicator, that the *Love's Labour's Won* listed in Francis Meres's 1598 *Palladis Tamia* among Shakespeare's plays was the one now known—probably in a revised version—as *All's Well that Ends Well*. Bishop Percy first suggested the identification in a letter to Richard Farmer, who included it in his 1767 *Essay on the Learning of Shakespeare*.[2] Malone was persuaded and assigned *All's Well* to 1598 in the 1778 Johnson–Steevens edition, but later changed his mind and in the 1821 Boswell edition placed the play in 1606 on the basis of its mature style and the anti-Puritan satire of Act 1 Scene 3, which Malone thought accorded well with the aversion of James himself. Coleridge in an 1813 lecture advanced a theory that pleased both those who believed *Love's Labour's Won* had to exist in some form, since a well-received play of Shakespeare's could hardly be lost completely, and those who saw the strong links between *All's Well* and later plays such as *Hamlet* and *Measure for Measure*: *All's Well*, he said, was an early play, 'but afterwards *umgearbeitet*, especially Parolles'.[3] The judgement was presumably based on his sense, reported by Collier, of 'two distinct styles' in the play, 'not only of thought, but of expression'.[4] While some nineteenth-century scholars stay with the early date, most others give one in the 1590s for the original and another in the early 1600s for the supposed revision.

[1] *Textual Companion*, pp. 126–7. The tests cited are discussed in the 'Canon and Chronology' section of the introduction, pp. 93–109.

[2] Thomas Percy to Richard Farmer, 28 February 1764, in *The Percy Letters*, vol. ii, ed. Cleanth Brooks (Baton Rouge, La., 1946), p. 68; Farmer, p. 16.

[3] T. M. Raysor, ed., *Coleridge's Shakespearean Criticism* (1930), i. 237.

[4] Collier, iii. 203.

The chief evidence for an 'early' style was the passages of formal rhymed couplets in Helen's first encounter with the King and the husband-choosing scene (Act 2 Scenes 1 and 3): others saw marks of the immature Shakespeare in Paroles (viewed as an early study for Falstaff), in the colourless Clown and his lack of connection to the main action, and in Helen's conversation with Paroles on virginity (1.1), not only as showing a lack of mature taste but as closely related to the Sonnets usually dated in the early 1590s. The observed hiatus in the text at 1.1.167 also pointed to revision.[1]

But more recent considerations defend the couplet passages as functional in their context, to lift the dramatic discourse out of the ordinary and invoke the folk-tale mystery that Shakespeare needs at certain key moments. They discard the other tokens of immaturity as speculative, non-definitive, or culture-biased. The Clown's comments, as I have already suggested, seem at times to have more to do with the main action than with his own situation. Paroles can hold his own as a comic creation quite separate from Falstaff; Coleridge, we recall, saw this character as a mark of the *later* style. Helen's sexual banter is a problem for Victorians rather than Shakespeare. If the Sonnet connections, of which there are probably more than the older critics thought, represent anything more than Shakespeare's usual habits in drawing on his own past as well as current work, there may be a better explanation in speculations that have recently been advanced on Shakespeare's reworking of these poems some years after most of them were first written (see below, p. 23 n. 1). Signs of revision in the playtext (including others recently demonstrated by Fredson Bowers, discussed below) do not in themselves imply a lapse of several years from the original. A more general argument against identifying *All's Well* with *Love's Labour's Won*, as Albert Tolman notes, is the play's lack of alignment in structure or tone with its supposed companion piece, *Love's Labour's Lost*.[2] In sum, Meres's tantalizing ghost-title remains to be explained, and there are no good grounds for seeing *All's Well* as an early play incompletely revised.

[1] Albert H. Tolman, 'Shakespeare's *Love's Labour's Won*', in *The Views about 'Hamlet' and Other Essays* (Boston and New York, 1904), pp. 274–6.

[2] Tolman, pp. 279–80.

Topical allusions have been observed in the text, although their import for dating is a matter for dispute. The glance at Puritan resistance to ecclesiastical vestments that Malone noted in the Clown's resolve to 'wear the surplice of humility over the black gown of a big heart' (1.3.94–5) might refer to the enforcement of the surplice in 1604, as Dover Wilson suggests (Cambridge edn., p. 105), but this struggle was a long-standing one. The Clown's prefatory lament 'That man should be at woman's command, and yet no hurt done' perhaps points to Puritan restiveness under Elizabeth rather than under James. On the other hand, the more relevant such a complaint was to the current head of Church and State, the more dangerous it was to voice on the stage. The same might be said of Paroles' scornful picture of 'old virginity', withered, out of fashion, and not in demand (1.1.157–65), which can easily be seen as satirizing the royal myth of eternal and eternally desirable virginity, even while gesturing at the actual gauntness and wrinkles of a woman in her sixties. Supporting the revision theory, Dover Wilson found an additional trace of the supposed early version that pertained to the Queen. Kept by his sovereign from fighting in foreign wars as he longs to, Bertram's situation recalls that of Elizabeth's young courtiers, and his angry phrase 'fore-horse to a smock' (2.1.30), Wilson thinks, though risky on the Elizabethan stage would have no point on the Jacobean (pp. 105–6). I see no reason why audience members would not pick up this hint, as well as those previously noted, a year or two after the Queen's death: a change of reigns does not, after all, produce total amnesia. On balance, the probable allusions to Elizabeth suggest a date after—but not long after—her death in March 1603 and the immediate mourning period: 1604–5 fits in this respect, and accords with the stylistic tests.

The Oxford editors see evidence that the sequence of Shakespeare's poems that was eventually published in 1609—the Sonnets and 'A Lover's Complaint'—developed over a decade or so, from the early 1590s to 1603–4.[1] If Shakespeare was

[1] They cite the well-supported connections between Sonnet 107 and the death of Queen Elizabeth and the accession of King James in 1603; the hints from manuscript variants of four sonnets that Shakespeare revised individual poems some years after their first composition when shaping them into a sequence; and the evidence from stylistic tests that places the sequence's

indeed revising and reordering the Sonnets at this time, and almost by necessity reprocessing the experience and emotions that inform them, their close connection with *All's Well*, discussed below, makes chronological sense. The date of 1604–5 is also that usually assigned to *Measure for Measure*, which in its plot and situation, its admixture of gritty realism, and its elaborately staged revelations at the close, shows a close relationship to *All's Well*. If, as most editors have thought, *All's Well* was the earlier of the two, the record in the Revels Accounts of a performance of *Measure for Measure* at Whitehall on St Stephen's night (26 December) 1604[1] would make early 1604 a likely date for *All's Well*. But, as the Oxford editors observe, the assumption that *All's Well* came first seems to derive mainly from a general critical preference for *Measure for Measure* as the more solid achievement (*Textual Companion*, p. 127). The stylistic tests agree in making *All's Well* later rather than earlier, a conclusion that was reached independently by Alice Walker on different grounds. She argues that the nonce-use in *All's Well* of names more prominent in *Measure*—Mariana, Escalus, Lodowick, Isbel—indicates that *All's Well* came later. To those who would place *Measure* afterward because the bed-trick, added by Shakespeare to his source story, was probably derived from the Boccaccio tale behind *All's Well*, Walker replies sensibly that Shakespeare could have been familiar with the Boccaccio story well before he made it the basis for an entire play.[2] Accepting this order of the two plays, we are back in the larger circumference of 1604–5, with no reliable guides to further pinpointing; references to underminers and blowers-up (1.1.122–3) and traitors who attain their abhorred ends (4.3.23–4) seem to me too general to call up, as Wilson's notes speculate, the discovery and disposition of the Gunpowder Plot and its aftermath in late 1605 and 1606.

companion poem 'A Lover's Complaint' in the early seventeenth century, close to *All's Well*, *King Lear*, and *Hamlet*: *Textual Companion*, pp. 123–4, and Gary Taylor, 'Some Manuscripts of Shakespeare's Sonnets', *Bulletin of the John Rylands Library*, 68 (1985), 210–46.

[1] E. K. Chambers, *William Shakespeare: A Study of Facts and Problems*, 2 vols. (Oxford, 1930), ii. 331.

[2] Alice Walker, 'The Text of *Measure for Measure*' (Appendix), *RES*, 34 (1983), 19–20.

3. An overdressed, posturing Keith Michell in Noël Willman's 1955 production at Stratford-upon-Avon demonstrates the comic vitality that made Paroles the centre of the play for eighteenth-century audiences.

'Is not this Helen?': The Fortunes of an Unorthodox Heroine

All's Well that Ends Well has never been a favourite with audiences and readers. No allusions to it from Shakespeare's own time have been found, and evaluations by nineteenth- and early twentieth-century critics tend to be at best defensive; more often their tone is embarrassed or denunciatory, and some, like Quiller-Couch, Tillyard, and Josephine W. Bennett, do not hesitate to label the play a failure. Eighteenth-century audiences enjoyed the Paroles plot, but the Garrick version they saw displaced and dimmed the heroine and her trials of love to highlight the braggart soldier. Though nineteenth-century productions restored Helen to centre stage, it was in adaptations designed to distance her from sexual aggressiveness, and indeed from sexuality itself; yet in spite of all this anxious care, the play was performed only seventeen times in the entire century, considerably less than the fifty-one performances of the preceding century. Recent decades, however, have seen frequent productions: *Shakespeare Quarterly* records fifty-six since World War II. In the best of these—notably those by Tyrone Guthrie (1953 at Stratford, Ontario, and 1959 at Stratford-upon-Avon), Elijah Moshinsky (BBC Shakespeare series, filmed 1980), and Trevor Nunn (Stratford-upon-Avon 1981, London and New York 1982)—the script survives without distorting cuts; pain, farce, and social constraints all find their places in a dramatic experience of considerable complexity.[1]

This popularity of *All's Well* on stage both reflects and furthers an upswing in critical interest in the play and a new respect for its power and subtlety as drama. Tillyard, significantly, thought he might have had to qualify his label of 'interesting failure' if he had seen *All's Well* performed. That he had not had the opportunity, and assumed that no one else had either,[2] speaks perhaps as much to the tenacity of Victorian distaste for the indecencies of the play's plot as to stageworthiness *per se*. The current vogue on stage of *All's Well*, and of the other 'problem plays' *Measure for Measure* and *Troilus and Cressida*, in turn owes something to the modernist penchant for irony and to more recent post-structuralist trends in criticism, which value the very dislocations and gaps that distressed earlier organicist critics. Critics and directors alike see opportunity in the discord of modes, the signs of class and gender ideologies in conflict, that were only defects for earlier generations.

Besides objections to the incomplete blending of the 'mingled yarn', detractors of *All's Well* have sometimes located its problem in Bertram, an unsatisfactory figure not worthy of the hero's role or of Helen's love. Queasiness about the bed-trick recurs as well. Generally speaking, however, unease about *All's Well* has focused on Helen herself.

Samuel Johnson summed up Bertram's nature and behaviour as a serious stumbling-block to enjoying the play as a comedy:

---

[1] Joseph G. Price thoroughly canvasses the stage history of *All's Well* in *The Unfortunate Comedy* (Toronto, 1968); J. L. Styan examines twentieth-century productions in '*All's Well that Ends Well*', Shakespeare in Performance series (Manchester, 1984).

[2] 'Fail the play does, when read; but who of its judges have seen it acted? Not I at any rate; and I suspect that it acts far better than it reads': Tillyard, p. 89.

I cannot reconcile my heart to *Bertram*; a man noble without generosity, and young without truth; who marries *Helen* as a coward, and leaves her as a profligate: when she is dead by his unkindness, sneaks home to a second marriage, is accused by a woman whom he has wronged, defends himself by falsehood, and is dismissed to happiness.[1]

And many after Johnson, whether officially espousing poetic justice or not, feel that Bertram deserves casting out rather than reincorporation with his wife at the play's end. As Hugh Richmond points out, Bertram is given none of the charm that renders the offences of other adolescent heroes more tolerable to the audience.[2] Nor, although we seem meant to accept him as penitent at the play's end, has Shakespeare given him words to compel our belief in his change of heart. There is a limit to how much transformation the actor can project into his brief 'Both, both. O pardon!', his lines of conditional acceptance addressed to the King, and his subsequent silence, even with assistance from stage business (5.3.308–end).

Those who nevertheless find grounds for hope in this graceless character stress his youth. Immature Bertrams work best on the stage (Guthrie's Edward de Souza and Nunn's Philip Franks, in London and New York, are good examples), and the line of criticism that does most to rehabilitate him concentrates on problems of maturation. In this line, Richard Wheeler demonstrates clearly the difficult situation of a young man who escapes from a feminine family context, is immediately forced into a marriage that sucks him back into that orbit before he has attained real autonomy or confirmed his masculine sense of self, and understandably if reprehensibly runs off once more to the scene of male comradeship and achievement in battle.[3] Such arguments tend to put considerable weight on Bertram's military success as a sign of his maturing—more weight, probably, than the text can support, in view of its problematic presentation of martial honour.

---

[1] *Johnson on Shakespeare*, ed. Arthur Sherbo, *The Works of Samuel Johnson*, vol. vii (New Haven, 1968), p. 404.

[2] Hugh Richmond, *Shakespeare's Sexual Comedy* (New York, 1971), pp. 152–3.

[3] *Shakespeare's Development and the Problem Comedies*, pp. 35–45.

4. John Gunter's wonderfully versatile set for Trevor Nunn's 1981 production, here as Edwardian men's club: standing at left, Second Lord (Philip Franks) and First Lord (Peter Land) attend the invalid King (John Franklyn-Robbins), seated in a bath chair, while Lafeu (Robert Eddison) at right introduces young Bertram (Mike Gwilym) to the scene of manhood.

5. In Tyrone Guthrie's 1959 production at Stratford-upon-Avon, Helen (Zoë Caldwell) turns away from the willing court lords to choose the reluctant Bertram (Edward de Souza).

6. Edward de Souza kneels to Zoë Caldwell at the end of Guthrie's 1959 Stratford-upon-Avon production, filling out with gesture Bertram's too-brief words of penitence.

Finally seeing through Paroles is advanced as another step in his education (although critics like Evans and Leggatt point out that this supposed turning-point in fact brings him no discernible self-knowledge or alteration of behaviour). Karl Elze thought that we should see *All's Well* as a companion piece to *The Taming of the Shrew*: Bertram, like Kate, is a wayward young animal being tamed into his social role. As she is likened to a falcon in training, so he is a colt being broken.[1]

[1] Elze builds on suggestions from Kreyssig and Schlegel: '*All's Well that Ends Well*', *Essays on Shakespeare*, trans. L. Dora Schmitz (1874), pp. 118–50. Bertram is several times associated with horses: he complains at being 'fore-horse to a smock' (2.1.30), is threatened with 'the staggers' for disobeying the King (2.3.164), is encouraged in revolt by Paroles' comparison between 'jades' who remain in France and 'Mars's fiery steed' in Italy (2.3.283–5), is soon made general of the horse for Florence (3.3.1), is to be sold off at market like an unsatisfactory horse when found unworthy of Lafeu's daughter (5.3.148–9), is seen to 'boggle' like a horse taking fright when Diana produces the ring (5.3.232).

In Elze's view, Bertram's character—headstrong, unripe and unformed—is what it must be to carry out Shakespeare's major decision, which was to have in this version of the taming motif a woman as the tamer. In this case as in others, the roads of critics' disapprobation have a way of leading back to the main character, Helen. She is set up by the play for their admiration, but they cannot truly admire her: her actions require this peculiar kind of hero, the bed-trick—which causes extreme unease both as a deception of Bertram and as a degradation of Helen—is her doing. Critics after Johnson, while variously displeased with the hero, have by and large given to their dissatisfaction the local habitation and name of the heroine. Their text might in unexpurgated form run like this:

I cannot reconcile my heart to Helen: a woman who pursues and captures, not once but twice, a man who doesn't want her; uses trickery in order to force herself on him sexually; and finally consolidates her hold on her husband to a chorus of universal approbation.

Such a straightforward expression of distaste is rare, however. In the face of indications that Shakespeare (as well as his characters) approves of Helen, resentment tends to be suppressed; and that suppressed resentment may energize a view of Helen at the opposite extreme, as a selfless saint who degrades herself to redeem her husband.

When the rejuvenated King enters with Helen after she has cured him, there is an odd exchange between Paroles and Lafeu:

> PAROLES *Mort du vinaigre!* Is not this Helen?
> LAFEU Fore God, I think so.
>
> (2.3.45–6)

Lafeu's response is as puzzling in its way as Paroles' nonsensical oath. How can he be learning for the first time that the King's deliverer is the young woman he had met earlier at Roussillon, when he himself introduced her into the royal presence in Act 2 Scene 1? Commentators have had to posit irony, or a change in dress and mood after her success that transforms the Helen of old; I have in this edition adopted Taylor's attractive suggestion that the 'Doctor She' who presents herself at court in Act 2 Scene 1 is in disguise and therefore not recognized at that time by Lafeu (*Textual Companion*, p. 495). But the immediate sense this passage generates, that Lafeu is seeing a completely different woman from the one he sponsored just two scenes earlier, may stand as an emblem for the critical history of this play, which projects at least two quite different heroines.

The key to both the major versions of Helen is the upsetting of the gender role system created by having the woman rather than the man take the sexual initiative. Objections to the 'indelicacy' of Helen's banter with Paroles on virginity have tended to fade along with Victorian standards of propriety, but her appropriation of the male role as sexual aggressor has continued to give offence. No other heroine in Shakespearian comedy goes after the man she wants without some prior attachment initiated by the man. Even Helena in *A Midsummer Night's Dream*, whose pursuit of the unwilling Demetrius as well as her name links her with the Helen of *All's Well*,[1] is trying to win back a man who initially courted her (*Dream*, 1.1.106–8). Portia in *The Merchant of Venice*, in other ways as aggressive as the Helen of *All's Well* and a bigot to boot, attracts neither the chorus of disapprobation nor the nervous defences that Helen does, perhaps because in the crucial area of initiating marriage she lets Bassanio take the lead. However spirited and ready to take control, the Portias and Rosalinds wait to be wooed. If they love before they are asked, they nevertheless further their desires by strategies of reception and encouragement that are in keeping with their traditional gender role. Both heroines of *The Two Gentlemen of Verona* follow the men they love, but only after they have been courted and won. Silvia is bridging distance rather than reversing sexual initiative when she goes after the banished Valentine; Julia is doing the same as far as she knows, thinking herself sure of Proteus' welcome. Even in male disguise (assumed for protection rather than as conferring male aggressive prerogatives, and maintained as a means of

---

[1] See Susan Snyder, '*All's Well that Ends Well* and Shakespeare's Helens: Text and Subtext, Subject and Object', *English Literary Renaissance*, 18 (1988), 66–77; some of the material following is also adapted from this article.

access to Proteus), she is not a pursuer but an object of pursuit waiting for renewed attention. Helen alone makes her beloved a sexual object.[1]

Anxiety on this score may be as old as the story itself. Giletta, we are told, fell in love with Beltramo 'more than was meet for a maiden of her age' (Painter, p. 225; Boccaccio, '*oltre al convenevole della tenera età*'). No one voices such a reservation in the play, where only Bertram and Paroles hold out against the universal admiration of Helen. Yet we may wonder if the misogynistic ramblings of the Clown in Act 1 Scene 3 were not called forth by some anxiety felt by Shakespeare at his own transgressions of gender convention. The Clown elsewhere is one of Helen's admirers (4.5.17–18), but sometimes, as we have seen, he speaks for others besides himself. Perhaps in this third scene not only the sexual nausea noted in my previous discussion but the following ballad of Troy with its antifeminist commentary were generated by nervousness about Helen's actions, distant as they are from the accepted norm for good women.

In any case, patriarchal anxieties are unmistakable in the concerns of some adapters and critics. In refining the playtext in the last years of the eighteenth century, John Philip Kemble disallowed for his heroine not only unseemly banter about virginity and competence with fistulas but also husband-hunting initiative: he ends the first scene with Helen's passive, despairing words of love for the 'bright particular star' who is impossibly far above her, and delays the contrasting soliloquy of energetic resolve that should end the first scene, 'Our remedies oft in ourselves do lie', for inclusion in the third scene, so that Helen appears to be acting under the Countess's sanction rather than striking out on her own. Helen does not in his version flaunt her prerogative as chooser of her mate by speaking with each of the King's wards in

[1] The patriarchal discomfort this creates receives clarification in Laura Mulvey's study of the way films in directing the 'curious gaze' enact a gendered active/passive division of labour. 'According to the principles of the ruling ideology and the psychical structures that back it up, the male figure cannot bear the burden of sexual objectification. . . . Hence the split between spectacle and narrative supports the man's role as the active one of forwarding the story, making things happen': 'Visual Pleasure and Narrative Cinema', *Screen*, 16, no. 3 (1975), 6–18; p. 12.

turn but presents herself directly, and meekly, to Bertram. Critics show the same anxieties. E. K. Chambers's assumption that women should be ancillary to male activities rather than initiating action on their own is apparent when he finds Helen degraded by an inordinate desire, which 'turns man's tender helpmate . . . into the keen and unswerving huntress of man'. John Masefield thinks Shakespeare shared his outrage at 'a woman who practises a borrowed art, not for art's sake, not for charity, but, woman fashion, for a selfish end', who puts 'a man into a position of ignominy quite unbearable, and then plot[s] with other women to keep him in that position'. Andrew Lang hoots at Hazlitt's contention (see below) that Helen, whom he calls 'this female D'Artagnan', does not violate modesty. His effort at evenhandedness, asserting that her behaviour would be just as reprehensible in a man, does not convince: do we expect modesty in a male D'Artagnan?[1]

Since patriarchalism shapes women's values as well as men's, it is no surprise to find Charlotte Lennox as an early (1753) denouncer of Helen. Her indictment has many counts, but the main charges of arrogance, cruelty, and guile are informed by a sense that Helen violates feminine propriety. The same is true for the hard, predatory figure discerned by Helen's most fervent recent attacker, Bertrand Evans: while he rails against her deceptions, a deeper antipathy emerges in assertions like 'her pilgrimage was never meant for [Saint] Jaques, but for Priapus'. Dismay at Helen's sexual aggressiveness also lurks in the background of other charges: ambition (Clifford Leech), religious hypocrisy (Cole), conspiracy (Richard Levin), even quackery (Henry Yellowlees).[2]

Masefield and Lang take particular exception to Coleridge's frequently-quoted pronouncement that Helen is 'Shakespeare's loveliest character'. But Coleridge is in fact a good

[1] Chambers, *Shakespeare: A Survey* (1925), p. 203; Masefield, *William Shakespeare* (New York, 1911), p. 148; Lang, '*All's Well that Ends Well*', *Harper's New Monthly Magazine*, 85 (1892), 213–27.

[2] Lennox, *Shakespear Illustrated* (1753), i. 190–2; Evans, *Shakespeare's Comedies* (Oxford, 1960), pp. 145–66, quotation from p. 157; Leech, 'The Theme of Ambition in *All's Well that Ends Well*', *ELH*, 21 (1954), 23–9; Cole, pp. 114–37; Levin, '*All's Well that Ends Well* and "All Seems Well"', *Shakespeare Studies*, 13 (1980), 131–44; Yellowlees, in *More Talking of Shakespeare*, ed. John Garrett (1959), pp. 175–7.

example of the ambivalence called forth by this masterful heroine. In a more private moment, he sympathized with Bertram at being forced to marry Helen, and added, 'Indeed, it must be confessed that her character is not very delicate, and it requires all Shakespeare's skill to interest us for her.'[1] Even the 'loveliest character' tag occurs in a problematic context: commenting on Helen's statement to the Florentine women (3.5.50–1) that she knows Bertram by reputation only, he asks, 'Shall we say here that Shakespeare has unnecessarily made his loveliest character utter a lie?'[2] Should we perhaps also say that Coleridge's 'loveliest character' superlative is a kind of compensation, energized by the force of his own suppressed revulsion at Helen's indelicacy? Something of the sort is clearly at work in Hazlitt, who keeps defending Helen against unstated but persistent accusations:

> The character of Helen is one of great sweetness and delicacy. She is placed in circumstances of the most critical kind, and has to court her husband both as a virgin and a wife; yet the most scrupulous nicety of female modesty is not once violated. There is not one thought or action that ought to bring a blush into her cheeks, or that for a moment lessens her in our esteem.[3]

The gentleman protests too much. He also writes as if the plot of the play were imposed from outside on an unwilling protagonist, and not generated by her own desire. Anna Jameson too sees Helen 'placed' by her marriage in a degrading situation, glossing over the fact that it was Helen's own initiative that brought about the marriage against Bertram's will.[4] Separating the character from her plot in this manner allows critics to bury their doubts in superlatives of veneration. It is one way to 'save appearances', in the scientific as well as the

[1] Raysor, ii. 356–7.

[2] Raysor, i. 113; he goes on to pose an alternative question about the necessity of deceit but never resolves the doubt.

[3] *Collected Works of William Hazlitt*, ed. A. R. Waller and Arnold Glover (London and New York, 1902–4), i. 329. A. P. Rossiter noted similar signs in comments by Dowden and Tillyard of 'holding something down'—something negative about Helen. He himself advises us not to look too closely at her character, but goes on to do just that, and to find her virtue is really 'virtù', a strong will and an aptitude for scheming: *Angel With Horns*, ed. Graham Storey (1961), pp. 82–107.

[4] Jameson, *Characteristics of Women*, 2nd edn. (1833), i. 109.

social sense: they account for troublesome phenomena and behaviour outside the code by manoeuvres that resemble in their complication those of the pre-Copernican astronomers.

Saving appearances has been a major motivation for critics of Helen, and the anxious idealization first displayed by Coleridge and Hazlitt in the early nineteenth century was long the favoured method. Dowden, who first finds Helen the embodiment of will and energy, recuperates her from this potentially amoral position by demonstrating how she shapes the double action of the play through her role as providential healer, first of the King's sick body and then of Bertram's sick spirit. Helen's unseemly desire is thus obliterated by altruistic love, and her dubious actions are justified by their purpose (asserted by Dowden with no textual evidence) of serving her husband. H. B. Charlton too, backing off from an initial vision of Helen as a 'nymphomaniac' who casts decency aside to get her man, eventually comes up with a combination saint and social worker. Wilson Knight pushes the sanctification further, allying Helen in purity with Joan of Arc and in her salvific function with Christ. Her assuming, 'for once, the male prerogative of action' is vindicated allegorically in that 'she goes out as a Saint Joan to fight for the female values, for the female honour, for "virginity" as a conquering power'. The potentially interesting notion of 'female values' posed against the male valourizing of prowess in battle is thus completely desexualized to equate with religious spirituality.[1]

Knight is, nevertheless, more comfortable with Helen when she is grovelling to Bertram: 'the woman is at her finest in submission'. The recurrent position of self-abasement before her 'bright particular star' that we see in Helen's first soliloquy, in the careful phrasing by which she turns 'I choose you' into 'I give myself into your power', in her humble acceptance of his dismissive cruelty, and in her blame of herself for endangering his well-being by driving him away to the wars, offers all-important support to the sanctifiers. Several point to the bed-substitution as itself a self-humbling act, thus resourcefully turning a potential negative to positive

<hr />

[1] Dowden, *Shakspere: A Critical Study of His Mind and Art* (1875), p. 86; Charlton, *Shakespearian Comedy* (1938), pp. 217, 258–65; Knight, *The Sovereign Flower* (1958), pp. 95–160.

advantage.[1] It must be observed, however, that even in the most generous interpretation Helen's submissive posture is recurrent, not constant. It alternates with episodes of self-assertion, so that the passivity of her first soliloquy is, after her conversation with Paroles, replaced by the confident plans of her second soliloquy, still in the same scene. Her submission to Bertram follows hard upon the unmaidenly forwardness of choosing her own husband, and indeed may well be a reaction to it. Her announced withdrawal to leave the scene clear for Bertram's return somehow takes her to the very place where he is; and her passive mode quickly converts to active as she arranges and carries out her stratagem for getting Bertram's ring and conceiving his child. Confronting Bertram in the last scene, she both pleads and asserts her claim. Schücking and others have judged these pendulum-swings as internal contradiction, a basic compositional flaw;[2] perhaps we should see them rather as deliberately constructed to render the waverings of a woman driven to transgress gender proprieties by overpowering desire, but embarrassed by that transgression and trying to cover or redeem it with extreme humility—another version of the compensatory mechanism I have observed variously in the Clown's misogyny and the critics' beatification.

That beatification also draws support from the eulogies of Helen we hear from the Countess, the King, Lafeu, the French lords, and even the Clown. Indeed, this universal approval, unqualified by any character whose opinion we are invited to trust, seems to forbid reservation or mixed reaction on the part of the audience. On the other hand, they praise her for the quality of her being rather than specifically for her actions. Their summations present her as good in herself and as good

---

[1] Frances M. Pearce sees another parallel to Christ, who employed humiliating means to save mankind as Helen does to save Bertram: 'In Quest of Unity: A Study of Failure and Redemption in *All's Well that Ends Well*', *SQ*, 25 (1973), 71–88; pp. 84–5. See also William B. Toole, *Shakespeare's Problem Plays: Studies in Form and Meaning* (The Hague, 1966), p. 150.

[2] Levin L. Schücking, *Character Problems in Shakespeare's Plays* (London, Calcutta, Sydney, 1922), pp. 195–6. Donald Stauffer agrees that the inconsistency between Helen's Patient Griselda side and 'the ruthless self-made woman' makes her fail as a character: *Shakespeare's World of Images* (New York, 1949), p. 119.

7. An intense Helen (Martha Henry) confides in a sympathetic Countess (Margaret Tyzack): Stratford Festival, Ontario, 1977, production directed by David Jones.

for Bertram, if only he would value her properly. That is, they tend to redefine Helen out of the subject-position she has appropriated in such an unorthodox way, back into a more ideologically acceptable role as valuable object—or, viewed as a channel of heavenly grace, as a vehicle for a more exalted Subject rather than acting in her own interest.

The idealized Helen is ultimately just as inadequate in expressing our experience of this complex play as the debunked and degraded one. Indeed, the action of *All's Well* itself, as Joseph Westlund reminds us, 'fully reveals the danger of inventing what one wants' in displaying the nature and consequences of Helen's uncritical adoration for Bertram. Idealization of Helen by the other characters and by critics, though applied to less intractable material, should be suspect too, when we see how her obsession creates the perfect love object by neglecting all his qualities except high birth and good looks. In order to achieve their ends, the sanctifying critics must in turn neglect this very obsessiveness, which renders inoperable where Bertram is concerned the moral judgement and good sense she applies to everyone else, and drives her to focus totally on her own feelings with no attention to his.[1] It is worth noting that, while the haloed Helens created by some actresses are remembered only for their beauty, if at all, obsessiveness and intensity help to make Helen a compelling figure on the stage; they were at the centre of two highly successful recent performances, by Angela Down on television, and by Harriet Walter in the Royal Shakespeare Company production of 1981.

Psychological approaches to Helen's situation, working apart from the extremes of moral evaluation that have distorted much past criticism, have recently been more fruitful. Robert Ornstein sees her as a figure comparable to Angelo, uneasy with her own desire and striving to repress it. He stresses her initial psychological isolation as one who has grown up on the fringes of a noble household with no assured place in it. Only later in her alliance with the Widow and Diana does she learn to reach out to others; her experience also engenders a more realistic attitude to sexual passion.[2] To Ornstein's we may add several other readings in which Helen grows in the course of the action, her development being in some sense parallel to that of Bertram. Some of these are attractive, for example the notion advanced by John Russell Brown and later Michael Shapiro that Helen must get beyond the arrogance that tries to compel love. But developmental readings of Helen, like those of Bertram, tend to crumble at the resolution stage, unable to show either of them as clearly arrived at a new and better understanding.[3]

[1] Westlund, *Shakespeare's Reparative Comedies: A Psychoanalytic View of the Middle Plays* (Chicago and London, 1984), pp. 121, 128–9, 134. R. A. Foakes also sees Helen as 'in her own way . . . as self-centred as Bertram and Parolles', pursuing Bertram without reference to what he really is or whether he wants her; but he sidesteps any judgement by likening Helen to Ann Whitefield in pursuit of Jack Tanner in Shaw's *Man and Superman*, a natural force allied with the vigour of life itself: *Shakespeare: The Dark Comedies to the Last Plays; From Satire to Celebration* (Charlottesville, Va., 1971), pp. 16, 29.

[2] Robert Ornstein, *Shakespeare's Comedies: From Roman Farce to Romantic Mystery* (Newark, Del., London, and Toronto, 1986), pp. 172–94.

[3] James L. Calderwood, 'The Mingled Yarn of *All's Well that Ends Well*', *JEGP*, 62 (1963), 61–76; Price, pp. 137–72; Ruth Nevo, 'Motive and Meaning in *All's Well that Ends Well*'. On compelling love, see J. R. Brown,

Another approach to the contradictions in Helen's stance—not only between aggressive and submissive lover but between miracle-worker and down-to-earth arranger of the sexual rendezvous—is through the demands of the hybrid plot rather than the nuances of psychological portraiture. Carol Thomas Neely notes that in the folk-tale analogues 'the entire burden of sexual union is symbolically placed on the woman, who must contrive to fill both halves of it. In order to do so, she must be . . . both "clever" [in gaining access to her husband] and a "wench" [unformidable and seduceable, thus allaying her husband's sexual anxieties].'[1] Peter Ure would have Helen as well as Shakespeare aware of the contradictory roles required of her, so that the passionate woman consciously transforms herself into the 'remote, thaumaturgic heroine' required to win Bertram against all mundane probabilities.[2] But it is Shakespeare, according to a popular line of reasoning, who has effected the main transformation: fearing that Helen's descent from working miracles in Act Two into something like procuring in Acts Three and Four may lose her the audience's sympathy, he displaces her from the centre of attention in this second phase. We are variously invited to concentrate on Diana and her mother, Paroles, and Bertram, while Helen operates more in the background, offering no access to her thoughts and motives.[3] The shift from the early, soliloquizing Helen to the later, more reticent one certainly calls for attention. A crucial question of motivation is left in doubt when Shakespeare has Helen apparently announce a

Shakespeare and his Comedies (1957), p. 187, and Michael Shapiro, ' "The Web of Our Life": Human Frailty and Mutual Redemption in *All's Well that Ends Well*', *JEGP*, 71 (1972), 514–26. Brown, trying to see an evolution away from pushiness, hedges on the question of how and why Helen gets to Florence; Shapiro thinks Helen repeats her error of trying to win love by force in engineering the bed-trick, but has to lean on her 'untriumphant entry' in 5.3 to show she has attained humility.

[1] Neely, *Broken Nuptials in Shakespeare's Plays* (New Haven and London, 1985), p. 78.

[2] Ure, p. 14.

[3] The case is argued most fully in Harold S. Wilson, 'Dramatic Emphasis in *All's Well that Ends Well*', *Huntington Library Quarterly*, 13 (1950), 217–40. 'It is the *idea* of Helena [as noble, humble, virtuous] that sustains our impression of the consistency of her character in the second episode, up to the moment when she reappears in her old role of the humble and devoted wife' (p. 226).

pilgrimage to Santiago de Compostela in Spain and then arrive in central Italy in the town where she knows Bertram to be. The very silence of the text on her intentions has encouraged contrasting critical inscriptions; the detractors suspect that the penitent pilgrimage is a ruse from the beginning, veiling an intention to hunt down and capture Bertram, while the sanctifiers are enabled to see divine providence once more assisting Helen, leading her where she may further the larger plan of Bertram's redemption. It is not clear, though, that Shakespeare found this 'de-characterization' of Helen neces- sary to deflect audience disapproval of her doings and thus save the schematic happy ending.[1] Such readings are also suspect in tending to play down or gloss over Helen's consid- erable aggressiveness in the earlier acts, highlighting only the self-abnegating side of her pendulum swings.

Seeking the Generic Fix

The internal inconsistency of *All's Well* is sometimes conceived by critics in generic terms, for example as a disjunction between the miracle tale of the play's first part and the intrigue comedy of the second. From this angle *All's Well* seems structurally parallel to *Measure for Measure*, which also apparently breaks in the middle. The second parts of both plays deny us the access to characters' psyches that the early acts afforded and focus on plot machinery rather than the attitudes that generate events. These two 'dark comedies' may represent an experiment in genre, challenging the usual pre- sumption in favour of maintaining a single dramatic centre and a predominant dramatic 'kind'. A failed experiment, some would say, tried again with new means and better success in *The Winter's Tale*.[2]

---

[1] This position is argued or assumed by Kenneth Muir in *Shakespeare's Sources*, vol. i (1957), pp. 100–1, and R. L. Smallwood in 'The Design of *All's Well that Ends Well*', *Shakespeare Survey* 25 (Cambridge, 1972), pp. 52–5, as well as Elze, Wilson, and others. De-characterization is often a strategy for 'saving appearances'.

[2] For the ferment of generic innovation in the early seventeenth-century English theatre and its attitudinal and commercial context, see Lee Bliss, *The World's Perspective: John Webster and the Jacobean Drama* (New Brunswick, NJ, 1983), introd. and chs. 1–2.

In any event, many have sought to establish the proper perspective on *All's Well* by placing it in the right generic context. Genres are lenses of interpretation: what Rosalie Colie has called ' "frames" or "fixes" on the world'.[1] Situating this troublesome play within such a frame should enable us to make sense of its peculiarities, its departures from the romantic mode that usually defines Shakespearian comedy for us. Michael Benthall's 1953 production at the Old Vic, which presented two-dimensional characters framed in a brightly pretty décor, imposed coherence on the play by reducing it to something like its fabliau source.[2] But few critics trying to come to terms with Shakespeare's full text have been able to follow Frye in finding *All's Well* a 'fairly typical' romantic comedy, 'where the chief magical device used is the bed-trick instead of enchanted forests and identical twins' (*Myth of Deliverance*, p. 3), as if the bed-trick posed no problems apart from improbability.

If *All's Well* is not a romantic comedy, what is it? We have already seen a few answers proposed. Elze conceived of the play as a reverse *Taming of the Shrew*, but believed that in spite of Shakespeare's best efforts *All's Well* could not achieve full comic effect because in having a woman do the courting and taming it flouted nature, where *The Taming of the Shrew* only exaggerated the natural relation of the sexes (p. 124). A more seminal notion, Dowden's formula of the double healing action—Helen's physical cure of the King followed by her spiritual cure of Bertram—stands behind several more recent attempts to place *All's Well* generically.

For these, the relevant context one way or another is medieval religious drama. The bed-trick has a model in the mystery plays: its combination of self-humbling and trickery makes sense theologically as a parallel to Christ's outwitting of the devil by taking on human flesh. Miracle plays, especially those in which the Virgin Mary is the mediating force in bringing erring humanity to redemption, offer another generic frame. R. G. Hunter sees *All's Well* superimposing such a

[1] Colie, *The Resources of Kind: Genre Theory in the Renaissance*, ed. Barbara K. Lewalski (Berkeley, Los Angeles, and London, 1973), p. 8.

[2] Richard David, 'Plays Pleasant and Unpleasant', *Shakespeare Survey 8* (Cambridge, 1955), pp. 134-6.

pattern on the folk-tale source, shifting the emphasis from the need for the lower-class girl to prove herself worthy of marriage into the aristocracy into the need for a strayed Bertram to 'be made worthy of his wife'. In this process, Helen's charity is what counts rather than Bertram's worthiness: from the theological perspective, all men are undeserving of their salvation, which comes about through the generous mediation of the Virgin. Helen's function in *All's Well* parallels in secular form that of the Virgin in the *Miracles de Notre Dame*.[1] This argument for *All's Well* as a 'comedy of forgiveness', though skilfully conducted, runs into difficulty on the near-absence of exactly what ought to stand out at the end—Bertram's recognition of his sin and repentance for it. Yet though parallels with Christ and the Virgin cannot finally explain Helen's actions, they do usefully highlight the mysterious, absolute core of this play: her arbitrary, gratuitous love and its radical conjunction with the flesh.

The morality play has been advanced by Tillyard, Muriel Bradbrook, G. K. Hunter, Jonas Barish, and others as one shaping influence on *All's Well*. In this scheme, Helen and Paroles operate like the Good and Bad Angels, struggling for the allegiance of Bertram. Helen's unwavering love and Bertram's faultiness have their obvious functions in this configuration, which also finds a place for the rogue character whom Shakespeare so emphatically introduced into his plot. The dynamics of *All's Well* do not match the morality mode, however—Helen does not influence Bertram at all, and Paroles does so only to a limited extent; and the black–white moral opposition may encourage oversimplification of both characters.

Yet if we do not press it too hard (as indeed most of its proponents have not), the morality model has value for clarifying structure, if not spiritual significance. It brings out, for example, the unexpected parallelism between Helen and Paroles as lower-class opportunists seeking entry to the world of the nobility. Is the impact one of forceful moral contrast, as the morality pattern suggests, or of successful trickery as

[1] Hunter, *Shakespeare and the Comedy of Forgiveness* (New York and London, 1965), chs. 2 and 5; quotation from p. 112. For the mystery play, see Cox, pp. 128–50.

opposed to unsuccessful, sanctioned ambition as opposed to pretensions exploded?[1] The morality scheme that casts Bertram as contested ground rather than contestant helps Tillyard to justify the ending, in which a 'heavy series of blows to Bertram's confidence' climaxes in accusations of fornication and murder. In the resulting panic, the reappearance of Helen both overwhelms him and bails him out. The fight, unequal from the beginning, was not between Helen and Bertram but between the solidly arrayed forces out to save him and his single ally in jejune depravity.[2] Paroles is better construed apart from moral absolutes, as the symptom rather than the cause of Bertram's waywardness,[3] embodying superficial courtly and martial values.[4] From another point of view, his struggle with Helen is like the rivalry between Antonio and Portia in *The Merchant of Venice* or between Don Pedro (and Claudio) and Beatrice in *Much Ado About Nothing*: on the one hand is the male bond, detaining Bertram—or Bassanio, or Benedick—in adolescent same-sex attachment and thus resisting the move into heterosexual commitment represented by the women. (By *commitment* I mean to separate true emotional engagement from the marriages that Antonio and Don Pedro do promote for their young men friends, while expecting, or at least trying, to keep possession of their first loyalties.) Bertram does not feel the counter-pull of desire in the same way that the other two do, but the general psychological dynamic of rivalry is similar.

More contemporary generic categories proposed for *All's Well* include the prodigal-son group, the 'Patient Griselda' dramas of long-suffering wives and the plays about enforced marriage (the categories overlap to some degree), and Italian tragicomedy. In still other readings, action and characters are controlled by a central idea, or ideas in debate—merit as opposed to inherited nobility, virtue in action, the Life Force— or by a perspective of the old upon the young.[5] Each has some

[1] G. K. Hunter, Arden introd., p. xxxiii.

[2] Tillyard, pp. 113–17.

[3] R. G. Hunter likens him to the King's fistula, pp. 121–2.

[4] Alan Dessen, *Shakespeare and the Late Moral Plays* (Lincoln, Neb., 1986), pp. 113–33.

[5] On the overlapping categories, see Robert Y. Turner, 'Dramatic Convention in *All's Well that Ends Well*', *PMLA*, 75 (1960), 497–502; Wilson,

value, none comes anywhere near a comprehensive view, and in the most thoughtful approaches this or that subgenre is presented as an addition to a rich mix rather than as a single sufficient frame for the play. The more models that are found to contribute genuine insight, the less likely it is that any single generic key to the play will be discovered.

Anatomy of Desire: (I) *'All's Well' and the Sonnets*

Indeed, the most promising approach to the tensions and dislocations of *All's Well* that has emerged of late connects them with works of a distinctly different literary kind, Shakespeare's own lyric poems. The collection published in 1609 by Thomas Thorpe, 154 sonnets followed by 'A Lover's Complaint', probably took shape in ten or so years extending from the 1590s sonnet-vogue to the opening years of James's reign when Shakespeare was writing *All's Well* (see p. 22 above and p. 23 n. 1). Without canvassing in detail the vexed question of the Sonnets as autobiography (John Kerrigan[1] reminds us that autobiography in the modern sense of tracing the development of the individual self hardly existed in Shakespeare's time), it seems reasonable to guess that the situations and attitudes refracted in these poems had their roots in Shakespeare's own experience. These situations and attitudes recur in *All's Well,* which also centres on 'a provincial gaining entrée to court circles by virtue of a rare skill', passionately attached to a handsome, shallow, self-centred

'Dramatic Emphasis'; Marilyn L. Williamson, *Patriarchy in Shakespeare's Comedies* (Detroit, 1986), pp. 58–74. On the similar clash of tones in Italian tragicomedy, G. K. Hunter, 'Italian Tragicomedy on the English Stage', *Renaissance Drama VI* (Evanston, Ill., 1975), pp. 123–48. On ruling ideas, Muriel C. Bradbrook, 'Virtue is the True Nobility: A Study of the Structure of *All's Well'*, *RES*, 1 (1950), 289–301; Warner Berthoff, ' "Our Means Will Make us Means": Character as Virtue in *Hamlet* and *All's Well'*, *New Literary History*, 5 (1973), 38–51; Robert Hapgood, 'The Life of Shame: Parolles and *All's Well that Ends Well'*, *EIC*, 15 (1965), 269–78. On the sympathetic but distanced perspective of age on youth's desperation, Josephine Waters Bennett, 'New Techniques of Comedy in *All's Well that Ends Well'*, *SQ*, 18 (1967), 337–62.

[1] Kerrigan, Introduction to New Penguin edition, *The Sonnets and A Lover's Complaint* (Harmondsworth, New York, etc., 1986), p. 11.

young nobleman who does not respond in kind.[1] Bradbrook and Roger Warren speculate that this nexus of social and emotional inequality in love might have been what drew Shakespeare to the Giletta story in the first place. In any event, the terms of Boccaccio's tale could easily accommodate Shakespeare's reworking of an intense, unsatisfactory, unresolved relationship. The insight offered by the Sonnets and their companion poem of love's distress is not a set of conventions (although *All's Well* does include persuasions to eros and declarations of idolatrous love familiar from sonnet discourse) but a matrix of enthralled love, enthralled both as obsessively attracted and as unwillingly imprisoned.

How does *All's Well* play out the fervours and anxieties of that painful relationship? Warren shows that Helen recapitulates the intensity, self-abnegation, and suffering of the sonnet-speaker, and that Bertram, whose portrayal in harsher terms than Boccaccio's Beltramo now assumes new significance, corresponds in his weakness and cold indifference to the muted reproaches directed at the beloved young man in the Sonnets. He believes that Shakespeare meant the play to 'end well', presenting Bertram as not beyond redemption and celebrating the power of Helen's love even in full awareness of Bertram's faults. That this ending does not come off in a fully satisfactory way he attributes to the public nature of their final freighted confrontation, which precludes the intense personal expression of this love that is necessary to convince us of its power. But he also notes that Shakespeare, by clinging to the truth of his own experience and refusing to falsify or mitigate the young man's defects in Bertram, 'has imperilled the impression of reconciliation he needs at this point' (p. 88). This hint that the actions and attitudes of *All's Well* may be shaped by Shakespeare's resentment as well as

[1] Parallels with the Sonnets are noted by Bradbrook, 'Virtue is the True Nobility', p. 290; Knight, *Sovereign Flower*, pp. 157–8; Roger Warren, 'Why Does it End Well?: Helena, Bertram, and the Sonnets', *Shakespeare Survey 22* (Cambridge, 1969), pp. 79–92; Cyrus Hoy, 'Shakespeare and the Revenge of Art', *Rice University Studies*, 60 (1974), 71–94 , pp. 86–7; Wheeler, *Shakespeare's Development*, pp. 57–75; Sheldon P. Zitner, '*All's Well that Ends Well*', Harvester New Critical Introductions to Shakespeare (New York, London, Toronto, Sydney, Tokyo, 1989), pp. 23–39; the quotation is from Zitner, p. 30.

8. Helen (Claire Bloom) against a fairy-tale backdrop in Michael Benthall's 1953 Old Vic production.

by his selfless love is not developed by Warren, but Richard Wheeler rounds out the picture with considerable attention to the play's enactment of negative feelings about the young man that the Sonnets sought to suppress.

In this psychoanalytic approach, Shakespeare in *All's Well* is not just recollecting the relationship that informed the Sonnets but attempting, after a passage of time, to 'work it through'. Though Wheeler does not mention 'A Lover's Complaint', the Sonnets' companion-poem which internal dating tests place in the early 1600s, it supports his hypothesis of Shakespeare's returning to old preoccupations at this time by portraying yet another lovely, faithless young man who is idolatrously loved by the one he betrays.[1] Moving from the

---

[1] Roger Warren spells out the links in detail in 'A Lover's Complaint, All's Well, and the Sonnets', *N&Q*, 215 (1970), 130–2; grounds for attributing the poem to Shakespeare in his maturity are carefully set forth by MacDonald P. Jackson, *Shakespeare's 'A Lover's Complaint': Its Date and Authenticity* (Auck-

lyric genre, with its single perspective of the still-adoring speaker, to the multi-perspective mode of drama in *All's Well* enables Shakespeare to put his conflicting feelings into play through separate figures. He can give vent, in the harsh criticism of Bertram by both the elder authority figures (including his own mother) and his own contemporaries (the French lords), to the resentment that the speaker of the Sonnets must keep stifled, and still preserve his devotion unsullied in Helen's adoration. The almost universal praise of Helen that balances the equally widespread condemnation of Bertram serves to repair the lover's self-esteem, so damaged by his social and emotional disadvantage in this relationship. 'Much of the power of *All's Well* derives from the release in its dramatic action of trends precariously held in check in the *Sonnets* by the idealizing love for the friend' (p. 65).

Approaching the play through the poems thus suggests a basis for its peculiar emotional intensity and for the intractable baseness of its hero that makes the happy ending feel not inherent but imposed by fiat. The dramatic machinery may creak here precisely because the material is not entirely under the dramatist's conscious control. Paroles, the despicable toady who nevertheless attracts with his verbal energy, may also be shaped by this same construction, a projection of the self-contempt that sometimes unsettles the sense of his own worth as devoted lover in Shakespeare's sonnet-speaking 'I'. As the loser in the contest for his 'sweet heart' Bertram, Paroles stands in the speaker's place in the love triangle of

land, 1965). Apart from the situation of the Sonnets, but offering further reason to connect the volume of poems with *All's Well*, is the resonance between 'Complaint' 148–329 and Bertram's seduction of Diana in *All's Well* 4.2, which Wilson Knight noted without elaboration (*Sovereign Flower*, p. 157). His passing observation can be fleshed out with several parallels of detail: seduction likened to duelling through talk of 'distance' ('Complaint' 148–54, *All's Well* 5.3.212); the seduced woman imaged as a plant stripped of the flower and left with only the stalk (ll. 146–7, 4.2.18–20); precedents of the ruin of other women as insufficient to deter the current prey of seduction (ll. 155–6, 3.5.20–5); vows offered as honest and never given wholeheartedly to anyone before (ll. 179–82, 4.2.14–17), which are in fact brokers to negotiate seduction (l. 173, 3.5.69–72; 4.2.70–1); and possession of the seduced maiden imaged in terms of the hunt—'amorous spoil', in a context of bleeding (ll. 153–4, 4.3.16).

the Sonnets, and as a low-born man trying to curry favour with fine words and a gallant show, he parodies the situation of his creator as playwright and actor.[1] The uniqueness of Helen, so driven and intense in comparison with earlier comic heroines, becomes understandable if she is carrying the additional weight of Shakespeare's own powerful and troubled feelings. If she is kept apart from the general condemnation of Bertram, she nevertheless enacts in her alternation between despairing passivity and energetic, cunning pursuit the ambivalences of the sonnet-speaker: caught between protest and prostration, abject in love but self-assertive in poetic creation.[2]

The critics who relate the Sonnets to *All's Well* have little to say about the male Shakespeare's investing a woman with his own urges and conflicts, but it is easy to imagine that the aggressive, unorthodox heroine that resulted may have caused some concern to the dramatist himself. Since mapping his relationship with the young man on to a heterosexual romantic action must result—with or without any intention to upset the gender system—in a revolutionary heroine who appropriates male prerogatives of desire and sexual initiative, the compensatory impulse that I have posited in Helen's episodes of shame and withdrawal may speculatively be attributed to Shakespeare as well as (or rather than) his heroine. If Fredson Bowers is correct in his hypotheses of revision based on variant speech prefixes and misplaced stage directions (see below, 'The Text and its Evolution'), at least one of these episodes was an authorial second thought: Helen's speech in the husband-choosing scene apologising for putting herself forward in this unmaidenly way, along with some reassuring validations of her conduct from the royal wards and the King (2.3.64–74).

[1] Wheeler is anticipated up to a point by G. P. Krapp, who characterized Paroles as 'like a French novel, vicious but tolerated for its style', and as parallel to Shakespeare in attempting to use his skill with words for social advancement: 'Parolles', in *Shakespearean Studies*, ed. Brander Matthews and Ashley H. Thorndyke (New York, 1916), pp. 294–5.
[2] Wheeler, pp. 57–75; see also Zitner, p. 110.

Anatomy of Desire: (II) All's (?) Well (?) that Ends (?) Well (?)

The title of *All's Well that Ends Well* makes an apparently straightforward statement. With this directive, it seems that the plays should be easy to interpret: the title proverb shows how to view the action and directs us to look especially at the ending for its significance. But what does the proverb mean? Helen first advances it, with the emphasis of a scene-concluding couplet, trying to hearten Diana and the Widow for the arduous journey to Marseilles and the embarrassment of Diana's appeal to the King by telling them to keep their eye on the final happy result: 'All's well that ends well; still the fine's the crown. | Whate'er the course, the end is the renown' (4.4.35–6). When they miss the King at Marseilles, she repeats it in the same hopeful spirit, rallying them for further effort: 'All's well that ends well yet, | Though time seem so adverse, and means unfit' (5.1.25–6). The primary meaning seems to be the same, something like 'As long as our efforts end in success, it will be worth all we have had to endure.' But the proverb can also carry a message more Machiavellian, that the desirable end justifies the questionable means used to achieve it.[1] In fact, the play's title in its dual possibility replicates the schizophrenia of critical reaction to *All's Well*: should the emphasis fall on the persevering, loving wife winning her husband in a conclusion that redeems all suffering, or on the dubious methods she used to achieve her desire? And, if we opt for the second of these, do we take the maxim at face value (Leggatt thinks Shakespeare is attempting through the familiar saying to defuse uneasiness about the bed-trick), or do the repetitions and variations—there are two more in the last scene, offered with increasing tentativeness by the King—serve to raise a question rather than forestall it?

It is not clear, then, how we should interpret the title summation as a whole. Beyond that, each term in it is problematic in its own right. *All*: how can one ending, no matter

---

[1] The parallel proverb also cited by Helen ('still the fine's the crown': Tilley E116, the end crowns, or tries, or proves, all) is open to the same ambiguity: everything about the process, including its moral rightness or wrongness, is to be judged by the presumably good outcome.

how elaborate, resolve both the fairy-tale quest and the serious social issues that have complicated it—marriage crossing class barriers, marriage imposed by a guardian on an unwilling ward, the lack of compatibility between an excessively loving woman and a man too shallow to deserve that love or to requite it? 'The frog prince remains a frog until the end and the princess chooses to overlook his slimy skin.'[1] Even in the realm of the conventional tale, as Stephen Booth observes, *All's Well* starts too many hares to finish off in one kind of ending: a 'Patient Griselda' plot, a story of the virtuous child and the proud stepmother, a story of the prodigal misled by bad companions, a story of enforced marriage to a 'loathly lady', and a plot in which the young folks outwit the old folks, as well as the basic tale of the gifted young person who is rewarded by marriage to the King's own child. Having raised generic expectations that have to do with all of these, Shakespeare gives us 'a happy ending of a kind appropriate to any one of them but disconcertingly unsatisfying as a conclusion to the chimeralike play in which they coexist'.[2]

Well is not a straightforward term in *All's Well*. The Clown holds it up for examination in Act 1 Scene 3, turning the Countess's meaningless prompter, 'Well, sir', into an occasion for grievance: 'No, madam, 'tis not so well that I am poor' (l. 16). And even that significance is muddled by the qualification that follows, 'though many of the rich are damned'. It is not well (comfortable, appropriate) to be poor, but perhaps it *is* well in another sense, if it offers a better chance to escape damnation. The Clown's quibbling goes into high gear a few scenes later, when Helen's inquiry whether the Countess is 'well' elicits an elaborate double response (2.4.2–13). What is 'well' according to one system (the Countess is in health and good spirits) may not be 'well' according to another (she is not yet in Paradise, the real locus of well-being for any Christian). The maxim so insisted on in the latter part of the play perhaps needs to be interpreted from the perspect-

[1] Carolyn Asp, 'Subjectivity, Desire, and Female Friendship in *All's Well that Ends Well*', *Literature and Psychology*, 32 (1986), 48–63 ; p. 48.

[2] Booth, '*King Lear*,' '*Macbeth*,' *Indefinition, and Tragedy* (New Haven and London, 1983), p. 166n.

ive thus set up earlier, of competing systems: the plot can come out 'well' in an external way analogous to the possession of goods and health without resolving more complex issues of psyche and society. The last scene itself, which at once offers a complicated tying up of plot threads and withholds a true resolution, is also the site of more quibbling that recalls the Clown's scrutiny of 'well': Diana is a maid and not a maid, Paroles says Bertram loved her and loved her not. While these are resolvable, the technique keeps calling attention to clashing truth systems.

Ends is a problematic notion too, as several critics have noted.[1] Not only does the King seem about to begin the action all over again by proposing to reward Diana with the husband of her choice, but the whole conclusion is hedged with conditionals and deferrals. The King's affirmations grow tentative: 'All yet seems well, and if it end so meet, | The bitter past, more welcome is the sweet.' It is not unusual for Shakespeare to put off to a post-play future full explanations of events already familiar to the audience (some have criticized him for not doing just that at the end of *Romeo and Juliet*), but here he defers beyond the boundaries of the stage action what would seem to be the very foundations of any happy ending—full understanding and rapprochement between principals and full validation by authorities. Bertram's promise of love is notoriously conditional: 'If she, my liege, can make me know this clearly, | I'll love her dearly, ever, ever dearly.' Will a complete accounting really dispose him to cherish Helen, even in the mood of resignation and relief that some infer in him? Or does his clinging to the letter here match Helen's earlier when she shows that she has met each of his angry stipulations: 'here's your letter. . . . This is done.' Even the baby who is to meet one of those stipulations is not, as in the source story, there to offer visible confirmation of his

---

[1] For example Ian Donaldson, '*All's Well that Ends Well*, Shakespeare's Play of Endings', *EIC*, 27 (1977), 34–55; Thomas Cartelli, 'Shakespeare's "Rough Magic": Ending as Artifice in *All's Well that Ends Well*', *Centennial Review*, 27 (1983), 117–34; Neely, *Broken Nuptials*, pp. 58–104; Kastan, 'Limits of Comedy'. The following discussion draws on the insights of these articles as well as on my own essay, ' "The King's not here": Displacement and Deferral in *All's Well that Ends Well*', *SQ*, 43 (1992), 20–32.

parentage. This child, who should represent dramatically the joined future of Helen and Bertram, is promised rather than fully present.

I have written elsewhere of *All's Well*'s pronounced rhythm of displacement and deferral. In its inability to arrive at closure and complete presence—an inability that may derive from the fusion of its action with the playwright's own unresolved love experience—the play enacts the Lacanian notion of desire, a fundamental lack co-engendered with self-hood that can never be filled. We may also find in this ending that does not end, or end well, a deflation of the 'happily ever after' conventions of romance: the final ironies definitively cut off the marriage of Helen and Bertram from idealization and refound it on disillusioned reality, like the new situation of the exposed Paroles. It is tempting as well to see a meta-theatrical dimension here: the divergence between the neat formula-title *All's Well that Ends Well* and the play's actual wayward characters and tentative, flawed conclusion is for some critics so striking as to thematize the inadequacy of comedy as a genre—or of art itself—to make sense of life's messiness. As at the end of *Measure for Measure*, the stubborn persistence of human needs and limitations, the unaddressed ethical problems posed by high-handed intervention resist the superficial dispositions achieved by intrigue. But whatever our final evaluation, the best way of approaching this play is not to patch over its clashes of tone and mode with ingenious or defensive explanations, but to take those very dislocations and deferrals as the point of entry.

The Text and its Evolution

The First Folio of 1623 provides the only authoritative text of *All's Well that Ends Well*. According to Hinman's analysis, the text was set by Compositor B except for the first formes, V3–V4^v, set by Compositors A and C. Using more refined criteria (arrangement of turned-over verse lines and treatment of contractions with *'ll* and *th'*), Howard-Hill assigned V3^v and V3 (almost all of Act 1 Scene 3 and the opening few lines of Act 2 Scene 1) to D rather than A. D's characteristic errors are misreadings, with occasional omission of a line or phrase;

those of B and C are more likely to derive from faulty memory.[1]

The copy from which they worked seems to have offered ample opportunity for both. Features that mark 'foul papers' survive abundantly in the printed text: varying forms for speech prefixes (see Appendix C), casual and permissive entry directions (*Enter 3 or 4 Lords* at 2.3.52.1, *Enter one of the Frenchmen, with fiue or sixe other souldiers* at 4.1.0.1), divergences between these and subsequent speech prefixes (the *Messenger* specified by the entrance direction at 4.3.74.1 is *Ser.* in the ensuing speech prefix, the entry allowing either three or four lords prefaces dialogue that requires four), entries directed for ghost characters or characters who have no function in the scene (*Violenta* in Act 3 Scene 5, perhaps *the two French Lords* in Act 5 Scene 3), entries duplicated for the same character (Paroles at 5.3.157, and then, correctly, at 5.3.230.1), omitted exits, commentary in stage directions that suggests the author's hand (*She addresses her to a Lord*; *Parolles and Lafew stay behind, commenting of this wedding*).

Greg considers the proposal that 'the foul papers had been transcribed by a rather incompetent literary scribe'—necessarily literary because 'anyone connected with the theatre must have done more to tidy them up'. The main support for this hypothesized transcription is the lack in the Folio text of spellings accepted as typically Shakespearian.[2] But Taylor points out that a handful of these do survive—*on* for one (2.5.29), *in* for e'en (3.2.18), *ton tooth* for t'one to th' (1.3.177), *Angles* for angels (3.2.126),[3] and Bowers observes that the smoothing out of eccentric spellings is to be expected from compositors working with a manuscript some twenty years old.[4] Some of the other features thought by Greg to

[1] Charlton Hinman, *The Printing and Proof-Reading of the First Folio of Shakespeare*, 2 vols. (Oxford, 1963), ii. 457–70, 480–2; Trevor Howard-Hill, 'The Compositors of Shakespeare's Folio Comedies', *SB*, 26 (1973), 61–106; John O'Connor, 'A Qualitative Analysis of Compositors C and D in the Shakespeare First Folio', *SB*, 30 (1977), 57–74; Alice Walker, *Textual Problems of the First Folio* (Cambridge, 1953).

[2] Greg, *The Shakespeare First Folio: Its Bibliographical and Textual History* (Oxford, 1955), p. 353.

[3] *Textual Companion*, p. 492.

[4] Bowers, 'Foul Papers, Compositor B, and the Speech-Prefixes of *All's Well that Ends Well*', *SB*, 32 (1979), p. 81n.

indicate the transcriber actually altering, and 'botching,' the original Shakespearian manuscript are better understood as traces of the author's own revising hand (see below).

Two sorts of minor later addition are likely, however. The division into five acts, highly untypical of foul papers and of pre-Blackfriars plays in general, was presumably done by the company in anticipation of a revival or of the Folio printing itself. Perhaps the first is more likely in view of the other presumable late additions, two calls in the stage directions (1.2.0.1 and 2.1.0.1) for cornetts. So unusual was this instrument in the pre-1609 public theatre that its prescription in *All's Well* was probably added after 1609 in preparation for a revival. Taylor conjectures that the original prompt book of *All's Well* was lost and that before a new one was made 'the foul papers were read and sporadically annotated by the book-keeper (as happened to Fletcher's *The Mad Lover*)'.[1] Stanley Wells notes that the music cues—besides the two directions for cornetts, additional 'Flourish' notations marking exits by the King in 1.2 and 2.1 and his entrance in 5.3, as well as entrances by the Duke of Florence in 3.1 and 3.3, and his exit in 3.1, a 'tucket' direction in 3.5, and a cue in the spoken text of 5.2 for trumpets—are more numerous than one would expect in a foul-papers text, another possible indication of later annotation.

From the evidence of misassigned speeches and speech-prefixes repeated within the same speech, or shifting into alternative forms from one speech to another, it can be deduced that the manuscript from which *All's Well* was printed contained marginal additions or alterations that would further complicate the compositors' work. This process has been most extensively explored and documented by Bowers, to whose work the following analysis is heavily indebted.[2] In Act 1 Scene 3, the repeated speech prefix for the Countess at Helen's entrance along with the change in form for that prefix from *Cou.* to *Old Cou.* or *Ol. Cou.* through the next sixty lines or so can best be explained by the theory that Shakespeare

---

[1] *Textual Companion*, p. 492.

[2] Bowers, 'Speech-Prefixes', and 'Shakespeare at Work: The Foul Papers of *All's Well that Ends Well*', in *English Renaissance Studies Presented to Dame Helen Gardner*, ed. John Carey (Oxford, 1980), pp. 56–73.

added these lines (the Countess's musing on her own youthful passion and the dialogue with Helen on the daughter–mother relation) some time after first composing the scene, marked the opening line of the insert to show who was speaking, and used a different designation for the Countess from the one used throughout the first form of the scene.

As Bowers observes, it is unlikely that the original scene began with the abrupt question 'Do you love my son?' which is the first of her speeches after Helen's entrance which is once again headed *Cou.* Presumably some of the lines first written were crossed out when the new sixty lines were added. Another discrepancy, the stage direction in the husband-choosing scene *She addresses her to a Lord* (2.3.63.1), placed some twelve lines before Helen in fact turns from general address to the group to an encounter with a single lord, points, in contrast, to simple expansion. It would not be out of character for Helen to make a false start at her business, an embarrassingly public marriage proposal that reverses conventional gender roles, and then to retreat into general discourse for a while before trying again. But if Bowers is right in speculating that the intervening lines 64–77a were a marginal addition (which B then set after rather than before the stage direction), it is interesting that Shakespeare's second thoughts included the need for more maidenly modesty in his heroine: the speech in question first gives the credit for the King's cure to God, then proclaims her own humble estate, and tries to withdraw from the whole selection ritual, seen as immodest in itself and threatening even worse consequences if she is refused. Perhaps Shakespeare himself, anticipating the later critics and stage adapters, had occasional qualms about the unconventional heroine he had created.

Also probably misplaced is Lafeu's question 'How understand we that?' (1.1.60; discussed in Appendix A), which should more logically respond to the riddling speech of Helen (line 54) or that of the Countess (lines 57–8) than to what it actually follows, Bertram's simple request for his mother's blessing. The error of placement, hard to understand if Compositor B was working from a clean manuscript, makes sense if Lafeu's question was added in the margin and B mistook its proper position. Of course, it is not inconceivable that Lafeu *is* responding to Bertram, not to his wish for parental blessings but to his rudeness in interrupting the conversation to speed his own departure. No such justifications of the text as it stands are possible in another passage in Act 4 Scene 3, where two short speeches are given to what are clearly the wrong speakers. The first, 'Hush, hush', B tags on to Bertram's 'A plague upon him, muffled! He can say nothing of me', but it belongs, not with Bertram's self-centred unease but with the following warning of First Lord, infused with game-playing spirit: 'Hoodman comes' (ll. 119–20). A few lines later, 'All's one to him' is hitched on to the end of a panicky vow by Paroles, when it is in fact a comment on his behaviour and must belong with Bertram's disgusted judgement that follows (ll. 140–1). The likeliest cause of these misplacements is again that the phrases were later insertions in the manuscript, written between the lines or on the side, causing B to misunderstand their relation to the context.

To these traces of revision and addition we may add other textual indications of authorial second thoughts, one of which is the apparent renaming of the Widow's daughter. Her first scene, Act 3 Scene 5, has the entrance direction *Enter old Widdow of Florence, her daughter, Violenta and Mariana*. The scene offers no lines for Violenta, and lines 93–5 suggest that only the Widow, her daughter Diana, and Mariana are present in addition to Helen. Violenta may be a vestigial first idea, a figure for whom Shakespeare found no use when actually writing the dialogue but whom he forgot to revise out completely. On the other hand, while naming this extra figure the entrance direction does *not* name Diana, although she is the focus of the scene that follows and takes an active part in the dialogue, with speeches headed *Diana*, *Dia.*, or *Dian*. Taken together, these facts suggest that we should ignore the comma after *daughter* in the stage direction,[1] that *Violenta* is not a rejected first thought for a separate character but a rejected first idea for the name of the character who came to be called Diana, which Shakespeare forgot to alter when he changed the speech prefixes. The dialogue of the scene does not name the daughter but certainly suggests that even on

[1] As we do in the 2.1 entrance direction, which lists Bertram as *Count, Rosse* (Bowers, 'Foul Papers', p. 65n).

first writing he was thinking of this character primarily as 'maid': the frequency of 'maid,' or 'maidenhood', or 'virgin' in this first introduction (lines 12, 20, 23, 67, 72, 93, 96) suggests what is most important about her and her situation. Abandoning 'Violenta' to ally the daughter more firmly with maidenhood by rechristening her after the 'queen of virgins' (1.3.114) seems a natural progression. There is support for this hypothesized rethinking process in her next scene (Act 4 Scene 2), with its oddly emphatic entrance direction *Enter Bertram and the Maide called Diana* and the additional emphasis on her name in the opening exchange:

> *Ber.* They told me that your name was *Fontybell.*
> *Dia.* No my good Lord, *Diana.*

The heroine's own name did some evolving of its own: she is *Helena* only once in the dialogue, in the opening scene, and only three times in stage directions, all in the first two acts. All other references in dialogue and stage directions are to *Hellen* or *Helen*; indeed, that form is probably present from the beginning as an alternative, if we take it that the speech prefix *Hell.*, in Act 1 Scene 1 and later scenes, abbreviates only the shorter form of the name. In any case, the emergence of Diana from Violenta and the less dramatic but significant shift from Helena to Helen together bring out some mythic resonances of the action in the interplay of the principles represented by Venus, patroness of Helen of Troy, and her traditional opposite Diana.[1]

Signs of evolution of a more local sort appear elsewhere. *Enter a Messenger* at 4.3.74.1 heralds Bertram's own servant, designated as such subsequently in the speech prefix *Ser.*, who in response to a question tells what his master has been doing but bears no message. As Bowers says, 'inadvertence in a change of plan not corrected appears to be as good an explanation as possible revision, although revision can certainly not be ruled out'.[2] The entrance of Paroles with the

---

[1] 'Violenta' does not work well in this opposition: it suggests the passion associated with Venus and Helen rather than its self-contained opposite. For working out of the Venus–Diana substructure, see my article 'Naming Names in *All's Well that Ends Well*' (see p. 8 n. 1).

[2] 'Foul Papers', p. 65. If the 'messenger' label is a trace of an earlier plan, it is tempting to speculate that before revision the script called for a messenger

Widow and Diana at 5.3.157, inappropriate for the scene as we have it, may also be a vestigial trace of an earlier plan, abandoned when Shakespeare returned to his writing (Bowers speculates on the basis of changed speech prefixes for both Bertram and the Countess in this part of the scene that the time lapse was considerable). Perhaps we should include with these possible second thoughts Act 3 Scene 3, where the entrance direction calls for Paroles, but out of the usual sequence: *Flourish. Enter the Duke of Florence, Rossillion, drum and trumpets, soldiers, Parrolles.* If the tacking on of Paroles after the general directions rather than among the named individuals does not represent Compositor B rectifying a memory slip, it may indicate an addition by the author some time after writing the original entrance direction; if so, the second thought that Paroles might be useful in this scene was abandoned in its turn, since he has no lines or action in the brief encounter between Bertram and the Duke.

A knottier textual problem arising from the use of authorial working papers for printers' copy is presented by the two French lords, who appear in seven scenes. In Act 1 Scene 2, the entrance direction presumably includes them among the *diuers Attendants* following the King, and their speech prefixes designate them as 1. *Lo.G.* and 2. *Lo.E.*;[1] in Act 2 Scene 1 they are among the *diuers yong Lords, taking leaue for the Florentine warre* and their prefixes are mainly 1. *Lo.G.* and 2. *Lo.E.* (occasionally without the numeral); in Act 3 Scene 1 they enter with the Duke of Florence as *the two Frenchmen*, with speech prefixes *French G.* (1.*Lord.*) and *French E.*; in Act 3 Scene 2, at Roussillon, they enter with Helen as *two Gentlemen*, and their prefixes are *Fren.G.* (1.*G.*) and *Fren.E.*; in Act 3 Scene 6 the entrance direction is *Enter Count Rossillion and the Frenchmen, as at first*, and their speeches are headed *Cap.E.* and *Cap.G.*; 4.1.0 calls permissively for the entrance of *one of the Frenchmen*, but the prefixes identify him specifically first as 1.*Lord E.* and then as *Lor.E.*; the Act 4

---

to arrive with news of Helen's pilgrimage and death. This way of supplying information is less awkward and more plausible than First Lord's unexplained knowledge of Helen's affairs (ll. 47–53, 55–9), though time problems remain.

[1] I have not included non-substantive variants in this and other scenes; for a complete list, see Appendix C.

Scene 3 entrance direction is *the two French Captaines*, and their prefixes are *Cap.G.* and *Cap.E.*; the entrance direction for Act 5 Scene 3 designates them for the first and only time as modern editors usually do throughout, *the two French Lords*, but they have no lines in this final scene.

Even for a text set from foul papers, this is a bewildering array of character designations. One problem is partly evident just in the listing. Can these labels all refer to the same pair of characters? How can the 'gentlemen' of Act 3 Scene 2, called so not only in stage directions and speech prefixes but three times in dialogue by the Countess, be the same as the 'lords' of the French court scenes? And even at court, there is some discrepancy between the young lords of Act 2 Scene 1, eager for military adventure and treating Bertram as a contemporary whose wishes will naturally be the same, and the apparently older pair of Act 1 Scene 2, who seem much in the King's confidence and privy to state affairs, who see the advantage of war as a 'nursery' where the young may gain some seasoning and discipline, and who introduce Bertram as 'Young'. What leads editors to treat these somewhat disparate pairs as one is their linkage through the initials G and E, repeated in their speech prefixes; but what do these letters mean, and how did they get into the text? Furthermore, there is some confusion of line distribution *between* the two Frenchmen in the sequence 3.6–4.3. In Act 3 Scene 6, they both promote to Bertram a scheme to expose Paroles, with E taking the lead in planning the false ambush and capture; E later has an apparent exit line, 'I must go looke my twigges, | He shall be caught', but the response is an obscurely directed line by Bertram followed by what sounds even more like an exit line from G:

> *Ber.* Your brother he shall go along with me.
> *Cap.G.* As't please your Lordship, Ile leaue you.

Bertram and E then remain on stage to talk of Diana and plan a visit to her. In Act 4 Scene 1, then, the one of the Frenchmen who is presumably free to direct Paroles' ambush and capture ought to be G, but the speech prefixes designate E (who, to compound the confusion, is initially also called 1. *Lord*, although earlier numerical prefixes had given that number to G). In Act 4 Scene 3, however, it is E who tells G about Bertram's activities with Diana, including the bartering of his family ring and the rendezvous he is keeping that very night. While this seems to restore E as the one who accompanied Bertram rather than the leader of the ambush, it is E who tells Bertram what has been happening to Paroles in captivity; but in yet another shift, after Paroles' entrance it is G who plays the part of the enemy general that E assumed in the capture scene (Act 4 Scene 1).

W. T. Hastings thought that the G and E initials were a later, non-Shakespearian addition that has obscured Shakespeare's intention of not one but three sets of characters: the counsellor–lords of Act 1 Scene 2, the gentlemen who bring Bertram's letter in Act 3 Scene 2, and the young lords Dumaine of the other five scenes.[1] One-appearance characters are not untypical of Shakespeare, though they tend to be single rather than paired; more importantly, they usually have an immediate function, comic, historical, allegorical, choric, or whatever, that is best served by a figure who is not part of the ongoing dramatic situation. But it is difficult to make such a case for either the mature lords or the gentlemen–messengers. When the latter do reveal a touch of personal feeling, it is sympathy for Helen and disapproval of Paroles—just the attitudes we are soon to see in the supposedly separate young French lords. In fact, there is considerable continuity between the supposedly distinct pairs. In Act 1 Scene 2 they discuss the war as an arena for martial adventure, in Act 2 Scene 1 they depart to fight for Florence. In Act 3 Scene 1 they are in Florence, and G echoes E's earlier observation at the French court about the young French gentry's need for military exercise (E's claim not to know why the King of France has not backed the Duke's side is not evidence that he must be different from the lord in 1.2 who heard the King's reasons, since the dramatic occasion here dictates evasive speech). In Act 3 Scene 2 they have returned from Italy to the French court and are in Roussillon on their way back to the war, and as might be expected from our view

[1] 'Notes on *All's Well that Ends Well*', *Shakespeare Association Bulletin*, 10 (1935), 232–9. Capell earlier worked out the three different pairs (*Notes*, pp. 13–14).

of the three young men together in Act 2 Scene 1, they know Bertram's plans and bear his letter. (They have covered a good deal of ground since Act 3 Scene 1, but this is not the only point in the play where the time-logic will not bear close scrutiny.) From Act 3 Scene 6 onwards there are no disparities of character or circumstance to remark, though the assignment of lines and actions gives trouble. In any case, the assignment of all these parts to the same two actors which Hastings took to be the import of the added letters would in performance make it hard to keep these pairs distinct.

Nevertheless, the disparities Hastings expounded are real, especially the difference between 'gentlemen' in Act 3 Scene 2 and 'lords' elsewhere, which can hardly be attributed to carelessness. In formal labelling like this, 'lords' denotes superior status within the larger general category of the well-born ('gentlemen'); no one in Shakespeare's time would be likely to muddle such class distinctions. Since the source story in Painter mentions two knights who take Giletta's message to Bertram and bring back in response his impossible stipulations, Shakespeare may on first writing have simply been following his source without thought for connecting these characters to others. Presumably written very early, the second scene may also have been created before Shakespeare was clear on exactly which characters would be necessary for the play as a whole. My guess is that, at some point as the writing proceeded, Shakespeare reviewed the text with an eye to dramatic economy and found that these pairs of lesser characters could be amalgamated with the French lords. He may have done a little revising, to bring the messengers of Act 3 Scene 2 in line with the knowledge and attitudes of the young lords as they were developing later in Act 3 and in Act 4, but complete consistency was not a major concern. He did, however, have to show in the speech prefixes that these lords, gentlemen, Frenchmen, etc. were all the same two characters; and rather than regularize each one he took a short cut, marking their speeches with the initials G and E.

This hypothesis assumes that G and E indicate actors' names, as Capell conjectured,[1] but as a means of tying

---

[1] See previous note. Actors' lists for the period of *All's Well* are sparse, but Samuel Gilburne is named in the will of one of the King's Men, Augustine

together various speech prefixes into one continuing pair of characters rather than of indicating how separate roles were to be doubled. Speech prefixes that designate actors instead of characters appear a few times in Shakespearian texts thought to be derived from the author's working papers: 'Sincklo' in Q *2 Henry IV* 5.4, and at F *Shrew* Ind.1.86, 'Sinklo' and 'Humfrey' throughout *3 Henry VI* 3.1, 'Kemp' and 'Cowley' in *Much Ado* 4.2, 'Will Kemp' at Q2 *Romeo* 4.5.127.1. There is no example of actor designation throughout a script; but these other occurrences presumably represent the playwright thinking of a particular player in the act of creating the scene, while if I am right the G and E labels are more conscious and more functional, annotating scenes already composed so that whoever transcribes the manuscript into a prompt-book will understand that only two characters are involved. Working back through several scenes and intending mainly a guide for the transcriber of where to regularize speech prefixes would explain the other unique practice posited here, Shakespeare's use of initials rather than full names or shortened forms of them.

Editors in the past have tended to agree with Chambers and Hastings that the initials indeed indicate actors but are the book-keeper's designations rather than Shakespeare's.[1] Given the text as we have it, in which the initials are in several scenes the only way of differentiating the two characters, it is certainly unlikely, as Hunter says (p. xv), that Shakespeare should have left it to the book-keeper to sort out which speech to assign to which character. In fact, even if Shakespeare added the initials after some of the scenes had been written, as I am suggesting and as Hunter speculates briefly (pp. xv–xvi) without addressing this problem, it is hard to imagine that the members of these character-pairs were only occasionally differentiated. If my theory is to hold, one must suppose that in the process of adding G and E Shakespeare crossed

Phillips, in 1605, and by 1611 the company included William Ecclestone and Robert Gough (Chambers, ii. 212, 214, 216). Like 'Humfrey' in *3 Henry VI* 3.1 (noted below), the speech prefixes may refer to first names, but the lists we have offer no candidates.

[1] Chambers, *William Shakespeare*, i. 450; Hastings (see p. 60 n. 1) works out the idea more fully.

out the 1 and 2 which he had originally used to distinguish his lords, gentlemen, etc., but was not consistent in this process of deletion: the numerals are still there throughout Act 1 Scene 2 and a large part of Act 2 Scene 1, and there are single instances in the first and second scenes of Act 3 and Act 4 Scene 1. There is no evidence for these deletions, but quite a lot *against* the alternatives.

It is not possible to determine at what point Shakespeare coalesced his pairs into one. The peculiar entrance direction of Act 3 Scene 6 for *the Frenchmen, as at first* might indicate that these are the same two Frenchmen we first saw, that is, the courtiers of Act 1 Scene 2, the emphasis of the stage direction pointing, like '*the Maide called Diana*' in Act 4 Scene 2, to a recent change of plan. On the other hand, the direction may have intended the opposite effect of keeping the pairs distinct, noting that these are not the Frenchmen we have seen most recently, the gentlemen–messengers of Act 3 Scene 2, but those shown earlier (Act 2 Scene 1), urging Bertram to go with them to the wars. In any case, a subset of confusions begins at the end of this scene, where for the first time the two French lords do not operate as a pair but have separate functions. One is to accompany Bertram to Diana's, and the other is to set up the ambush of Paroles, but the general scheme is clearer than who does what. While both lords try to persuade Bertram of Paroles' baseness, E is the one who presents the ambush plan and when Bertram has agreed prepares to go off and carry it out; Bertram follows this departure-line with a command that 'your brother' shall accompany him; and, while this should select G for the Diana expedition, G then agrees and takes leave, while E remains to hear Bertram's confidences. Since Act 4 Scene 1 calls for E as leader of the ambush, most editors alter the speech prefixes at the end of Act 3 Scene 6 so that it is E who exits after agreeing with Bertram's request for his brother's companionship and G who stays to talk with Bertram. But when the lords meet again in Act 4 Scene 3, it is E who is in Bertram's confidence and knows about his affair with Diana, and after the entrance of Paroles it is G who carries on from Act 4 Scene 1 the part of the enemy 'general'. This suggests that perhaps we ought to read the end of Act 3 Scene 6 a different way rather than reassigning the speeches. Bertram outranks the lords both as a peer and as a cavalry general, and it would be quite in keeping with his peremptory way with inferiors to insist that E change his own plans to suit Bertram's wishes. That both lords should defer to him is also consistent with their usual behaviour: their censure of Bertram is expressed to each other and indirectly through the exposure of his favourite Paroles, but they do not cross or criticize him directly. It is unnecessary to switch the speeches between G and E throughout the scene to put G in charge of the Paroles plot from the beginning; he has been pressing it just as enthusiastically as E and can easily be supposed to step in as leader. It is the speech prefixes placing E at the ambush of Act 4 Scene 1 that call for emendation. The entrance direction for *one of the Frenchmen* suggests that Shakespeare had lost track of which lord was to do what, a confusion that would be all the more understandable if he had set it up in Act 3 Scene 6 for one and then transferred it to the other.[1] It is unlikely that it mattered much to him which lord enacted which function. The prefix 1. *Lord* for the first speech correctly puts G in the scene, but when Shakespeare added the defining initial—whether when first writing or when later annotating—he forgot that it was G that was always marked 1 and marked the speeches E. Some have suspected the same confusion after Bertram's entrance in Act 4 Scene 3, when E is the one who tells Bertram of Paroles' behaviour in captivity; but this prominence balances that assumed by G in the interrogation that follows, and E has had ample time to observe the captive Paroles while Bertram was keeping his assignation with Diana.

This explanation of the various and occasionally contradictory operations of G and E in the text is only a hypothesis, but whether one accepts this theory or goes the opposite way, altering prefixes to leave G as Bertram's companion and E in charge of the Paroles plot, the rationalizations in either case assume some kind of rethinking and revising on Shakespeare's part. The evidence of the French lords, albeit unclear in detail,

---

[1] Bowers speculates that Shakespeare originally had G go with Bertram 'but at some point recognized his mistake and clumsily repaired the error': 'Foul Papers', p. 70.

thus supports the impression that the *All's Well* manuscript had been considerably worked over after the first writing.[1] So does the occasional stretching of text, by generous spacing or by printing prose as verse, that fills out some Folio pages, the compositors making up for miscalculations of length that were probably caused by written-over copy (see Appendix D).

[1] It is tempting to ascribe other textual peculiarities to disruptions caused by alterations and marginal additions: the repeated speech prefixes *Lady* in the middle of an uninterrupted speech by the Countess at 2.2.40 and *Clo*[*wn*] in the same position at 2.4.36. Could the celebrated crux at 4.2.38–9 have resulted from Compositor B's misreading a line that was written in over the original, another second thought? Unfortunately, such a theory helps not at all in emending.

9–12. From Geoffrey Whitney, *A Choice of Emblems* (Leyden, 1586). 9. 'Since I nor wax nor honey can bring home ...' (1.2.65–7): bees returning to the hive, with verses celebrating their commonwealth ruled by the 'maister bee', fo. b4ᵛ.

10. 'this cap'cious and intenible sieve ...' (1.3.202–4): sieve, with verses on the Danaïds, fo. B2ᵛ.

11. 'will you eat / No grapes, my royal fox?' (2.1.67–8): the fox and the grapes, fo. N1ᵛ.

12. 'Let's take the instant by the forward top' (5.3.39): Occasion bald at the back with hair only in front, fo. Z3.

EDITORIAL PROCEDURES

THIS text of *All's Well that Ends Well* is based on the 1623 Folio and modernized according to the principles set forth by Stanley Wells in *Modernizing Shakespeare's Spelling* (Oxford, 1979), and by Gary Taylor in his edition of *Henry V* (Oxford, 1982). In particular, the spelling of French personal and place names has been normalized: *Roussillon, Paroles, Gérard de Narbonne, Marseilles* (this last still allows for the three syllables indicated in the Folio spellings *Marcellus* and *Marcellae*). Speech prefixes have been silently normalized from several variants: for example the headings *Countess, Mother,* and *Lady* all appear as *Countess,* and a considerable range of designations centring on '1' and '2', *G* and *E*, are reduced to *First Lord* and *Second Lord*. Only significant reassignments from one character to another are included in the collations. Appendix C gives a complete listing of variations in speech prefixes; their implications are discussed in Appendix C and in the Text section of the Introduction.

The list of Persons of the Play is an editorial addition, as are all *aside* and *to* stage directions. Scene divisions, also absent in the Folio text, have been added: these are traditional and uncontroversial. Stage directions in this apparently foul-papers text are often incomplete as well as ambiguous and discursive. Additional directions supplementing these are not marked in the text if they are clearly indicated by the dialogue. Where action or agency is debatable, the added full or partial stage direction is enclosed in half-brackets. Occasional italicizations for emphasis in the dialogue are editorial.

Collations record verbal departures from the Folio text. Typographical errors with no possibility of alternative readings are silently corrected, as are non-debatable expansions of contractions. Earlier editors' 'emendations' that are now recognized as simple modernizations or variant spellings are also not recorded. In citing variant and rejected readings in the collations, I have regularized ligatures, digraphs, and long *s* without comment, unless the original typography is relevant to emendation. Changes in punctuation are recorded in the collations only when the sense is at issue. Speech-prefix variations for single characters are pooled in Appendix C; the collations record rejected readings only for significant reassignments. Alternations in lineation do not appear separately in the collations but are grouped together in Appendix D; these variations are discussed in the commentary when they bear on meaning or circumstances of printing. The name after the lemma identifies the edition where that reading first appeared; a name in parentheses indicates an earlier scholar who first suggested the reading. Emendations which have not been adopted in this text but which deserve serious consideration are also collated; these are usually discussed in the commentary.

Commentary on the text is primarily interpretative, though it occasionally includes observations on productions (which may, of course, expand interpretation) and attention to textual questions. I have tried to respond to Shakespeare's rich indeterminacy by opening up possibilities rather than closing them down, ruling out all but a single definition. Analogues and contexts for the language and references of *All's Well* are provided by general cultural sources, such as proverbs, emblem collections, the Bible and church liturgy, as well as Shakespeare's other works and those of contemporary writers, mainly dramatists and poets.

Shakespeare is cited from *William Shakespeare: The Complete Works*, gen. eds. Stanley Wells and Gary Taylor. For ease of reference, citations of the disintegrated scenes they place among 'Additional Passages' are followed by act, scene, and line references keyed to the 1951 Alexander *Complete Works*. Contemporary dramatists are cited from Revels editions, where they exist for the play in question; exceptions are Jonson, quoted from *The Complete Plays of Ben Jonson*, ed. G. A. Wilkes, based on the Herford and Simpson edition, 4 vols. (Oxford, 1981–2); Massinger, from *The Plays and Poems of Philip Massinger*, ed. Philip Edwards and Colin Gibson, 5 vols. (Oxford, 1976); Middleton, from *The Works of Thomas Middleton*, ed. A. H. Bullen, 8 vols. (1885–6). The source for Biblical quotations and references is the Bishops' Bible (1568). When quoting early printed books, except in the case of Spenser, in the commentary and the Introduction, I have modernized the spelling.

Editions of *All's Well* and other works appearing more than once in the critical apparatus are cited by name of editor or author; full publication material appears in the 'Abbreviations and References' section which follows.

Abbreviations and References

Place of publication is London unless otherwise noted. Titles of early texts are given in modern spelling. Seventeenth-century editions of Shakespeare are listed in chronological order; editions after the first four folios are listed in alphabetical order.

EDITIONS OF SHAKESPEARE

F, F1	The First Folio, 1623
F2	The Second Folio, 1632
F3	The Third Folio, 1663
F4	The Fourth Folio, 1685
Alexander	Peter Alexander, *Complete Works* (1951)
Barish	Jonas Barish, *All's Well that Ends Well*, The Pelican Shakespeare (Baltimore, 1964)
Bevington	David Bevington, *Complete Works* (Glenview, Ill., 1980)
Boswell	James Boswell, *Plays and Poems*, 21 vols. (1821)
Brigstocke	W. O. Brigstocke, *All's Well that Ends Well*, Arden Shakespeare (1904)
Cambridge	W. G. Clark and W. A. Wright, *Works*, The Cambridge Shakespeare, 9 vols. (Cambridge, 1863–6)
Capell	Edward Capell, *Comedies, Histories, and Tragedies*, 10 vols. (1767–8)
Case	Arthur E. Case, *All's Well that Ends Well*, The Yale Shakespeare (New Haven and London, 1926)
Clarkes	Charles and Mary Cowden Clarke, *Plays*, 3 vols. (1864–8)
Collier	John Payne Collier, *Works*, 8 vols. (1842–4)

Collier 1858	John Payne Collier, *Comedies, Histories, Tragedies, and Poems*, 6 vols. (1858)
Craig	Hardin Craig, *Works* (Chicago, 1951)
Delius	Nicolaus Delius, *Shakespeares Werke*, 2 vols. (Elberfeld, 1854)
Delius 1872	Nicolaus Delius, *Werke*, 2 vols. (Elberfeld, 1872)
Dyce	Alexander Dyce, *Works*, 6 vols. (1857)
Dyce 1864	Alexander Dyce, *Works*, 9 vols. (1864–7)
Everett	Barbara Everett, *All's Well that Ends Well*, New Penguin Shakespeare (Harmondsworth, 1970)
Fraser	Russell Fraser, *All's Well that Ends Well*, New Cambridge Shakespeare (Cambridge, 1985)
Gentleman	Francis Gentleman, *All's Well that Ends Well*, adaptation ascribed to David Garrick (1774)
Globe	W. G. Clark and W. A. Wright, *Works*, Globe edition (Cambridge, 1864)
Grant White	Richard Grant White, *Works*, 12 vols. (Boston, 1857–66)
Halliwell	James O. Halliwell[-Phillipps], *Works*, 16 vols. (1853–65)
Hanmer	Thomas Hanmer, *Works*, 6 vols. (Oxford, 1743–4)
Harrison	G. B. Harrison, *All's Well that Ends Well*, Penguin Shakespeare (Harmondsworth, 1955)
Hunter	G. K. Hunter, *All's Well that Ends Well*, new Arden Shakespeare (1959)
Johnson	Samuel Johnson, *Plays*, 8 vols. (1765)
Keightley	Thomas Keightley, *Plays*, 6 vols. (1864)
Kemble	J. P. Kemble, ed. and adapt., *All's Well that Ends Well* (1793)
Kittredge	George Lyman Kittredge, *Complete Works* (Boston, 1936)
Knight	Charles Knight, *Works*, Pictorial Edition, 8 vols. (1838–43)
Malone	Edmond Malone, *Plays and Poems*, 10 vols. (1790)
Neilson	W. A. Neilson, *Works*, Cambridge edition (Boston, 1906)
Neilson–Hill	W. A. Neilson and Charles J. Hill, *Plays and Poems* (Cambridge, Mass, 1942)

Oxford	Stanley Wells and Gary Taylor (general editors), *The Complete Works* (Oxford, 1986)
Pope	Alexander Pope, *Works*, 6 vols. (1723–5)
Rann	Joseph Rann, *Dramatic Works*, 6 vols. (Oxford, 1786–94)
Reed	Samuel Johnson, George Steevens, and Isaac Reed, *Plays*, 15 vols. (1785)
Riverside	G. Blakemore Evans (textual editor), *The Riverside Shakespeare* (Boston, 1974)
Rolfe	William J. Rolfe, *All's Well that Ends Well* (New York, 1890)
Rowe	Nicholas Rowe, *Works*, 6 vols. (1709)
Rowe 1714	Nicholas Rowe, *Works*, 8 vols. (1714)
Schlegel–Tieck	A. W. von Schlegel and Ludwig Tieck, *Dramatische Werke*, 9 vols. (Berlin, 1825–33)
Singer	Samuel W. Singer, *Dramatic Works*, 10 vols. (Chiswick, 1826)
Singer 1856	Samuel W. Singer, *Dramatic Works*, 10 vols. (1856)
Sisson	C. J. Sisson, *Complete Works* (1954)
Staunton	Howard Staunton, *Plays*, 3 vols. (1858–60)
Steevens	Samuel Johnson and George Steevens, *Plays*, 10 vols. (1773)
Steevens 1778	Samuel Johnson and George Steevens, *Plays*, 10 vols. (1778)
Steevens–Reed	George Steevens and Isaac Reed, *Plays*, 15 vols. (1793)
Theobald	Lewis Theobald, *Works*, 7 vols. (1733)
Theobald 1740	Lewis Theobald, *Works*, 8 vols. (1740)
Warburton	William Warburton, *Works*, 8 vols. (1747)
Wilson	Arthur Quiller-Couch and John Dover Wilson, *All's Well that Ends Well*, The New Shakespeare (Cambridge, 1929)

OTHER WORKS

Abbott	E. A. Abbott, *A Shakespearian Grammar*, second edition (1870)
Bowers, 'Foul Papers'	Fredson Bowers, 'Shakespeare at Work: The Foul Papers of *All's Well that Ends Well*', in *English*

	Renaissance Studies Presented to Dame Helen Gardner, ed. John Carey (Oxford, 1980), pp. 56–73
Bowers, 'Speech-Prefixes'	Fredson Bowers, 'Foul Papers, Compositor B, and the Speech-Prefixes of *All's Well that Ends Well*', *SB*, 32 (1979), 60–81
Brissenden	Alan Brissenden, *Shakespeare and the Dance* (Atlantic Highlands, NJ, 1981)
Brook	G. L. Brook, *The Language of Shakespeare* (1976)
Capell, *Notes*	Edward Capell, *Notes and Various Readings to Shakespeare*, Part I (1774)
Chambers	E. K. Chambers, *The Elizabethan Stage*, 4 vols. (Oxford, 1923)
Colman	E. A. M. Colman, *The Dramatic Use of Bawdy in Shakespeare* (1974)
Cotgrave	Randle Cotgrave, *A Dictionary of the French and English Tongues* (1611; facsimile, Columbia, S. Carolina, 1950)
Dent	R. W. Dent, *Shakespeare's Proverbial Language: An Index* (1981)
Dowden MS	Edward Dowden, MS notes in Brigstocke, Folger Library copy
EIC	*Essays in Criticism*
Farmer	Richard Farmer, *An Essay on the Learning of Shakespeare* (Cambridge, 1767)
Florio	John Florio, *Queen Anna's New World of Words, or Dictionary of . . . Italian and English* (1611)
JEGP	*Journal of English and Germanic Philology*
Malone, *Order*	Edmond Malone, *An Attempt to Ascertain the Order . . . [of] Shakspeare's Plays*, in Steevens 1778, vol. i
Mason	John Monck Mason, *Comments on the Last Edition of Shakespeare's Plays* (1785)
MLR	*Modern Language Review*
N & Q	*Notes and Queries*
Noble	Richmond Noble, *Shakespeare's Biblical Knowledge and Use of the Book of Common Prayer* (1935)
Onions	C. T. Onions, *A Shakespeare Glossary*, third edition, rev. Robert D. Eagleson (Oxford, 1986)
Partridge	Eric Partridge, *Shakespeare's Bawdy* (1948)

Perring	Philip Perring, *Hard Knots in Shakespeare*, second edition (1886)
Price	Joseph G. Price, *The Unfortunate Comedy: A Study of 'All's Well that Ends Well' and its Critics* (Toronto, 1968)
RES	*Review of English Studies*
Ritson	Joseph Ritson, *Remarks, Critical and Illustrative, on . . . the Last Edition of Shakespeare* (1783)
SB	*Studies in Bibliography*
Schmidt	Alexander Schmidt, *A Shakespeare Lexicon*, third edition, revised G. Sarrazin, 2 vols. (1902; reprinted Berlin 1962)
SQ	*Shakespeare Quarterly*
Stewart	Charles D. Stewart, *Some Textual Difficulties in Shakespeare* (New Haven, 1914)
Textual Companion	Stanley Wells and Gary Taylor with John Jowett and William Montgomery, *William Shakespeare: A Textual Companion* (Oxford, 1987)
Theobald, *Letters*	Lewis Theobald, letters to Warburton, in John Nichols, *Illustrations of the Literary History of the Eighteenth Century*, vol. ii (1817)
Theobald, *SR*	Lewis Theobald, *Shakespeare Restored* (1726)
Thirlby	Styan Thirlby, MS notes in Theobald 1733 edition and Warburton 1747 edition, Folger Library copies
Thiselton	A. E. Thiselton, *Some Textual Notes on 'All's Well that Ends Well'* (1900)
Tilley	M. P. Tilley, *A Dictionary of the Proverbs in England in the Sixteenth and Seventeenth Centuries* (Ann Arbor, 1950)
Tyrwhitt	Thomas Tyrwhitt, *Observations and Conjectures upon Some Passages of Shakespeare* (Oxford, 1766)
Walker	W. S. Walker, *A Critical Examination of the Text of Shakespeare*, 3 vols. (1860)

All's Well that Ends Well

THE PERSONS OF THE PLAY

BERTRAM, Count of Roussillon

The COUNTESS OF ROUSSILLON, his mother

HELEN, an orphan in the Countess's protection, in love with Bertram

STEWARD (Rinaldo) ⎫
CLOWN (Lavatch) ⎭ servants of the Countess

PAROLES, Bertram's companion

The KING of France

LAFEU, an old lord

FIRST LORD (Dumaine) ⎫ brothers, later captains in the
SECOND LORD (Dumaine) ⎭ Florentine army

FIRST SOLDIER, interpreter

GENTLEMAN of the French court

The DUKE of Florence

A WIDOW of Florence

DIANA, her daughter

MARIANA, her friend

Lords, Attendants, Soldiers, Townspeople of Florence

The Persons of the Play

Names: in adopting *Helen* rather than the usual *Helena*, I follow the preference revealed in the Folio text, in which *Helena* occurs only once in dialogue and three times in stage directions, all before the end of Act Two, whereas *Helen* or *Hellen* is the only form used in the last three acts and overall decidedly outweighs the longer form with twenty-five occurrences. The form of Paroles' name conforms with the general principles in *Modernizing Shakespeare's Spelling*. There are a few 'nonce-names'—Dumaine, Lavatch, Rinaldo—which are not offered as part of the character but thrown in to meet the necessities of a single immediate situation, with no further use and no effect on stage directions and speech prefixes. I have preferred to stay with F's generic labels for these characters—Lords, Clown, Steward—to avoid the inadvertent overemphasis on those casual, sometimes borrowed names that constant repetition in stage directions creates, and to keep distinct the names that do have symbolic resonance, especially those of Helen and Diana.

Casting: no cast list survives in the Folio for *All's Well*, but the play could easily be done with no more than eleven players. The parts of characters who go from France to Italy are not easily doubled, but other actors in the French scenes could take on an additional role later in the play: Lafeu as the Duke of Florence, the Countess as Mariana, the Steward as the Gentleman of 5.1, the King as First Soldier. For the 'ghost' character Violenta, see note on 3.5.0.1–2.

All's Well that Ends Well

1.1 *Enter young Bertram Count of Roussillon, his*
mother the Countess, Helen, and Lord Lafeu, all
in black

COUNTESS In delivering my son from me, I bury a
second husband.

BERTRAM And I in going, madam, weep o'er my
father's death anew; but I must attend his majesty's
command, to whom I am now in ward, evermore in 5
subjection.

LAFEU You shall find of the King a husband, madam;
you, sir, a father. He that so generally is at all times
good must of necessity hold his virtue to you, whose
worthiness would stir it up where it wanted rather 10
than lack it where there is such abundance.

COUNTESS What hope is there of his majesty's amend-
ment?

LAFEU He hath abandoned his physicians, madam,
under whose practices he hath persecuted time with 15
hope, and finds no other advantage in the process
but only the losing of hope by time.

1.1.0.1–3 Envisioning the group in
mourning, including orphaned son,
widowed mother, and counsellor, may
have activated the reminiscences of
Hamlet that cluster in this scene opening: the Countess's allusion to a second husband (l. 2), Lafeu's assurance
that she will find one in the King (a
hint not developed later) as Bertram
will find a substitute father (ll. 7–8),
warnings to Helen against excessive
filial grief (49–58), aphoristic parental
advice to the son departing for Paris
(61–8).
1 **delivering** giving up, with a pun on
'giving birth to': Bertram's 'birth' into
the world, entailing separation from
her, is akin to her husband's death.
Robertson Davies's observation (*Renown
at Stratford* (Toronto, 1953), p. 59)

that the Countess is the only female
character to open a Shakespearian
play is accurate if we except the First
Witch in *Macbeth*, and suggests the
importance of women and their initi-
atives in this play.
7 **of** in
8 **generally** to everyone
9 **hold** maintain
10–11 **stir ... abundance** stimulate virtue in one who lacks it, sooner than
find a deficiency in one so amply en-
dowed with it
15–16 **under ... hope** under whose pro-
fessional treatments he has made his
days painful in hope (of a cure)
17 **losing** F's spelling is normal for this
meaning, but possibly *loosing* is also
intended (the two words were not
always distinguished), with the idea of

COUNTESS This young gentlewoman had a father—O,
that 'had', how sad a passage 'tis!—whose skill was
almost as great as his honesty; had it stretched so   20
far, would have made nature immortal, and death
should have play for lack of work. Would for the
King's sake he were living! I think it would be the
death of the King's disease.

LAFEU How called you the man you speak of, madam?   25

COUNTESS He was famous, sir, in his profession, and it
was his great right to be so: Gérard de Narbonne.

LAFEU He was excellent indeed, madam. The King very
lately spoke of him admiringly, and mourningly. He
was skilful enough to have lived still, if knowledge   30
could be set up against mortality.

BERTRAM What is it, my good lord, the King languishes
of?

LAFEU A fistula, my lord.

BERTRAM I heard not of it before.   35

LAFEU I would it were not notorious.—Was this
gentlewoman the daughter of Gérard de Narbonne?

COUNTESS His sole child, my lord, and bequeathed to
my overlooking. I have those hopes of her good that
her education promises her dispositions she inherits,   40

1.1.40 promises‿] F; promises; ROWE 1714

time's passage finally removing hope
of cure from the King who had clung
to it.

19 **passage** i.e. from the present tense
appropriate for the living to the past
tense, a specific application of *passage*
= death as in *Hamlet* 3.3.86 and
5.2.352

27 **great right** right resulting from greatness (Abbott, §4)
Narbonne This southern French city
near the Mediterranean coast is just to
the north of the province of Roussillon.

30 **still** probably 'now, as before'; but
perhaps 'always'

31 **mortality** i.e. the necessity for all men
to die

34 **fistula** Commentators who link the
King's disease with impotence presumably are thinking of an abscess near
the genitals; but Bucknill in *Medical
Knowledge of Shakespeare* (1860) distin-

guishes the meaning current in his
own time, an abscess external to the
rectum, from the more general Elizabethan use of the term for 'a burrow-
ing abscess in any situation' (p. 96).
While there are certainly sexual suggestions in Lafeu's introduction of
Helen as 'medicine' for the ailing old
King (see 2.1.70–6 and 95–6), the text
does not clearly locate the fistula, and
the King's implication that the disease
is properly owned by his heart (2.1.8–
10) suggests that Shakespeare was
probably following his source, in
which the fistula derives from a swelling on the King's breast.

39 **overlooking** superintendence

40–1 **promises ... fairer** F's punctuation,
though lacking authority, gives a marginally better sense than Rowe's widely accepted emendation. In the latter,
inheriting (good) tendencies makes the
gifts (= 'graces acquired by education')

which makes fair gifts fairer—for where an unclean
mind carries virtuous qualities, there commendations
go with pity: they are virtues and traitors too. In
her they are the better for their simpleness. She
derives her honesty and achieves her goodness.   45

LAFEU Your commendations, madam, get from her
tears.

COUNTESS 'Tis the best brine a maiden can season her
praise in. The remembrance of her father never
approaches her heart but the tyranny of her sorrows   50
takes all livelihood from her cheek.—No more of this,
Helen. Go to, no more, lest it be rather thought you
affect a sorrow than to have—

HELEN I do affect a sorrow indeed, but I have it too.

52 Helen] F (*Helena*)   53 have—] F; have it. THEOBALD

fairer; in the former, the antecedent
of *which* is more likely to be *education*,
which brings to full expression Helen's
gifts (= 'natural endowments'). Shakespeare frequently uses *gifts* in this
sense, but only once (*Twelfth Night*
1.3.121) with the unambiguous meaning of 'learned acquirements' that
Rowe's emendation requires. 'Her
education promises her dispositions
(which) she inherits'—the omitted
relative pronoun being common in
Shakespeare—with no break of phrasing between nurture and nature,
expresses well the Countess's stress on
their harmonious interaction.

42 **virtuous qualities** commendable accom-
plishments, conceived of as at odds
with the inborn bad disposition (*unclean mind*). For *virtuous* here and
virtues at l. 43 signifying learning
without reference to morality, compare Italian *virtuoso*, and *Pericles*
19.207; and for this usage as well as
the thought as a whole, compare
Othello on Desdemona's social accom-
plishments: 'Where virtue is, these are
more virtuous' (3.3.190). Virtue =
'power' may also be implied, the effective ability that makes such virtues traitors as well (l. 43) when serving evil
ends.

43 **go with pity** are mixed with regret.
OED does not record pity = 'regret',

but the meaning is implicit in *sb.* I. 3,
'regrettable fact'.

44 **simpleness** being unmixed (with inborn vice)

48 **season** temper by admixture

51 **livelihood** vitality, animation

53 **have—** If the Countess has finished her
speech, elliptic but clear in intent, the
dash suggests a pause while she waits
for a response from an embarrassed
Helen, as at 1.3.156. If the dash indicates that her speech is cut short, the
cause, as Hunter says, is likely to be
the newly widowed Countess's own
emotion as she speaks of grief that is
inwardly felt rather than 'affected'.
Helen's social inferiority and general
reticence in groups make improbable
the dash's frequent meaning of interruption by the next speaker.

54 **I do . . . too** Helen appears to say that
affecting, or making a display of, sorrow does not obviate truly feeling it;
her private meaning, revealed only in
the soliloquy beginning at l. 81, is that
she pretends grief for the loss of her
father while actually feeling it for the
loss of Bertram. *Affect* thus reinter-
preted goes beyond exaggeration and
artificial display to = 'counterfeit', predating *OED*'s 1661 first citation of this
sense (*v.* 1.6) without a following infinitive or gerund.

LAFEU Moderate lamentation is the right of the dead,   55
  excessive grief the enemy to the living.
COUNTESS If the living be enemy to the grief, the excess
  makes it soon mortal.
BERTRAM Madam, I desire your holy wishes.
LAFEU How understand we that?   60
COUNTESS

Be thou blessed, Bertram, and succeed thy father
In manners as in shape. Thy blood and virtue
Contend for empire in thee, and thy goodness
Share with thy birthright. Love all, trust a few,
Do wrong to none. Be able for thine enemy   65
Rather in power than use; and keep thy friend
Under thy own life's key. Be checked for silence,
But never taxed for speech. What heaven more will,
That thee may furnish and my prayers pluck down,
Fall on thy head. (*To Lafeu*) Farewell, my lord.   70

55–60 LAFEU Moderate . . . that?] F;   *Lafeu* Moderate . . . *living. Countess* If . . . *mortal.*
Lafeu How . . . that? *Bertram* Madam . . . wishes. KITTREDGE (*conj.* Theobald, *Letters*);
Lafeu Moderate . . . *living. Helena* If . . . *mortal. Bertram* Madam . . . wishes. *Lafeu* How . . .
that? KNIGHT, *after* Schlegel–Tieck

57–8 **If . . . mortal** The Theobald emendation, presupposing a common compositorial omission (see Gary Taylor,
' "Praestat difficilior lectio": *All's Well
that Ends Well* and *Richard III*', *Renaissance Studies*, 2 (1988), p. 32), has
the Countess agree with and extend
Lafeu's terms. Excessive grief is hostile
to the survivor, and if the survivor
does not evince a matching hostility
by casting it out, it will cause her
death. But F makes sense if the Countess is introducing another idea about
excess and using *mortal* to mean
not 'deadly' but 'subject to death',
'doomed to immediate death' (*OED* 1.
b): let Helen strive to conquer her
grief, and its very magnitude will
hasten its end. Compare Q2 *Hamlet* 4.7
after line 96: 'goodness, growing to a
plurisy, | Dies in his own too much';
and, for sorrow killing itself, *Winter's
Tale* 5.3.52–3. Lafeu's puzzlement
(l. 60), if responding to this thought,
favours the knottier F version over
Theobald's straightforward one.
60 **How . . . that?** See Appendix A.
62–4 **Thy . . . birthright** Having praised

Helen for the inherited goodness that
turns her education to best advantage,
the Countess reverses her emphasis in
advising Bertram to match his inherited beauty and nobility (*shape, blood,
birthright*) with qualities achieved by
his own efforts (*manners, virtue, goodness*). In Moshinsky's TV production,
the Countess presented Bertram with
a ring at *birthright,* giving the notion
of inheritance an additional dimension
by introducing the 'monumental ring'
on which the later plot will turn.
63 **empire** dominion
65–6 **Be able . . . use** have the potential to
defeat your adversary without always
acting on it
67 **checked** rebuked
68 **taxed** censured
69 **furnish** equip
70 **Farewell** Several editors follow Capell
in having the Countess address her
farewell to Bertram, concluding her
formal blessing before she turns to
Lafeu. But she would naturally take
some formal leave of the old lord, and
Bertram receives his farewell at l. 74.
The short line allows time for the

'Tis an unseasoned courtier. Good my lord,
Advise him.

LAFEU   He cannot want the best
That shall attend his love.

COUNTESS Heaven bless him.—Farewell, Bertram.

BERTRAM The best wishes that can be forged in your   75
    thoughts be servants to you.   ⌈*Exit Countess*⌉
    (*To Helen*) Be comfortable to my mother, your mistress,
    and make much of her.

LAFEU Farewell, pretty lady. You must hold the credit
    of your father.   *Exeunt Bertram and Lafeu*   80

HELEN

O, were that all! I think not on my father,
And these great tears grace his remembrance more
Than those I shed for him. What was he like?
I have forgot him. My imagination
Carries no favour in't but Bertram's.   85
I am undone. There is no living, none,
If Bertram be away. 'Twere all one
That I should love a bright particular star
And think to wed it, he is so above me.
In his bright radiance and collateral light   90
Must I be comforted, not in his sphere.

76 *Exit Countess*] NEILSON–HILL; *not in* F 1; *at l.* 74 F2· 77 *To Helen*] WILSON (*conj.* Nicholson); *not in* F; *at l.* 75 ROWE 80 *Exeunt Bertram and Lafeu*] *not in* F 89 me.] ROWE (~:); me‸ F

Countess to bless her son before turning to Lafeu.

73 **his love** love of him; cf. 2.3.74. Presumably *the best* = 'advice', which Bertram will not lack because it will naturally accompany the love he inspires—or should strive to inspire. If Lafeu's poor opinion of Bertram (2.3.101–2) is germinating already (see Appendix A), his reassurance to the Countess is also an admonition to Bertram to be sure his conduct is worthy of love.

75–6 **The best . . . to you** Rowe and subsequent editors understood this speech as addressed to Helen along with ll. 77–8. But the radical shift this supposes from courtly compliment to something approaching an order is unlikely, and the likelihood of some

wish from Bertram to answer his mother's blessing also supports Nicholson's conjecture that Bertram speaks first to his mother.

77 **comfortable** supportive, consoling

79 **hold the credit** keep up the good reputation

82–3 **And . . . him** and these tears I weep (for Bertram) do more apparent honour to my father's memory than those I actually wept at his death

85 **favour** countenance, with a pun on 'lover's token'

90–1 **In . . . sphere** In Ptolemaic astronomy, the spheres in which heavenly bodies were set revolved collaterally, in parallel motion. From her lower level, Helen can see Bertram's light and follow his career, but her sphere will never touch his.

Th'ambition in my love thus plagues itself:
The hind that would be mated by the lion
Must die for love. 'Twas pretty, though a plague,
To see him every hour, to sit and draw   95
His archèd brows, his hawking eye, his curls
In our heart's table—heart too capable
Of every line and trick of his sweet favour.
But now he's gone, and my idolatrous fancy
Must sanctify his relics. Who comes here?   100
        Enter Paroles
One that goes with him. I love him for his sake,
And yet I know him a notorious liar,
Think him a great way fool, solely a coward.
Yet these fixed evils sit so fit in him
That they take place when virtue's steely bones   105
Looks bleak i'th' cold wind. Withal, full oft we see
Cold wisdom waiting on superfluous folly.

PAROLES Save you, fair queen.

HELEN And you, monarch.

PAROLES No.   110

HELEN And no.

PAROLES Are you meditating on virginity?

HELEN Ay. You have some stain of soldier in you; let

95 hour,] POPE; houre‸ F   106 cold wind] F; wind *conj.* This edition

93 **hind ... lion** The disparity of rank on
the chain of being between the valor-
ous king of beasts and the timorous
hind is reinforced by *hind* = 'servant
or menial'.

96 **hawking** keen, either because like a
hawk's (Schmidt) or as having the
sharpness needed in the sport of hawking

97–8 **capable | Of** able to take in (heart
as receptacle) and have drawn on it
(heart as *table*, i.e. tablet)

99 **idolatrous** as worshipping the image in
her heart and other traces of his
presence (*relics*), and perhaps also as
adoring a star; compare Helen as sun-
worshipper, 1.3.204–7.

103 **a great way** largely
solely altogether

105 **take place** (a) find acceptance (b)
take precedence, in contrast to unat-
tractive virtue's position 'out in the

cold' or subordinate to (*waiting on*)
folly. Warburton's reading of *cold* as
'naked' and *superfluous* as 'overdressed' is supported by *sit so fit*—lies
and foolishness seen as becoming
clothes—as well as later references
to Paroles' overelaborate dress; the
clothing contrast develops the idea of
austere virtue as *steely bones*, lacking
the attractive covering of rounded
flesh.

106 **i'th' cold wind** Did Compositor B pick
up *cold* from the next line and attach
it by natural association to *wind*?
Without it the line is regular and the
force of *cold wisdom* is not weakened
by anticipation.

108 **fair queen** Paroles' joking address
probably is based on the name she
shares with Helen of Troy.

113 **stain** tinge or trace; *OED* cites only
Shakespeare for this meaning, but con-

84

me ask you a question. Man is enemy to virginity.
How may we barricado it against him?   115
PAROLES Keep him out.
HELEN But he assails; and our virginity, though
valiant in the defence, yet is weak. Unfold to us some
warlike resistance.
PAROLES There is none. Man setting down before you   120
will undermine you and blow you up.
HELEN Bless our poor virginity from underminers and
blowers-up. Is there no military policy how virgins
might blow up men?
PAROLES Virginity being blown down, man will quick-   125
lier be blown up. Marry, in blowing him down again,
with the breach yourselves made you lose your city.
It is not politic in the commonwealth of nature to
preserve virginity. Loss of virginity is rational increase, and there was never virgin got till virginity   130
was first lost. That you were made of is mettle to
make virgins. Virginity by being once lost may be
ten times found; by being ever kept, it is ever lost.
'Tis too cold a companion. Away with't.

118 valiant in the defence,] REED (*conj.* Thirlby); valiant, in the defence‸ F   130 got]
F2; goe F1

text makes the meaning clear in its
other appearance, *Troilus* 1.2.25.

116 **Keep him out** This hardly responds
to Helen's need for a barricade, unless
Paroles' verb glances at the noun *keep*
in its military meaning (*OED*, *sb*. 3):
fortify yourself in a stronghold.

118 **valiant in the defence,** The F punctuation, as the *Textual Companion* says,
'is not only awkward, but could imply
that virginity would not be weak "in
the offence" '. The emendation brings
out the contrast between strong resistance in the spirit and fleshly vulner-
ability to seduction.

120 **setting down before** laying siege to
(compare 3.7.18)

121–7 The bawdy play on *blow up* with
woman as object carries on, with
undermine and *breach*, the equation of
war and sex: destruction (of virginity)
involves swelling in pregnancy. The

blowing down of maidenly resistance
blows up (= 'sexually excites') the
man, and in blowing him down again
by inducing his orgasm, the virgin
gives up what she had been defending.

122 **Bless** (may God) keep safe

123 **policy** stratagem

129–30 **rational increase** sensible profit-
making; *rational* in this sense predates
the first *OED* entry (1635) for *adj.* 4.

131 **mettle** (F mettall) includes with 'substance' or 'stuff' the notion of generation as coinage (cf. *Measure* 2.4.45),
according with Paroles' ongoing commercial metaphor; *metal* and its figurative extension *mettle* were not yet
discriminated in spelling or meaning.

133 **ten times found** i.e. by producing ten
(virgin) children. Hunter sees an allusion to 'the allowed ten per cent interest on moneys invested', but the rate
Paroles offers is, at one child a year, a
usurious 100 per cent.

HELEN I will stand for't a little, though therefore I die   135
a virgin.

PAROLES There's little can be said in't, 'tis against the
rule of nature. To speak on the part of virginity is
to accuse your mothers, which is most infallible
disobedience. He that hangs himself is a virgin: 140
virginity murders itself, and should be buried in
highways, out of all sanctified limit, as a desperate
offendress against nature. Virginity breeds mites,
much like a cheese, consumes itself to the very
paring, and so dies with feeding his own stomach.   145
Besides, virginity is peevish, proud, idle, made of
self-love—which is the most inhibited sin in the
canon. Keep it not, you cannot choose but lose by't.
Out with't! Within ten year it will make itself two,
which is a goodly increase, and the principal itself   150
not much the worse. Away with't.

HELEN How might one do, sir, to lose it to her own
liking?

PAROLES Let me see. Marry, ill, to like him that ne'er
it likes. 'Tis a commodity will lose the gloss with   155

149 ten year . . . two] F; ten year . . . ten HANMER; the year . . . two DELIUS 1872 *(conj.*
Anon.); t'one year . . . two RIVERSIDE

135 **stand for** defend (as a thesis)
137 **in't** in its defence
139 **infallible** certain
140-3 **He . . . nature** A virgin, by refusing
self-perpetuation in offspring, commits
a crime against nature tantamount to
suicide and should therefore be denied
burial in sanctified ground.
145 **his own stomach** its own stubborn
pride
147-8 **most inhibited sin in the canon** sin
most prohibited by canon law; *the
canon* could also mean canonical scrip-
ture, but *inhibited* was associated with
ecclesiastical interdiction (*OED, inhibit*,
1). The moral argument recalls Sonnet
3 ('Or who is he so fond will be the
tomb | Of his self-love to stop pos-
terity?') and the early sonnets in
general.
149 **Out with't** (a) cast it away (b) put it
out to interest
ten year . . . two The rate of increase
is less ample than at l. 133, here
matching the allowed ten per cent. Of

the emendations that would bring this
into accord with 'ten times found',
Riverside assumes the likeliest error, F
t'on misread. But Paroles, not strong
on consistency, may think here of one
child growing at the allowed rate until
at the end of her tenth year she is near
enough to puberty actually to replace
the nubile virgin (Dowden MS).
154-5 **ill . . . likes** Paroles' answer as
usually understood, 'you would do ill
to *like* one who *dis*likes virginity', does
not logically lead into his subsequent
advice to sell her personal wares before
they deteriorate with time (*lose the
gloss with lying*). If, however, he takes
Helen's *to her own liking* not only as
'to someone she likes' but as 'at a time
of her choosing', his answer cautions
her that she may deal badly by finally
choosing a man to whom she is not
attractive, having meanwhile refused
other offers when she was most
saleable.

lying; the longer kept, the less worth. Off with't
while 'tis vendible. Answer the time of request. Virginity like an old courtier wears her cap out of
fashion, richly suited but unsuitable, just like the
brooch and the toothpick, which wear not now. Your   160
date is better in your pie and your porridge than in
your cheek. And your virginity, your old virginity,
is like one of our French withered pears: it looks ill,
it eats drily, marry, 'tis a withered pear. It was
formerly better, marry, yet 'tis a withered pear. Will   165
you anything with it?

HELEN Not my virginity yet—
There shall your master have a thousand loves,
A mother, and a mistress, and a friend,
A phoenix, captain, and an enemy,   170
A guide, a goddess, and a sovereign,

160 wear] F (were)   167 virginity yet—] F (~:); virginity yet. You're for the Court:
HANMER; virginity; yet . . . HUNTER; virginity, yet at the court *conj.* Oxford

160 **toothpick . . . now** Toothpicks, introduced from Italy in the later sixteenth
century and worn in the hat to show
off travel experience or familiarity with
new imports, are a sign of affectation
in Overbury's 'A Courtier': *The Over-
burian Characters*, Percy Reprints XIII,
ed. W. J. Paylor (Oxford, 1936), p. 7.
wear not are not the fashion

161 **date** (a) fruit (b) season, to be put to
productive use while ripe; both
aspects of the image are extended in
the following *withered pear*. Dates were
used as a sweetener, e.g. in porridge.

167 **Not . . . yet—** The line is short, and
in sense does not lead naturally into
the following one. A few have seen
There (l. 168) as referring to *my virginity*—'in my virgin love, which is
not yet a withered pear, your master
will find all he ever wanted in a mistress'—but Helen would hardly reveal
her secret love to Paroles, of all people,
and some of the later epithets of Bertram's tyrannical mistress are quite at
odds with her subservient adoration.
Others fill out the line variously to
bridge the gap between meditations on
Helen's own virginity and imaginings
of Bertram's amorous adventures at
court. But both the incomplete line

and the sudden shift in subject may be
functional, like the breaks at ll. 177
(identically punctuated in F) and 179;
the more radical rupture here can convey Helen's inability to go on with the
game (notice the coinciding change
from prose to verse) after Paroles' joking references to the passing of youth
and beauty have struck home, and thus
prepare for her return to the obsession
with Bertram that she has been trying
to keep at bay. Hunter makes *yet* a
transition covering (inadequately) such
an abrupt shift in thought.

168–77 **There . . . he—** Imagining court
amours in the language of contemporary sonnet literature, Helen reproduces
that literature's central mode of oxymoron not only in the formal para-
doxes of ll. 173–5 but in the larger
alternation of epithets between bene-
volence and hostility, subjugation and
intimate affection, tutelary guidance
and violation of trust. *Mother* alone
looks odd in this context; Hunter's
suggestion that Helen modulates into
her list with a general formula encompassing 'every kind of love' is supported by Spenser's threefold division
in *Faerie Queene* IV. ix. 1: 'The deare
affection unto kindred sweet, | Or

A counsellor, a traitress, and a dear;
His humble ambition, proud humility,
His jarring-concord, and his discord-dulcet,
His faith, his sweet disaster; with a world   175
Of pretty, fond adoptious christendoms
That blinking Cupid gossips. Now shall he—
I know not what he shall. God send him well!
The court's a learning place, and he is one—
PAROLES What one, i'faith?   180
HELEN That I wish well. 'Tis pity—
PAROLES What's pity?
HELEN

  That wishing well had not a body in't
  Which might be felt, that we the poorer born,
  Whose baser stars do shut us up in wishes,   185
  Might with effects of them follow our friends
  And show what we alone must think, which never
  Returns us thanks.
        Enter Page
PAGE Monsieur Paroles, my lord calls for you. ⌈*Exit*⌉
PAROLES Little Helen, farewell. If I can remember thee,   190
  I will think of thee at court.
HELEN Monsieur Paroles, you were born under a char-
  itable star.
PAROLES Under Mars, I.
HELEN I especially think *under* Mars.   195
PAROLES Why *under* Mars?
HELEN The wars hath so kept you under that you must
  needs be born under Mars.
PAROLES When he was predominant.

---

174 jarring-concord . . . discord-dulcet] HUNTER; iarring, concord . . . discord, dulcet F
189 *Exit*] THEOBALD; *not in* F

raging fire of love to woman kind, |
Or zeale of friends combynd with ver-
tues meet'.

174 F's commas in this line seem to be
  equivalent to hyphens, as in *Troilus*
  3.2.22 (QF), 5.3.28 (F), and Add. Pass.
  B.2/5.11.33 (QF), and *Merchant*
  2.4.14 (Q).
176 **adoptious** adopted
  christendoms namings, as at baptism

177 **gossips** sponsors, acts as godparent to
185 **shut us up in** confine us to
187 **alone must think** must only think
  (not act out)
189 **Monsieur . . . you** F's pseudo-verse
  here and at ll. 204–5 (see Appendix
  D) and the generous spacing of the
  Page's entrance direction suggest that
  Compositor B was trying to stretch the
  copy at the end of the second column
  of page V2.

HELEN When he was retrograde, I think rather.   200
PAROLES Why think you so?
HELEN You go so much backward when you fight.
PAROLES That's for advantage.
HELEN So is running away, when fear proposes the
   safety. But the composition that your valour and fear   205
   makes in you is a virtue of a good wing, and I like
   the wear well.
PAROLES I am so full of businesses I cannot answer thee
   acutely. I will return perfect courtier, in the which
   my instruction shall serve to naturalize thee, so thou   210
   wilt be capable of a courtier's counsel and understand what advice shall thrust upon thee; else thou
   diest in thine unthankfulness, and thine ignorance
   makes thee away. Farewell. When thou hast leisure,
   say thy prayers; when thou hast none, remember   215
   thy friends. Get thee a good husband, and use him
   as he uses thee. So farewell.   *Exit*
HELEN

Our remedies oft in ourselves do lie
Which we ascribe to heaven. The fated sky

---

217 *Exit*] not in F

200 **retrograde** 'unfavorably disposed,
   going *backward* (hence prompting
   those born under his influence to run
   away)' (Barish)
203–6 **advantage . . . safety** Helen converts Paroles' military *advantage*
   ('superior tactical position') to the
   non-military meaning of 'personal
   benefit'.
205 **composition** perhaps just 'mixture',
   more likely with a quibble on 'treaty
   to end hostilities', continuing the military language; Paroles' valour, which
   goes backward for advantage, is easily
   brought into accord with his fear,
   which dictates running to safety.
206 **of a good wing** rapid in flight; Steevens 1778 cites Bacon's *Natural History*, experiment 886, in which *good
   wing* = 'strong wing'. He also notes a
   possible clothing allusion in the
   phrase, *wing* as shoulder lappet, as in
   Jonson, *Every Man Out of His Humour*
   3.5.5, which links with *I like the wear
   well* immediately following and with

Paroles' exaggerated dress in general.
209–14 **I will . . . away** Paroles returns to
   the bawdy of his earlier conversation
   with *naturalize* (release from conven-
   tionality into the natural state),
   capable, understand and *thrust upon
   thee*, again linked to persuasion
   against virginity (ll. 212–14).
215–16 **when . . . friends** Paroles' construction could mean either 'think of
   your friends no matter how busy you
   are' (as opposed to thinking of God
   only when you have nothing better to
   do), or 'don't think of them at all'
   (because your lack of leisure will prevent it).
218–31 **Our remedies . . . leave me**
   Helen's soliloquy differs from her earlier one before Paroles' entrance not
   only in its active resolve but in its
   form: rhymed verse, as she exhorts
   herself with *sententiae*.
219 **fated** 'invested with the power of destiny' (Bevington)

Gives us free scope, only doth backward pull   220
Our slow designs when we ourselves are dull.
What power is it which mounts my love so high,
That makes me see, and cannot feed mine eye?
The mightiest space in fortune nature brings
To join like likes and kiss like native things.   225
Impossible be strange attempts to those
That weigh their pains in sense and do suppose
What hath been cannot be. Who ever strove
To show her merit that did miss her love?
The King's disease—my project may deceive me,   230
But my intents are fixed and will not leave me.

Exit

I.2   *Flourish cornetts. Enter the King of France with
letters, First Lord, Second Lord, and divers
attendants*

KING

The Florentines and Senois are by th'ears,
Have fought with equal fortune, and continue
A braving war.

FIRST LORD   So 'tis reported, sir.

225 like likes] F4; like. likes F1
    1.2.0.2 *First Lord, Second Lord,*] *not in* F

224–5 **The mightiest . . . things** Though
    the meaning is clear, the syntax is not,
    with the object of *brings*, which in turn
    governs the next line, unclear or ab-
    sent. Perring and Abbott suggest that
    space (= something like *difference* at
    1.3.112) is an error for *spaces*, and cite
    examples in Shakespeare of the plural
    or possessive *s* missing after an *s*
    sound; but following this theory we
    still have to bend the hypothetical
    spaces to mean 'those separated by
    space'. Alternatively, we must supply
    an object and read *space* as an 'accu-
    sative of measurement': 'nature
    brings [them] across, or through, the
    mightiest space' (Perring).
225 **native things** 'things formed by
    nature for each other' (Mason in
    Steevens–Reed), or 'parts of a single
    whole' as at *Hamlet* 1.2.47

227 **sense** rational calculation of prob-
    ability of success
229 **miss** fail to attain
1.2.0.1 The King was probably carried on
    in a chair, a conventional stage sign
    of weakness or infirmity. Productions
    with more modern settings by Tyrone
    Guthrie and Trevor Nunn brought him
    on in a wheelchair. For the cornetts,
    see Introduction, p. 54.
1 **Senois** Sienese; the French form may
    indicate transmission of Shakespeare's
    source through a French intermediary
    (see Introduction, p. 1, n. 1), but in
    any case it matches the French names
    (Lafeu, Paroles, etc.) and phrases
    (*Saint Jacques, Mort du vinaigre*) by
    which Shakespeare suggests his play's
    basic milieu.
3 **braving** marked by mutual defiance

KING

    Nay, 'tis most credible: we here receive it

    A certainty vouched from our cousin Austria,   5

    With caution that the Florentine will move us

    For speedy aid—wherein our dearest friend

    Prejudicates the business, and would seem

    To have us make denial.

FIRST LORD   His love and wisdom,

    Approved so to your majesty, may plead   10

    For amplest credence.

KING   He hath armed our answer,

    And Florence is denied before he comes.

    Yet for our gentlemen that mean to see

    The Tuscan service, freely have they leave

    To stand on either part.

SECOND LORD   It well may serve   15

    A nursery to our gentry, who are sick

    For breathing and exploit.

KING   What's he comes here?

    Enter Bertram, Lafeu, and Paroles

FIRST LORD

    It is the Count Roussillon, my good lord,

    Young Bertram.

KING   Youth, thou bear'st thy father's face.

    Frank nature, rather curious than in haste,   20

    Hath well composed thee. Thy father's moral parts

    Mayst thou inherit too! Welcome to Paris.

BERTRAM

    My thanks and duty are your majesty's.

KING

    I would I had that corporal soundness now

    As when thy father and myself in friendship   25

    First tried our soldiership. He did look far

    Into the service of the time, and was

18 Roussillon] F2 (*Rosillon*); *Rosignoll* F1

5 **cousin** fellow monarch
6 **move** put pressure on
8 **seem** think fit
11 **armed our answer** made our response a repelling one, fortified it against entreaties

16–17 **sick | For breathing** longing for exercise, out of condition for lack of it
20 **Frank** bounteous
    curious careful
26–7 **did look far | Into the service** had extensive knowledge of military matters

Discipled of the bravest. He lasted long,
But on us both did haggish age steal on,
And wore us out of act. It much repairs me   30
To talk of your good father. In his youth
He had the wit which I can well observe
Today in our young lords; but they may jest
Till their own scorn return to them unnoted
Ere they can hide their levity in honour.   35
So like a courtier, contempt nor bitterness
Were in his pride or sharpness; if they were,
His equal had awaked them, and his honour—
Clock to itself—knew the true minute when
Exception bid him speak, and at this time   40
His tongue obeyed his hand. Who were below him
He used as creatures of another place,
And bowed his eminent top to their low ranks,
Making them proud of his humility,
In their poor praise he humbled. Such a man   45
Might be a copy to these younger times,
Which followed well would demonstrate them now
But goers backward.
BERTRAM   His good remembrance, sir,
Lies richer in your thoughts than on his tomb.

27–8 **was | Discipled of** (a) had as fol-
lowers or (b) was taught by

30 **wore us out of act** wore us down till
we were past acting

33–4 **they ... unnoted** 'They jest, and
draw jests upon themselves again; so
much better than their own that they
hardly see they are laugh'd at' (Capell,
Notes, p. 6).

35 **hide their levity in honour** envelop the
frivolity of wit in a good name earned
by deeds (like Bertram's father)

36–7 **contempt nor** neither contempt nor.
F's punctuation may indicate no contempt or bitterness in his pride and no
sharpness either, but the sense suggests a more balanced formulation:
pride without contempt and sharpness
without bitterness.

41 **His tongue obeyed his hand** as the
hand of his honour's clock arrived at
the proper hour on the dial (*true*

minute, l. 39), his voice responded by
taking *exception* (l. 40)

42 **another place** i.e. a rank not below his
but above

43–5 **And . . . humbled** In a gesture of
rank-reversal, he made the humble
folk proud by his courteous bow, while
he humbled himself by accepting the
praise of inferiors. For the participle
with a nominative absolute, *he* (being)
humbled, see Abbott §376.

45–8 **Such . . . backward** i.e. (a) one man
who rightly imitated (*followed well*)
the model (*copy*) of Bertram's father
would show up the others as not advancing but falling off from the standard; or (b) perusing well this past
model would demonstrate the present
young men as retrogressing rather
than going forward in the perfection
of manhood.

47 **them now** either (a) 'the men of today'
or (b) *these younger times* (l. 46)

So in approof lives not his epitaph   50
As in your royal speech.

KING

Would I were with him! He would always say—
Methinks I hear him now; his plausive words
He scattered not in ears, but grafted them
To grow there and to bear. 'Let me not live'—   55
This his good melancholy oft began
On the catastrophe and heel of pastime,
When it was out—'Let me not live,' quoth he,
'After my flame lacks oil, to be the snuff
Of younger spirits, whose apprehensive senses   60
All but new things disdain, whose judgements are
Mere fathers of their garments, whose constancies
Expire before their fashions.' This he wished.
I, after him, do after him wish too,
Since I nor wax nor honey can bring home,   65
I quickly were dissolvèd from my hive
To give some labourer 's room.

SECOND LORD   You're lovèd, sir.
They that least lend it you shall lack you first.

52 him!] THEOBALD; ~ ʌ FI; ~: F2   56 This] F; Thus POPE   67 labourer 's] This
edition; Labourers F; labourer WARBURTON

50 **So . . . epitaph** his (laudatory) epitaph
is nowhere so confirmed (*in approof*)
53 **plausive** worthy of applause (?); *OED*
cites only Shakespeare for this meaning, this passage and Q2 *Hamlet*, Add.
Pass. B.14/1.4.30.
54 **ears** suggests not only the organs by
which words are heard but seed-
containers, picking up on *scattered*: a
more casual way of disseminating wisdom than the careful grafting imaged
in contrast
57 **catastrophe and heel** end (construed in
terms first of drama and then of anatomy): an example of Shakespeare's
fondness for pairing an abstract word
with a concrete one and a learned
word with an ordinary one.
58 **out** at an end; perhaps with a suggestion of 'no longer alight', anticipating
the lamp and candle metaphors of ll.
59–60
59 **snuff** burnt part of a candle wick,
which impedes its further burning

60–1 **whose . . . disdain** i.e. whose mental
faculties are quick to grasp what
comes along, and thus have only disdain for what was there before
61–2 **whose . . . garments** 'who have no
other use of their faculties, than to
invent new modes of dress' (Johnson)
66 **dissolvèd** detached, released
67 **labourer 's** F's *labourers* read as a plural makes general sense in the contrast
between productive work and inability
to contribute wax or honey, but the
room vacated when the king dies will
not be filled by more than one person
but by one alone (another 'king-bee',
in the Elizabethan misapprehension of
hive-society). If a plural is thus ruled
out by sense, F's final *s* probably indicates a contraction: 'labourer his'.
There are several F and Q examples of
final *s* without apostrophe meaning
'his' or 'us'; see especially *Troilus* Q
3.1.87, *makes* = 'make his'.
68 **it** May refer forward, as Delius

93

KING

  I fill a place, I know't.—How long is't, Count,

  Since the physician at your father's died?   70

  He was much famed.

BERTRAM   Some six months since, my lord.

KING

  If he were living, I would try him yet.

  —Lend me an arm.—The rest have worn me out

  With several applications. Nature and sickness

  Debate it at their leisure. Welcome, Count.   75

  My son's no dearer.

BERTRAM   Thank your majesty.

                                  Flourish. Exeunt

I.3   *Enter Countess, Steward, and Clown* ⌈*following*⌉

COUNTESS I will now hear. What say you of this
  gentlewoman?

STEWARD Madam, the care I have had to even your
  content I wish might be found in the calendar of my
  past endeavours, for then we wound our modesty   5
  and make foul the clearness of our deservings, when
  of ourselves we publish them.

COUNTESS What does this knave here? (*To Clown*) Get
  you gone, sirrah. The complaints I have heard of you
  I do not all believe. 'Tis my slowness that I do not,   10
  for I know you lack not folly to commit them and
  have ability enough to make such knaveries yours.

CLOWN 'Tis not unknown to you, madam, I am a poor
  fellow.

COUNTESS Well, sir.   15

76.1 *Flourish. Exeunt*] *after* F (*Exit* | *Flourish.*)
  1.3.0.1 *following*] *after* OXFORD; *not in* F

thought, to *lack you*, i.e. those who
least grant they will miss you will be
the first to do so; or may refer back
either to *room* or to *lovèd* (l. 67): those
who are now most grudging in according you love or your position will be
the first to miss you.

74 **several applications** separate treatments

1.3.0.1 A separate entrance of some sort
for the Clown is indicated by the
Countess's surprise at seeing him (l. 8).
3–4 **even your content** come up to your
desires, satisfy you
6 **clearness** purity
11–12 **I know . . . yours** The Countess
characterizes the Clown as both fool
and knave, as he will present himself
at 4.5.25–6.

CLOWN No, madam, 'tis not so well that I am poor,
   though many of the rich are damned. But if I may
   have your ladyship's good will to go to the world,
   Isbel the woman and I will do as we may.

COUNTESS Wilt thou needs be a beggar?   20

CLOWN I do beg your good will in this case.

COUNTESS In what case?

CLOWN In Isbel's case and mine own. Service is no
   heritage, and I think I shall never have the blessing
   of God till I have issue o' my body—for they say   25
   bairns are blessings.

COUNTESS Tell me thy reason why thou wilt marry.

CLOWN My poor body, madam, requires it: I am driven
   on by the flesh, and he must needs go that the devil
   drives.   30

COUNTESS Is this all your worship's reason?

CLOWN Faith, madam, I have other holy reasons, such
   as they are.

COUNTESS May the world know them?

19 I] F2; w FI

18 **go to the world** get married, as *Much
   Ado* 2.1.298–300; in the traditional
   medieval distinction, choose the secular way of the flesh rather than the
   chaste religious way. *World* as 'flesh'
   starts a chain of sexual suggestions:
   do (engage in sexual activity) in the
   next line, *case* at l. 23, *holy* (punning
   on hole = 'vagina') and *reasons* ('rais-
   ings') at l. 32.
19 **Isbel** One of several names apparently
   influenced by *Measure*, with Mariana
   (3.5), Escalus (3.5), and Lodowick
   (4.3): see Alice Walker, 'The Text of
   Measure for Measure', *RES*, NS 34
   (1983), p. 20.
   woman female servant
   do as we may In view of the Clown's
   penchant for proverbs in this scene,
   probably echoes the adage 'Men must
   do as they may, not as they would'
   (Dent M554), which lies behind passages in *Henry V* (2.1.13–15), *Titus*
   (2.1.107–8), and *Venus* (564). If so the
   emphasis is on compulsion, not elect-
   ing to marry but being driven to it;

compare ll. 28–30.
20 **Wilt . . . beggar?** The Countess's
   response may refer to his increased
   financial responsibilities after marriage, or she may be taking *go to the
   world* as 'appeal to the world for livelihood'.
23 **case** genitals—usually female, but
   applied to the male at *Romeo* 2.3.49
   and by Cotgrave glossing Fr. *cas*: 'also,
   the privities (of man, or woman)'
23–4 **Service is no heritage** This proverb
   (Tilley S253) appears in the Homily
   against Idleness as an argument for
   providing for old age by thrift and
   acquisition of new skills; the Clown
   here may thus want children not so
   much for generational continuity as
   for a future source of support.
26 **bairns are blessings** Proverbial (Tilley
   C331).
29–30 **he must needs go that the devil
   drives** Proverbial (Tilley D278).
34 **the world** we secular folk (set against
   the Clown's *holy reasons*)

95

CLOWN I have been, madam, a wicked creature, as you   35
and all flesh and blood are, and indeed I do marry
that I may repent.

COUNTESS Thy marriage sooner than thy wickedness.

CLOWN I am out o' friends, madam, and I hope to have
friends for my wife's sake.   40

COUNTESS Such friends are thine enemies, knave.

CLOWN You're shallow, madam, in great friends, for
the knaves come to do that for me which I am
aweary of. He that ears my land spares my team,
and gives me leave to in the crop; if I be his cuckold   45
he's my drudge. He that comforts my wife is the
cherisher of my flesh and blood; he that cherishes
my flesh and blood loves my flesh and blood; he that
loves my flesh and blood is my friend; *ergo*, he that
kisses my wife is my friend. If men could be contented   50
to be what they are, there were no fear in marriage;
for young Chairbonne the puritan and old Poisson
the papist, howsome'er their hearts are severed in
religion, their heads are both one: they may jowl

42 madam, in] F (Madam in); Madam; e'en HANMER   52 Chairbonne] F (*Charbon*)
Poisson] F (*Poysam*, interpreted as error for *Poyson* (Wilson))

37 **repent** Suggesting marriage as a pur-
gatorial experience, accords with the
implication of compelled entry into
wedlock at ll. 28–30 and the anticipation of sexual weariness at 43–4. The
Clown gives a mock-positive application of the proverb 'Marry in haste,
and repent at leisure' (Tilley H196).

42 **in** Hanmer reads *in* as a variant spelling of *e'en* (see 3.2.18), and Alexander
punctuates to break the sense after
madam. Both achieve a more direct
contradiction of the Countess's view
that friends with an eye to the wife are
enemies of the husband; but F makes
good sense and increases the Clown's
condescension toward his mistress by
linking her 'shallowness' to lack of
social knowledge: 'your notion of
great friends is superficial'. He carries
on this role of the court *habitué*
instructing the uninformed in 2.2.

44 **He that ears my land spares my team**
Proverbial (Tilley L57); for ploughing
another's land as replacing him sexu-

ally, see *2 Henry IV* 3.2.112.
ears ploughs

45 **in** gather in

46–50 **He ... wife is my friend** The Clown
achieves his paradox through the
truism that 'man and wife is one flesh'
(*Hamlet* 4.3.54). Noble hears an echo
of Ephesians 5: 28–9.

46 **comforts** gives pleasure to

51 **what they are** i.e. cuckolds

52–5 **young ... herd** The young Protes-
tant eater of meat (*chair*) and the old
Catholic eater of fish (*poisson*) invert
the saying 'hearts may agree though
heads differ' (Dent H431, though the
lack of references before Thomas Ful-
ler's 1732 collection renders doubtful
its proverbial status in Shakespeare's
time). Their hearts are far apart in age
and rival faiths but the heads of these
apparent opposites are identically
horned, sharing the fate common to
all men.

54 **jowl** knock

horns together like any deer i'th' herd.   55

COUNTESS Wilt thou ever be a foul-mouthed and calumnious knave?

CLOWN A prophet I, madam, and I speak the truth the
next way.

⌈*He sings*⌉   For I the ballad will repeat,   60
                 Which men full true shall find:
                 Your marriage comes by destiny,
                 Your cuckoo sings by kind.

COUNTESS Get you gone, sir. I'll talk with you more
anon.   65

STEWARD May it please you, madam, that he bid Helen
come to you. Of her I am to speak.

COUNTESS Sirrah, tell my gentlewoman I would speak
with her—Helen I mean.

CLOWN ⌈*sings*⌉

        'Was this fair face the cause,' quoth she,   70
            'Why the Grecians sackèd Troy?
        Fond done, done fond.
            Was this King Priam's joy?'
        With that she sighèd as she stood,
        With that she sighèd as she stood,   75
            And gave this sentence then:
        'Among nine bad if one be good,
        Among nine bad if one be good,
            There's yet one good in ten.'

72 done fond.] F (~ₐ); fond done;—for *Paris* he THEOBALD (*conj.* Warburton)

59 **next** nearest, most direct. What the Countess rebukes as abusive slander, the Clown implies, is in fact truth told without deviation or dressing up.

60–3 **For . . . kind** F's printing of ballad-lines as prose here and at ll. 76–9 (see Appendix D) is apparently an attempt by Compositor D to crowd material into this column; he also crams two ballad lines into one (72–3) and tacks on *bis* to line 74 to avoid taking up a line to repeat it.

62–3 Steevens noted a parallel in a poem in John Grange's *Golden Aphroditis* (1577), which concludes 'As cuckolds come by destiny, so cuckoos sing by kind' (R3ᵛ). But the distinction there seems to be between the individual (not universal) fate of being cuckolded and the bird's cry, which is prompted by nature only. In the Clown's version, it is marriage that comes by individual destiny (Tilley M682), fate joining a particular pair; but the common animal condition—quite apart from indi-vidual natures and circumstances—dictates that every man will be cuck-olded. One fate, *destiny*, is proper to the individual; the other, *kind* (na-ture), is proper to the species.

70–9 **Was . . . ten** Although the Count-ess's response at line 80 indicates that the ballad the Clown distorts is well known, no parallel has been found. The exchange following suggests that before corruption the numbers in the

COUNTESS What, one good in ten? You corrupt the 80
song, sirrah.

CLOWN One good *woman* in ten, madam, which is a
purifying o'th' song. Would God would serve the
world so all the year! We'd find no fault with the
tithe-woman if I were the parson. One in ten, quoth 85
a? An we might have a good woman born but or
every blazing star or at an earthquake, 'twould mend
the lottery well. A man may draw his heart out ere
a pluck one.

COUNTESS You'll be gone, sir knave, and do as I com- 90
mand you!

CLOWN That man should be at woman's command, and
yet no hurt done! Though honesty be no puritan,
yet it will do no hurt: it will wear the surplice of
humility over the black gown of a big heart. I am 95

86 but or] CAPELL; but ore F; but one COLLIER 1858   91 you!] ~? F

ballad referred to men and that their
proportion was reversed, nine good to
one bad. Warburton's speculation that
the sighing speaker was Hecuba, con-
templating her surviving sons and
finding Paris the one bad, is ingenious
but unproven. Line 72, which looks
too short for its position in the ballad
metre, matches the tetrameter well
when sung, four notes held longer.
Fond probably gathers in both 'enam-
oured' and 'foolish'.

76 **sentence** judgement, opinion

80-3 **corrupt the song . . . purifying o'th'
song** Presumably, as Theobald speculates (crediting Warburton), the Clown
has reversed the numbers, from nine
good in ten to only one. The Clown
explains that the apparent corruption
which decreases the total of good is
really an increase in that total,
because he is talking not of men but
of women—in whom a one in ten ratio
is an improvement over the status quo.

85 **tithe-woman** tenth woman, the one
good in ten, but also 'offered portion',
like the 'tithe-pig' apportioned to the
parson

86 **but or** F's *ore* has been read as *or* =
'before' or *ere*, but surely the comet,
signal of a wondrous event, ought to

precede the miraculous birth, not follow it. The usual modernization of *ore*,
o'er in Rowe and others, suffers from
a similar illogic: humans are born
under heavenly bodies, not over them.
Taking *or* as 'either' in the familiar 'or
. . . or' construction usefully emphasizes the balance of the two prodigious
phenomena, though it leaves *every
blazing star* without a preposition to
parallel *at an earthquake*.

87 **blazing star** comet

88 **lottery** alluding to the proverbial 'Marriage is a lottery' (Dent M681); the
metaphor also governs *draw* (l. 88) and
pluck (l. 89) for pulling lots.

92-5 **That . . . heart** The Clown adapts to
this new situation themes from his earlier patter: misogyny, in the implication that a woman who reverses the
natural hierarchy by commanding
men creates disruption, and his hypothetical role as parson. In this mode
his *honesty*—the faculty of speaking
truth 'the next way'?—though not a
puritan, will act like those puritans
who acceded under protest to government regulations on church vestments, wearing the prescribed surplice
in outward conformity but maintaining their independent spirit in the
black Geneva gown worn underneath.

going, forsooth. The business is for Helen to come
hither.   *Exit*

COUNTESS Well, now.

STEWARD I know, madam, you love your gentlewoman
entirely.   100

COUNTESS Faith, I do. Her father bequeathed her to me,
and she herself without other advantage may lawfully make title to as much love as she finds. There
is more owing her than is paid, and more shall be
paid her than she'll demand.   105

STEWARD Madam, I was very late more near her than
I think she wished me. Alone she was, and did
communicate to herself, her own words to her own
ears; she thought, I dare vow for her, they touched
not any stranger sense. Her matter was, she loved   110
your son. Fortune, she said, was no goddess, that
had put such difference betwixt their two estates;
Love no god, that would not extend his might only
where qualities were level; Dian no queen of virgins,
that would suffer her poor knight surprised without   115
rescue in the first assault or ransom afterward. This
she delivered in the most bitter touch of sorrow that
e'er I heard virgin exclaim in, which I held my duty
speedily to acquaint you withal, sithence in the loss
that may happen it concerns you something to know   120
it.

113 only_A] onelie, F   114 level; Dian no] CRAIG; leuell. F; level; *Diana* no THEOBALD

101–5 **Her . . . demand** Helen is first a
sum of money, bequeathed by her
father to the Countess and valuable in
herself without accrued interest (*advantage*), i.e. favourable circumstances
beyond her own nature and person;
then she is a claimant for payments of
love deserved in response.

110 **stranger sense** stranger's hearing

113–14 **only where qualities were level**
except where social positions were
equal

114 **Dian . . . virgins** Something is clearly
lacking in F, and O'Connor (*SB*, 30
(1977), p. 68) gives evidence of Compositor D's tendency to omit words.
Theobald's identification of the *queen
of virgins* is clearly right; Taylor ar-

gues for *Dian* rather than *Diana*, the
latter being reserved in this play for
the character while the former is
assigned to the goddess.

115 **surprised** (to be) captured suddenly

117 **touch** perhaps 'feeling' (*OED*, *sb*. III.
13. b), but more likely II. 8, 'note', in
the musical sense; at the beginning of
his speech and here (*delivered, heard*),
the Steward emphasizes his stance as
auditor.

119 **sithence** since
loss i.e. primarily Helen's failure to
gain the man she loves, which the
Steward would naturally assume, but
the word may encompass also the family's loss of Helen in consequence,
through her pining away.

COUNTESS You have discharged this honestly. Keep it to
   yourself. Many likelihoods informed me of this before,
   which hung so tottering in the balance that I could
   neither believe nor misdoubt. Pray you, leave me.   125
   Stall this in your bosom, and I thank you for your
   honest care. I will speak with you further anon.

                                     Exit Steward

     Enter Helen
COUNTESS (*aside*)

   Even so it was with me when I was young.
     If ever we are nature's, these are ours: this thorn
   Doth to our rose of youth rightly belong.   130
     Our blood to us, this to our blood is born;
   It is the show and seal of nature's truth,
   Where love's strong passion is impressed in youth.
   By our remembrances of days foregone,
   Such were our faults—or then we thought them
     none.   135
   Her eye is sick on't, I observe her now.
HELEN

   What is your pleasure, madam?
COUNTESS   You know, Helen,
   I am a mother to you.
HELEN

   Mine honourable mistress.
COUNTESS   Nay, a mother.

---

125 **believe nor misdoubt** accept as truth
   nor dismiss as probably false
127.2 *Enter Helen* F has Helen enter nine
   lines before she is given anything to
   say, considerably more than the
   couple of lines commonly given to
   cover an entrance on Shakespeare's
   large stage. At this point, too, a
   change in speech prefixes from *Cou.* to
   Old Cou. (ll. 128–67) suggests a later
   addition here, Shakespeare returning
   after the first writing to flesh out this
   scene and thinking of the Countess
   as 'Old' as he has her recall her own
   youth (see Randall McCloud, "UNEdi-
   ting Shak-speare," *Sub-Stance*, 33–4
   (1981–2), p. 49). Helen's early
   entrance may be a remnant of the
   original plan in which the dialogue
   began immediately. On the other

hand, the Countess in her meditation
talks as if she is looking at Helen,
seeing the external signs of love's
pain; and *Even so it was with me* is
more likely to refer to these outward
signs than to Helen's inner situation
of loving beyond her station. The awkwardness some editors have found in
Helen's silent presence actually works
well on stage, further defining her subordinate status as she hesitates to
interrupt her mistress.
129 **these** i.e. distresses of love and their
   outward manifestations
131 **blood** sexual appetite
135 **or then we thought them none** or not
   faults, as we didn't consider them so
   then
136 **observe** take notice of, look at with
   attention

Why not a mother? When I said 'a mother', 140
Methought you saw a serpent. What's in 'mother'
That you start at it? I say I am your mother,
And put you in the catalogue of those
That were enwombèd mine. 'Tis often seen
Adoption strives with nature, and choice breeds 145
A native slip to us from foreign seeds.
You ne'er oppressed me with a mother's groan,
Yet I express to you a mother's care.
God's mercy, maiden! Does it curd thy blood
To say I am thy mother? What's the matter, 150
That this distempered messenger of wet,
The many-coloured Iris, rounds thine eye?
—Why, that you are my daughter?

HELEN   That I am not.

COUNTESS

I say I am your mother.

HELEN   Pardon, madam.
The Count Roussillon cannot be my brother. 155
I am from humble, he from honoured name;
No note upon my parents, his all noble.
My master, my dear lord he is, and I
His servant live and will his vassal die.
He must not be my brother.

COUNTESS   Nor I your mother? 160

HELEN

You are my mother, madam, would you were—
So that my lord your son were not my brother—
Indeed my mother! Or were you both our mothers

145–6 **Adoption . . . seeds** Affections
toward an adopted child rival those
toward natural offspring, and the slip
selected for grafting on our own stock
becomes part of that stock, however
alien in origin.

151 **distempered** Gathers in, as Hunter
says, ideas of both emotional distress
and inclement weather: the balance of
the humours is upset on two levels.

152 **Iris** Puns on (a) the coloured part of
the eye surrounding the pupil and (b)
the rainbow, which refracts light from
drops of water (Helen's tears) into
many colours.

153 F's long dash seems to indicate a
pause while the Countess waits for an
answer to her question that the
shaken Helen is unable to make, before
prompting with an additional question. Elsewhere in F the dash most
frequently indicates interruption and
occasionally trailing off or groping
for words, but a few other instances
suggest a pause: e.g. *Merry Wives*
1.4.106, *Caesar* 3.1.76, *Cymbeline*
2.4.98.

157 **No note upon my parents** my fore-
bears undistinguished

163 **both our mothers** the mother of us

I care no more for than I do for heaven,
So I were not his sister. Can 't no other   165
But, I your daughter, he must be my brother?
COUNTESS
Yes, Helen, you might be my daughter-in-law.
God shield you mean it not, 'daughter' and 'mother'
So strive upon your pulse! What, pale again?
My fear hath catched your fondness. Now I see   170
The mystery of your loneliness and find
Your salt tears' head, now to all sense 'tis gross:
You love my son. Invention is ashamed
Against the proclamation of thy passion
To say thou dost not. Therefore tell me true,   175
But tell me then 'tis so—for look, thy cheeks
Confess it t'one to th' other, and thine eyes
See it so grossly shown in thy behaviours
That in their kind they speak it. Only sin
And hellish obstinacy tie thy tongue,   180

171 loneliness] THEOBALD; louelinesse F   177 t'one to th'] F2 ('ton); 'ton tooth to
th' F1

both. Logic requires *mother*, but in constructions like this the noun is apparently inclined to the plural by *both* and the plural pronominal adjective preceding, where usage might otherwise favour a singular, as at *Richard II* 3.3.106 or *Henry VIII* (*All is True*) 3.1.67.

164 **I care no more for** Editors strain to avoid the implication of the negative, *care no more for* = 'am indifferent to', by stressing the equation aspect: *care no more* as 'care as much, desire to the same extent'. Perhaps the negative meaning of *care* itself is preferable: *OED, v.* 2a, 'be troubled', or 1a, 'sorrow': your being our mother would be as little a cause of trouble or sorrow as heaven is.

165 **Can 't no other** can it come about in no other way

168 **God shield you mean it not** Here, in praying that Helen does not aspire to marry Bertram, and at ll. 170 and 182, suggestions of disapproval complicate the Countess's generally sympathetic stance in this scene. An

actress portraying her has several possible interpretations open to her: (1) she is in fact hostile to Helen's designs on her son till won over by later speeches—especially the appeal to her own youthful love experience at ll. 209–13, which reactivates the fellow-feeling of 128–35; (2) she favours the match herself but fears that Bertram cannot appreciate Helen; (3) she finds Helen's low rank an obstacle to the marriage no matter how adoring and worthy she is, until the King elevates her.

171 **loneliness** Theobald's emendation of F's *louelinesse*, supposing the easy mistaking of *n* for *u*, has been widely accepted; he paraphrases, 'I now find the mystery of your creeping into corners, and weeping, and pining in secret'.

172 **head** source
    gross evident

173 **Invention** i.e. the faculty for making up falsehoods

176–9 **thy cheeks . . . speak it** Helen's cheeks *confess* her love through blushes and her eyes speak it *in their kind*, their natural language of tears.

That truth should be suspected. Speak, is't so?
If it be so, you have wound a goodly clew;
If it be not, forswear't. Howe'er, I charge thee,
As heaven shall work in me for thine avail,
To tell me truly.
HELEN   Good madam, pardon me.   185
COUNTESS

Do you love my son?
HELEN   Your pardon, noble mistress.
COUNTESS

Love you my son?
HELEN   Do not you love him, madam?
COUNTESS

Go not about. My love hath in't a bond
Whereof the world takes note. Come, come, disclose
The state of your affection, for your passions   190
Have to the full appeached.
HELEN   Then I confess
Here on my knee, before high heaven and you,
That before you, and next unto high heaven,
I love your son.
My friends were poor but honest, so's my love.   195
Be not offended, for it hurts not him
That he is loved of me. I follow him not

---

181 **That truth should be suspected** Per-
    haps 'so that truth may be only sur-
    mised or guessed at' (not declared
    forthrightly); but more probably *sus-
    pected* carries the idea of contamina-
    tion. Compare *K. John* 4.2.26, 'Makes
    sound opinion sick, and truth sus-
    pected', and Honigmann's note (Arden
    edn.) on the phrase 'suspected places'
    for houses with plague.
182 **wound a goodly clew** Wilson's para-
    phrase, 'made a pretty tangle of it',
    keeps the metaphor of *clew* = 'ball of
    yarn'. Tilley compares 'You have spun
    a fine (fair) thread'—in all citations, as
    here, used ironically (T252).
188 **Go not about** don't speak circuitously
    (to evade direct answer)
191 **appeached** informed against you.
    If Helen has not already knelt to
    the Countess on asking pardon at
    l. 185, she kneels at this point for her

confession.
193–4 **That . . . son** There is no way to
    divide the overlong F line (see Appen-
    dix D) into two regular ones, but the
    short line that results is theatrically
    effective, emphasizing both Helen's
    simple monosyllabic confession after
    all her evasion, and her emotional
    inability to say any more.
197–200 **I follow . . . be** Helen is not
    necessarily disingenuous here in de-
    nying her pursuit of Bertram with
    marriage in mind, although in relating
    her plan to the Countess later in this
    scene she reveals only the part of it
    directed at curing the King and says
    nothing directly of her hope that suc-
    cess will win her Bertram. Here what
    she specifically denies is *presumptuous*
    suit, i.e. unfounded on right or war-
    rant; so Aragon in *Merchant* uses the
    verb in stressing that Portia's suitor

By any token of presumptuous suit,
Nor would I have him, till I do deserve him—
Yet never know how that desert should be.   200
I know I love in vain, strive against hope;
Yet in this cap'cious and intenible sieve
I still pour in the waters of my love
And lack not to lose still. Thus, Indian-like,
Religious in mine error, I adore   205
The sun that looks upon his worshipper
But knows of him nc more. My dearest madam,
Let not your hate encounter with my love
For loving where you do; but if yourself,
Whose agèd honour cites a virtuous youth,   210
Did ever in so true a flame of liking
Wish chastely and love dearly, that your Dian
Was both herself and Love, O then give pity
To her whose state is such that cannot choose
But lend and give where she is sure to lose;   215

---

202 cap'cious] F (captious)   intenible] F2; intemible F1; inteemable WILSON (*after* Mason *conj.,* unteemable)

should be worthy of her—'Let none presume | To wear an undeservèd dignity' (2.9.38–9). *Presumptuous* is thus opposed to *deserve* and *desert,* though Helen, evasive or lacking in confidence, keeps to herself the hoped-for grounds of that desert.

201 **hope** (reasonable) expectation
202 **cap'cious and intenible sieve** *cap'cious* highlights a meaning otherwise likely to be lost, while the echo of *captious* keeps in play the accompanying sense of 'deceitful'. From the Latin root *captare,* a frequentative and desiderative verb, Alice Walker argues for a stronger meaning, 'eager to take in or contain', rather than just 'capacious' ('Six Notes on *All's Well*', *SQ,* 33 (1982), p. 340). Wilson's return to F *intemible,* i.e. letting nothing teem, or pour, out (suggested originally by William Mason in a letter to Malone), seems to obviate the significance of the sieve, while the F2 reading underlines Helen's balanced paradox of a vessel measurelessly capable of (or desirous of) taking in and measurelessly incap-

able of retaining. Helen's leaky sieve image links her with the Danaïds, who killed their husbands on their wedding night and were condemned endlessly to pour water into containers that could not hold it—in reference not to their hostility to mating but to the loss of virginity signified in becoming unsealed vessels. See fig. 10, p. 66.

204 **lack not to lose still** have ever more waters of love to keep pouring in to drain out again
204–6 **Indian-like . . . worshipper** For the Indian, whether Asian or American, who worships the sun, compare *L.L.L.* 4.3.220–3.
208 **encounter** meet in battle
210 **cites** bears witness to
212–13 **Wish . . . Love** *Wish* and *love* in conjunction with *chastely* express verbally Helen's image of the patron of chastity encompassing the apparently antithetical divinity of love. Shakespeare may have known something of the figure of Venus–Virgo based on *Aeneid* i. 315 (Edgar Wind, *Pagan Mysteries in the Renaissance* (1958), pp. 74–5).

That seeks not to find that her search implies,
But riddle-like lives sweetly where she dies.

COUNTESS

Had you not lately an intent—speak truly—
To go to Paris?

HELEN   Madam, I had.

COUNTESS   Wherefore? Tell true.

HELEN

I will tell truth, by grace itself I swear.   220
You know my father left me some prescriptions
Of rare and proved effects, such as his reading
And manifest experience had collected
For general sovereignty; and that he willed me
In heedfull'st reservation to bestow them,   225
As notes whose faculties inclusive were
More than they were in note. Amongst the rest
There is a remedy approved set down
To cure the desperate languishings whereof
The King is rendered lost.   230

COUNTESS

This was your motive for Paris, was it? Speak.

HELEN

My lord your son made me to think of this.
Else Paris, and the medicine, and the King

223 manifest] F; manifold COLLIER 1858 (*conj.* Thirlby)   231 it? Speak.] F (it, speake?)

216–17 **That seeks . . . dies** i.e. that does
not actively pursue what her search
involves, its object, but instead stays
static: like a riddle in living where the
absence of Bertram undermines her life
(Diana's presentation of Helen as *riddle*
at the conclusion, 5.3.303), invokes
the same paradox of death coexisting
with life). Helen's shift to rhymed
couplets in lines 214–17 underlines
the sense of remoteness and enigma.
More than lines 197–200, this passage
seems designed to hide her plan for
Paris, but the Countess's questions immediately following indicate she is not
so easily taken in.
223 **manifest** Perhaps should be *manifold*,
as Thirlby speculates, which better
supports the necessary contrast
between *reading* and *experience* than
the applicable meaning of *manifest*,

'well-known'. Wilson highlights the
reading–doing contrast even more in
reading *manifest experience* as 'knowledge of manifestations or phenomena
he had actually seen', invoking a construction of an adjective in place of a
genitive seen in several of Shakespeare's other plays (Abbott §4 and
§374); but this sense of *manifest* or
manifestation in the English of Shakespeare's time gets no support from
OED.
224 **sovereignty** efficacy
225 **reservation . . . them** i.e. keeping
them back from ordinary use, to give
them out only in unusual need
226–7 **notes . . . note** 'receipts in which
greater *virtues* were *inclosed* than
appeared to observation' (Johnson)
230 **rendered lost** given up as incurable

Had from the conversation of my thoughts
Haply been absent then.

COUNTESS   But think you, Helen,   235
　If you should tender your supposèd aid,
　He would receive it? He and his physicians
　Are of a mind: he that they cannot help him,
　They that they cannot help. How shall they credit
　A poor unlearnèd virgin, when the schools,   240
　Embowelled of their doctrine, have left off
　The danger to itself?

HELEN   There's something in't
　More than my father's skill, which was the great'st
　Of his profession, that his good receipt
　Shall for my legacy be sanctified   245
　By th' luckiest stars in heaven; and would your
　　honour
　But give me leave to try success, I'd venture
　The well-lost life of mine on his grace's cure
　By such a day, an hour.

COUNTESS Dost thou believe't?   250

HELEN Ay, madam, knowingly.

COUNTESS
　Why, Helen, thou shalt have my leave and love,
　Means and attendants, and my loving greetings
　To those of mine in court. I'll stay at home
　And pray God's blessing into thy attempt.   255
　Be gone tomorrow, and be sure of this:
　What I can help thee to, thou shalt not miss.

　　　　　　　　　　　　　　　　　　　　Exeunt

235 Haply] F (Happily)   249 an] F1; and F3

234 **conversation** discourse
238 **Are of a mind** have the same opinion
240 **schools** (medical) faculty
241 **Embowelled** disembowelled, rendered
　empty of life-functions
　doctrine learning
244 **receipt** either prescription for a
　remedy or the remedy itself
247 **try success** find out what happens

248 **The well-lost life of mine** An unusual
　construction. Some editors emend *The*
　to *This*; but perhaps Helen means *of
　mine* to contrast with the much more
　important life of *his grace*.
251 **knowingly** i.e. my belief is based on
　real knowledge
255 **into** unto

2.1 *Flourish cornetts. Enter the King with divers*
young lords taking leave for the Florentine war,
Bertram, and Paroles

KING

Farewell, young lords; these warlike principles
Do not throw from you. And you, my lords, farewell.
Share the advice betwixt you. If both gain all,
The gift doth stretch itself as 'tis received,
And is enough for both.

FIRST LORD   'Tis our hope, sir,   5
After well-entered soldiers, to return
And find your grace in health.

KING

No, no, it cannot be. And yet my heart
Will not confess he owes the malady
That doth my life besiege. Farewell, young lords.   10
Whether I live or die, be you the sons
Of worthy Frenchmen. Let higher Italy—
Those bated that inherit but the fall
Of the last monarchy—see that you come
Not to woo honour but to wed it, when   15
The bravest questant shrinks. Find what you seek,
That fame may cry you loud. I say farewell.

2.1.0.1 *Flourish cornetts*] *at end of direction* F   0.3 *Bertram*] *Count, Rosse* F1 ; *Count*
Rosse F3   3 gain all,] CAPELL; gaine, all‿ F   15–16 it, when . . . shrinks.] F (shrin-
kes:); it; when . . . shrinks, POPE

2.1.0.1–2 The King's separate farewells
(ll. 1–2) as well as *betwixt* and *both*
(l. 3) suggest that the noblemen are in
two groups, those backing Florence
and those who will fight for Siena.

3–5 **If. . . both** This glosses *Share . . . be-*
twixt (l. 3). Unlike a material gift given
to two parties, with each receiving
only a fraction, this donation multi-
plies itself in being heeded and is thus
ample for both sides.

  3 **both gain all** both parties profit fully
from my advice

  6 **After well-entered soldiers** With pronoun as well as verb elided (*we are*),
a Latinate construction unusual in
Shakespeare. Abbott (§418) compares
Milton, *Paradise Lost* v. 247–8, 'nor
delay'd the winged Saint | After his
charge receiv'd'.

9 **owes** owns. See 1.1.34 and note.

12–16 **Let . . . shrinks** The King seems to
mean something like 'Let Italians of
the higher rank, now that those who
follow on the fall of the Roman empire
are diminished (i.e. fallen off from the
level of their Roman ancestors), see
that you (in contrast) come there not
to dally with honour but to win it truly
and wholly, when even the bravest
pursuer/suitor shrinks back in fear.'
Possibly *higher Italy* refers to geography rather than social eminence:
high was used of countries to denote
the inland area (*OED*, 3a). Hanmer
notes that ancient geographers divided
Italy along the Appennines into a
higher (Adriatic) side and a lower
(Tyrrhenian), and Shakespeare might
have been unaware that Florence and

SECOND LORD

Health at your bidding serve your majesty!

KING

Those girls of Italy, take heed of them.
They say our French lack language to deny   20
If they demand. Beware of being captives
Before you serve.

BOTH LORDS   Our hearts receive your warnings.

KING

Farewell. (*To some lords*) Come hither to me.
                        ⌈*Stands aside with lords*⌉

FIRST LORD (*to Bertram*)

O my sweet lord, that you will stay behind us!

PAROLES

'Tis not his fault, the spark.

SECOND LORD   O, 'tis brave wars!   25

PAROLES

Most admirable. I have seen those wars.

BERTRAM

I am commanded here, and kept a coil with:
'Too young', and 'the next year', and ''tis too early.'

PAROLES

An thy mind stand to't, boy, steal away bravely.

---

18 SECOND LORD] ROWE 1714; *L.G.* F   23 *To some lords*] HUNTER; *not in* F; *To Attendants* THEOBALD   23.1 *Stands aside with lords*] *Retires to a Couch* CAPELL; *not in* F; *Exit* POPE   27 with:] CAPELL (~;); with, F

Siena were both in the lower part. The Roman Empire was *the last monarchy* according to orthodox Christian interpretations of the four monarchies in Daniel 2.

17 **cry** extol (predating first *OED* entry for this meaning)

18 F assigns this line to First Lord, but if we are to make sense of the prefix *Both* (*Bo.*) for the second part of line 22 it seems likely that the F prefix *L.G.* here is an error for *L.E.*

23 Early editors had the King exit on this line, as the following conversation could not take place in his presence. But F indicates no exit and no re-entrance at l. 59, and Shakespeare's stage was large. The King probably

withdraws upstage instead and is seen in conversation with some of those who entered with him—perhaps the Sienese party, since he has been talking to the Florentine group as represented by First Lord. The King's illness might suggest a more dramatic withdrawal (Wilson directs that he swoon and be carried to a couch), but the lack of subsequent comment among the lords argues against this reading of *Come hither to me* as a call for help in extremity.

25 **spark** young gallant. In this sequence, as in the one beginning 2.3, Paroles intrudes on the conversation, answering remarks not addressed to him.

27 **kept a coil with** fussed over

BERTRAM

I shall stay here the fore-horse to a smock,   30
Creaking my shoes on the plain masonry,
Till honour be bought up, and no sword worn
But one to dance with. By heaven, I'll steal away!

FIRST LORD

There's honour in the theft.

PAROLES   Commit it, Count.

SECOND LORD

I am your accessary; and so farewell.   35

BERTRAM

I grow to you, and our parting is a tortured body.

FIRST LORD

Farewell, captain.

SECOND LORD   Sweet Monsieur Paroles.

PAROLES Noble heroes, my sword and yours are kin,
good sparks and lustrous, a word, good mettles. You
shall find in the regiment of the Spinii one Captain   40
Spurio with his cicatrice, an emblem of war, here on
his sinister cheek. It was this very sword entrenched
it. Say to him I live, and observe his reports for me.

---

41 Spurio with his cicatrice,] THEOBALD; *Spurio* his sicatrice, with F

30–3 **I . . . with** The basic contrast is
between courtly activities conducted in
fine clothes, especially dancing, and
the pursuit of honour in battle. The
level floor of the palace (*plain masonry*)
is opposed implicitly to the elevations
and difficulties of the battlefield, and
the ornamental dancing-rapier (see
Titus 2.1.39) to the active sword.

30 **fore-horse to a smock** vehicle at the
disposal of a woman, as in a dance.
The fore-horse, according to Staunton,
was ornamented with bells and rib-
bons. Wilson read 'the leader in a team
of horses driven by a woman', i.e. a
glance at Queen Elizabeth's habit of
preventing her young favourites from
seeking adventure in foreign wars. The
general image of bedecked but
degraded servitude to a *smock* easily
admits this specific application but
does not require it.

36 **I . . . body** i.e. I am as one body with
you, so that our separation is like torture of that body, dissevering parts

that belong together.

39 **a word** probably 'in a word', but
Moshinsky had the lords move away
from Paroles on their farewells so that
he had to call his *good sparks . . . good
mettles* after them, and *a word* begged
for their attention.

mettles F's *mettals* includes both
'metals', what the swords are made of,
and 'mettles', the combative spirits of
their owners. Modernization requires a
choice between what are now two distinct words, but election either way
loses the original balance.

41 **Spurio** The first concrete evidence
Paroles advances for his martial
experience has a name synonymous
with falsehood.

cicatrice scar

42 **sinister** left

43 **reports** The *OED* meaning that fits best
is 'response', in the musical sense, the
examples of which also support usage
in the plural.

FIRST LORD We shall, noble captain.

PAROLES Mars dote on you for his novices.   45

⌈*Exeunt First and Second Lords*⌉

(*To Bertram*) What will ye do?

BERTRAM Stay the King.

PAROLES Use a more spacious ceremony to the noble
lords. You have restrained yourself within the list of
too cold an adieu. Be more expressive to them; for   50
they wear themselves in the cap of the time, there
do muster true gait; eat, speak, and move under the
influence of the most received star; and, though the
devil lead the measure, such are to be followed. After
them, and take a more dilated farewell.   55

BERTRAM And I will do so.

PAROLES Worthy fellows, and like to prove most sinewy
swordmen.   *Exeunt*

Enter Lafeu to the King

LAFEU (*kneeling*)
Pardon, my lord, for me and for my tidings.

45.1 *Exeunt First and Second Lords*] CAPELL; *not in* F; *at l.* 44 COLLIER   46 *To Bertram*]
CAPELL; *not in* F   47 Stay₍] F1; Stay: F2   58.1 *to the King*] OXFORD; *not in* F   59
kneeling] JOHNSON; *not in* F

46–7 **What ... King** Paroles may be talking either to the Lords or to Bertram
(*ye* was used, in questions especially,
for either singular or plural). If to the
Lords, he means either 'where are you
going?' or, if the question mark is a
sign of emphasis, 'what (great feats of
war) will you achieve!' Bertram's line
thus breaks in to warn him that the
King is approaching, and should be
punctuated as in F2. But Paroles does
not *stay* (i.e. cease his talk): he goes
on for several more lines with no
acknowledgement of the King's presence or approach. It seems preferable
to take line 46 as a question addressed
to Bertram and line 47 as Bertram's
reply. Most editors assume that this
question is about running off to the
war, picking up on line 33, in which
case Bertram's resolve to *stay* may
mean 'support' or (with F2 punctuation) 'remain here'. But since Paroles
goes on to urge Bertram to an immediate action, pursuing the Lords for a
more elaborate leave-taking, both his
question and Bertram's answer prob-

ably have an immediate application—
'What are you doing hanging about
here when you should be following the
Lords?' 'I am awaiting the King.'

48 **spacious** ample

49 **list** limit

51 **wear themselves in the cap of the time**
i.e. are fashionable items displayed
with maximum visibility, as once were
the brooch and the toothpick
(1.1.159–60)

52 **muster true gait** Johnson's suggestion,
'they do *muster* with the *true gait*, that
is, they have the true military step', is
appropriate to Paroles' martial obsession, but the more general context
here of fashion (his other obsession)
supports Barish, 'set the right pace'.

53 **received** currently accepted, fashionable

55 **dilated** extended

56 **And** Asserts emphatic agreement
(Abbott §97), 'That's just what I will
do'; the underlining has more point if
Bertram is suddenly changing course,
swayed from his plan of awaiting the
King by a powerful new imperative.

KING

I'll fee thee to stand up.   60

LAFEU (*standing*)

Then here's a man stands that has bought his
    pardon.

I would you had kneeled, my lord, to ask me mercy,

And that at my bidding you could so stand up.

KING

I would I had, so I had broke thy pate

And asked thee mercy for't.

LAFEU   Good faith, across!   65

But, my good lord, 'tis thus: will you be cured

Of your infirmity?

KING   No.

LAFEU   O, will you eat

No grapes, my royal fox? Yes, but you will,

My noble grapes, and if my royal fox

Could reach them. I have seen a medicine   70

That's able to breathe life into a stone,

Quicken a rock, and make you dance canary

---

60 fee] THEOBALD; fee F   61 *standing*] *not in* F   bought] THEOBALD; brought F

60–1 **I'll . . . pardon** F's *I'll see thee to
stand up* may accord with usage as
Riverside suggests ('the infinitive with
to was common after verbs of perceiving'), but it responds in no way to
Lafeu's prayer for pardon. Theobald's
emendation, assuming the error of
'fee' for 'fee' that the long s made easy,
has the King provide money to the
pardon-seeker, who in turn uses it to
buy what he desires. As Taylor points
out, Theobald's second emendation of
brought to *bought*, besides according
with *fee*, avoids both the inconsistency
in Lafeu's first needing pardon and
then asserting he has brought it with
him, and the awkwardness of thus
presenting Helen and her cure *before*
his careful build-up in lines 66–85.

65 **across** Jokingly denigrates the King's
wit: in the joust, to break a lance
across rather than lengthwise from the
point backward showed ineptitude.

67–70 **O...them** The fox in Aesop's
fable, when he could not reach the
grapes, called them sour and denied he
wanted them. Lafeu hears such sour

grapes in the King's denial of desire to
be cured, and suggests that the grapes
he brings, the cure, may be within the
King's reach. See fig. 11, p. 67.

70 **medicine** Takes in both healing potion
and the doctor who administers it
(*OED, sb.* 1 and 2). The latter usage
(compare *Macbeth* 5.2.27 and *Winter's
Tale* 4.4.587) was presumably influenced by Fr. *médecin*. Helen's gender
brings the term even closer to Eng.
medicine: Cotgrave glosses *medecine* as
a physic or a 'she physician'. Lafeu
goes on to emphasize Helen herself as
the curative application, rather than
the prescription she carries. There are
suggestions, reinforced by lines 73–6
and 95–6 below, of the ancient practice of presenting a sexually attractive
young woman to an ailing king to
reanimate his potency and thus
his right to continue ruling; in the
case of the biblical David this device
was unsuccessful (1 Kings 1: 3–4),
but Lafeu hopes for a different outcome.

72 **canary** a dance 'fast, extravagant and

With sprightly fire and motion; whose simple touch
Is powerful to araise King Pépin, nay,
To give great Charlemagne a pen in 's hand   75
And write to her a love-line.

KING   What 'her' is this?

LAFEU

Why, Doctor She. My lord, there's one arrived,
If you will see her. Now, by my faith and honour,
If seriously I may convey my thoughts
In this my light deliverance, I have spoke   80
With one that in her sex, her years, profession,
Wisdom, and constancy, hath amazed me more
Than I dare blame my weakness. Will you see her—
For that is her demand—and know her business?
That done, laugh well at me.

KING   Now, good Lafeu,   85
Bring in the admiration, that we with thee
May spend our wonder too, or take off thine
By wond'ring how thou took'st it.

LAFEU   Nay, I'll fit you,
And not be all day neither.   ⌈*He goes to a door*⌉

KING

Thus he his special nothing ever prologues.   90

89 *He goes to a door*] HUNTER; *not in* F; *Exit* THEOBALD

even wild in its movement' (Brissen-
den, p. 54)

73 **simple** mere, perhaps playing also on
OED, *sb.* B6, 'medicine'
74–6 **Is powerful . . . love-line** Lafeu's
allusions to quickening inert matter
into lively action here become more
explicitly sexual: Charlemagne's *pen*
(slang for 'penis', as in *Merchant*
5.1.237) will enact desire for Helen;
Pépin, through the F spelling *Pippen*,
is also associated with the penis,
which Helen's powerful touch will
araise—raise from the dead, but specifically excite to an erection.
80 **light deliverance** frivolous way of
speaking; in view of the innuendoes
about Pépin and Charlemagne, probably *light* plays on 'wanton' as well.
81 **profession** that in which she professes
skill, i.e. medicine; amazing not in

itself but in conjunction with *her sex,
her years*. He is impressed well beyond
what can be ascribed to the suscepti-
bility of age (ll. 82–3).
86 **admiration** marvel
87 **take off** remove
88 **took'st** caught, as a disease
fit you 'furnish you with what you
need', perhaps with a glance at sexual
anatomy, and also 'pay you out, get
back at you'; Philip Edwards finds the
same double sense in *The Spanish Tragedy* 4.1.70, and adds that the latter
usage (*v.* 12) was well established before *OED*'s initial date for it of 1625
(Revels edn.).
90 **Thus . . . prologues** The King responds
to Lafeu's 'light deliverance' rather
than the serious thoughts of ll. 80–3.
The line functions mainly to cover
Lafeu's walk upstage to fetch Helen.

LAFEU

Nay, come your ways.

   Enter Helen, disguised

KING

This haste hath wings indeed.

LAFEU (*to Helen*)   Nay, come your ways.

This is his majesty. Say your mind to him.

A traitor you do look like, but such traitors

His majesty seldom fears. I am Cressid's uncle   95

That dare leave two together. Fare you well.

     ⌈ *Exeunt all but the King and Helen* ⌉

KING

Now, fair one, does your business follow us?

HELEN

Ay, my good lord.

Gérard de Narbonne was my father,

In what he did profess well found.

KING   I knew him.   100

HELEN

The rather will I spare my praises towards him.

Knowing him is enough. On 's bed of death

Many receipts he gave me, chiefly one

91.1 *disguised*] OXFORD; *not in* F   96.1 *Exeunt . . . Helen*] F (*Exit.*)

91.1 **Enter Helen, disguised** Taylor's proposal that Helen is in disguise avoids strained and awkward readings of 2.3.46, where Lafeu seems astonished to discover that the King's healer is the woman he met at Roussillon. The hypothesis that she is here cloaked or veiled so as to be unrecognizable is supported by Lafeu's talking as if he had only just met her (ll. 80–3), and not naming her when he presents her to the King (*Doctor She*) or when he comments on the cure at 2.3.42–3 (*I'll like a maid the better*) before her entrance in triumph.

92 **This haste hath wings indeed** The King may refer to Lafeu's speed in producing Helen so soon after broaching the subject, but more probably he comments on her hesitant entrance, as indicated by Lafeu's encouraging *Nay, come your ways*, which he has to repeat.

95 **Cressid's uncle** Pandarus, the first pander

96.1 **Exeunt . . . Helen** The Italy-bound lords who entered with the King at the opening of the scene have perhaps been still on stage, though withdrawn, during the intimate scene between the King and Lafeu, but in this meeting their continued presence seems inappropriate. The interchange between Helen and the King becomes itself increasingly intimate: by the end of the scene, she is addressing the monarch as *thou* (see note to line 191). The references that suggest a sexual aspect also point to a private encounter.

98–9 If F's lineation represents Shakespeare's intention, the short lines and pauses point to Helen's initial difficulty in presenting her case to the King.

100 **well found** *OED* 1, 'of tried goodness, merit, or value', cites only this example; possibly parallel to *well seen*, 'highly qualified', as in *Shrew* 1.2.132 and Marlowe, *Doctor Faustus* 1.1.38.

103 **receipts** formulas for remedies of diseases, prescriptions

Which as the dearest issue of his practice,
And of his old experience th'only darling,   105
He bade me store up as a triple eye,
Safer than mine own two. More dear I have so,
And, hearing your high majesty is touched
With that malignant cause wherein the honour
Of my dear father's gift stands chief in power,   110
I come to tender it and my appliance
With all bound humbleness.

KING   We thank you, maiden,
But may not be so credulous of cure,
When our most learnèd doctors leave us and
The congregated college have concluded   115
That labouring art can never ransom nature
From her inaidable estate. I say we must not
So stain our judgement, or corrupt our hope,
To prostitute our past-cure malady
To empirics, or to dissever so   120
Our great self and our credit to esteem
A senseless help, when help past sense we deem.

HELEN

My duty, then, shall pay me for my pains.
I will no more enforce mine office on you,
Humbly entreating from your royal thoughts   125
A modest one to bear me back again.

KING

I cannot give thee less, to be called grateful.

107 two. More dear] F (two:); two, more dear; STEEVENS

105 **old** long-time, plentiful
    only pre-eminent, chief
106 **triple** third
109 **cause** disease
    honour worthiness, 'quality for which
    it is esteemed' (Riverside)
111 **appliance** administering (of it)
114 **leave** give up on
115 **congregated college** i.e. of physi-
    cians; compare Massinger, *The City
    Madam* 4.2.21.
118 **stain** defile
    corrupt turn in a perverse direction
    (toward an amateur healer where the
    professional ones have failed)
119 **prostitute** surrender to degradation

120 **empirics** quacks
120-2 **or . . . deem** or to act in a way
    opposed to my good reputation by put-
    ting value on a cure not based on
    reason when I believe *any* cure is an
    unreasonable expectation
126 **A modest one** Primarily 'a thought of
    moderate approbation', with an under-
    current of 'one affirming I am modest'
    (compare *Much Ado* 4.1.37, *modest evi-
    dence* = 'evidence of modesty');
    Helen's word choice reflects the unease
    about overstepping the bounds of
    maiden modesty that comes through
    later in this scene (168-71) and in 2.3
    when choosing her husband.

Thou thought'st to help me, and such thanks I give
As one near death to those that wish him live.
But what at full I know, thou know'st no part;   130
I knowing all my peril, thou no art.

HELEN

What I can do can do no hurt to try,
Since you set up your rest 'gainst remedy.
He that of greatest works is finisher
Oft does them by the weakest minister.   135
So holy writ in babes hath judgement shown
When judges have been babes. Great floods have
    flown
From simple sources, and great seas have dried
When miracles have by the greatest been denied.
Oft expectation fails, and most oft there   140
Where most it promises; and oft it hits
Where hope is coldest and despair most fits.

142 fits] COLLIER (*conj.* Theobald); shifts F; sits ROWE 1714

128–208 As the King and Helen move
into real debate, blank verse yields to
couplets, which continue to the end of
the scene. That the effect is not so
much greater formality as increased
intensity is suggested by a simultan-
eous switch in the King's address to
Helen, from *you* to *thou*.

133 **set up your rest** take your final resolution (from the card game primero,
in which setting up one's rest is gam-
bling the reserved stake)

134–5 **He . . . minister** Malone cites Mat-
thew 11:25, where Jesus thanks God
for revealing to 'babes' what he hides
from the wise, and 1 Corinthians
1:27: 'But God hath chosen the foolish things of the world to confound the
wise; and God hath chosen the weak
things of the world to confound the
things which are mighty.'

136–7 **So . . . babes** Examples include the
young Daniel, who supported Susanna
while mature judges believed the
elders' false witness against her (Story
of Susanna 45–62), and the twelve-
year-old Jesus among the doctors of
the temple (Luke 2: 42–9).

137–9 **Great . . . denied** Both divine inter-
ventions involve Moses, who struck
water from a rock to quench the thirst
of the Israelites (Exodus 17), having
earlier led them through a miraculous-
ly dried Red Sea (Exodus 14). The
greatest who denied includes both Pha-
raoh, who hardened his heart against
earlier manifestations of the power of
Yahweh, and the elders of Israel who
joined the complaints against Yahweh
during the drought in the wilderness.

140 **Oft . . . there** Johnson's conjecture
that this line was once part of a
couplet, like all the other lines in this
section, is likely to be right; but speculation on what was in the omitted line
is difficult, since no gap in the sense
offers a lead.

expectation what is awaited

142 **fits** F's *shifts* makes a kind of sense,
and the faulty rhyme should not rule
it out in a passage that rhymes
finisher/minister, but the meanings of
shift do not suit the fixed quality seemingly required here for *despair*. Rowe's
sits meets that requirement, and is
strengthened by other instances of *sit*
with emotions, e.g. *Richard II* Add.
Pass. C.13/1.3.280, *Hamlet* 3.4.102;
but the likeliest hypothesis for the copy
behind F's error, *ffitts*, favours Theobald's emendation.

KING

I must not hear thee. Fare thee well, kind maid.
Thy pains, not used, must by thyself be paid.
Proffers not took reap thanks for their reward.   145

HELEN

Inspirèd merit so by breath is barred.
It is not so with him that all things knows
As 'tis with us that square our guess by shows.
But most it is presumption in us when
The help of heaven we count the act of men.   150
Dear sir, to my endeavours give consent.
Of heaven, not me, make an experiment.
I am not an impostor that proclaim
Myself against the level of mine aim,
But know I think, and think I know most sure,   155
My art is not past power, nor you past cure.

KING

Art thou so confident? Within what space
Hop'st thou my cure?

HELEN   The greatest grace lending grace,
Ere twice the horses of the sun shall bring
Their fiery torcher his diurnal ring;   160
Ere twice in murk and occidental damp
Moist Hesperus hath quenched her sleepy lamp;

153 impostor] F (Impostrue)   160 torcher] F; coacher HUNTER (*conj.* Thirlby)

144 **by thyself be paid** be their own reward
146 **breath** speech originating with humans, as opposed to divine breathing-in or inspiration; man creates obstacles in the way of what God offers as deserving of gratitude (*merit*).
148 **square our guess by shows** frame our hypothesis by observing appearances
153 **impostor** F's *Impostrue* looks like a transposition error for 'imposture', a variant spelling of 'impostor', here = 'swindler', cheat'. Contemporary uses of the word in its various forms frequently occur in a context of false magic or quackery.
153–4 **that ... aim** either (a) that publicly forecast my success before (*against*) my taking aim (Hunter's interpretation) or, if modifying not *I* but *impostor*, (b) that make claim for my skill in

opposition to (excess of) my ability to hit the target
158–66 **The greatest ... die** Helen's periphrases, as Hunter observes, 'are probably designed to produce an effect of incantation against sickness'—an effect intensified by the couplet form and the occasional poetic vocabulary. It has been so played in several modern productions, so that spectators sometimes speak of *seeing* the King's cure, which in fact takes place off-stage.
160 **torcher** torch-bearer
162 **Hesperus ... sleepy lamp** the evening star; *her* rather than the more usual 'his' may indicate that Shakespeare knew Hesperus was the planet Venus, or it may be influenced by the traditional imagining of night as female, opposite to day as male (*his diurnal ring*, l. 160).

Or four and twenty times the pilot's glass
Hath told the thievish minutes, how they pass,
What is infirm from your sound parts shall fly,   165
Health shall live free and sickness freely die.

KING

Upon thy certainty and confidence
What dar'st thou venture?

HELEN   Tax of impudence,
A strumpet's boldness, a divulgèd shame;
Traduced by odious ballads, my maiden's name   170
Seared otherwise; no worse of worst, extended
With vilest torture, let my life be ended.

KING

Methinks in thee some blessèd spirit doth speak:
His powerful sound within an organ weak.
And what impossibility would slay   175
In common sense, sense saves another way.
Thy life is dear, for all that life can rate
Worth name of life in thee hath estimate:
Youth, beauty, wisdom, courage, all
That happiness and prime can happy call.   180
Thou this to hazard needs must intimate
Skill infinite, or monstrous desperate.
Sweet practiser, thy physic I will try,
That ministers thine own death if I die.

169 shame;] THEOBALD; shame‸ F   170 ballads,] OXFORD; ballads: F   171 otherwise;] CAPELL; otherwise, F   no] F2; ne F1   173 speak:] CAPELL (~;); speak‸ F

163 **the pilot's glass** The nautical time-
keeper, customarily measuring a half-
hour, is conceived here as an
hourglass.
164 **Hath . . . pass** has counted over the
thievish minutes in their passage. This
sense is supported by F's comma after
minutes, which Rowe, followed by
many modern editors, deletes. The
result is the absurd reading, 'has
informed the thievish minutes of their
own passage'. For time as thief see
Sonnets 1–126 *passim*, and especially
77.7–8: 'Thou by thy dial's shady
stealth mayst know | Time's thievish
progress to eternity'.
165 **sound parts** parts that will be sound
166 **freely** readily
168–72 **Tax . . . ended** See Appendix B.

173–4 **in thee . . . weak** not 'speak his
sound', but a chiastic appositional
structure: *in thee = within an organ
weak, some blessèd spirit doth speak =
His powerful sound*
175–6 **And what . . . way** Against *common
sense*, which judges his cure impossible, the King sets a higher wisdom,
based not on hope for a miracle but
on rational apprehension of what
Helen is willing to hazard on her success.
178 **hath estimate** has a claim to be
counted in valuation
180 **prime** early womanhood, springtime
of life
182 **monstrous desperate** The words modify not *skill* but an understood 'thou'.
183 **practiser** (medical) practitioner

HELEN

>　If I break time, or flinch in property　　　　　　185
>　Of what I spoke, unpitied let me die,
>　And well deserved. Not helping, death's my fee.
>　But, if I help, what do you promise me?

KING

>　Make thy demand.

HELEN　　　　　　　　　　But will you make it even?

KING

>　Ay, by my sceptre and my hopes of heaven.　　　190

HELEN

>　Then shalt thou give me with thy kingly hand
>　What husband in thy power I will command.
>　Exempted be from me the arrogance
>　To choose from forth the royal blood of France,
>　My low and humble name to propagate　　　　　195
>　With any branch or image of thy state;
>　But such a one, thy vassal, whom I know
>　Is free for me to ask, thee to bestow.

KING

>　Here is my hand. The premises observed,
>　Thy will by my performance shall be served.　　　200
>　So make the choice of thy own time, for I,
>　Thy resolved patient, on thee still rely.
>　More should I question thee, and more I must,
>　Though more to know could not be more to trust:

190 heaven] THEOBALD (*conj.* Thirlby); helpe F

185–6 **flinch in property | Of** shrink or deviate from anything pertaining to

189 **make it even** meet my request with corresponding fulfilment

190 **heaven** Thirlby's emendation maintains the chain of rhymed couplets which begins at 128 and continues, with only one break at 140, to the end of the scene. It also underlines the solemnity of the vow to have the King swear not only by his high trust on earth but by his prospects of salvation beyond this life.

191 **thou** Helen here shifts from the conventional *you* to *thou* (maintained at ll. 192, 196, 197, 198), highly unusual in addressing a king. It may mark a special relationship, a kind of partnership in the attempted cure, or perhaps the licence of the miracle-bringer: Joan la Pucelle in *1 Henry VI*, when presented in 1.2 like Helen as a wonder-worker, uses the privileged 'thou' to the Dauphin.

196 **image** may mean 'representative', i.e. ruling out high court officials, but more probably it parallels *branch*: the royal children seen first as offshoots from the family tree and then as likenesses of their father. For *image* connected with offspring, see *Winter's Tale* 5.1.126, *2 Henry IV* 4.3.55, *3 Henry VI (Richard Duke of York)* 5.4.54, and *Lucrece* 1753.

From whence thou cam'st, how tended on—but rest   205
Unquestioned welcome, and undoubted blest.
—Give me some help here, ho!—If thou proceed
As high as word, my deed shall match thy deed.
                                          Flourish. Exeunt

2.2 *Enter Countess and Clown*

COUNTESS Come on, sir, I shall now put you to the
   height of your breeding.

CLOWN I will show myself highly fed and lowly taught.
   I know my business is but to the court.

COUNTESS To the court! Why, what place make you   5
   special, when you put off that with such contempt,
   'but to the court'?

CLOWN Truly, madam, if God have lent a man any
   manners, he may easily put it off at court. He that
   cannot make a leg, put off 's cap, kiss his hand, and   10
   say nothing, has neither leg, hands, lip, nor cap;
   and indeed such a fellow, to say precisely, were not
   for the court. But, for me, I have an answer will
   serve all men.

COUNTESS Marry, that's a bountiful answer that fits all   15
   questions.

CLOWN It is like a barber's chair that fits all buttocks:
   the pin-buttock, the quatch-buttock, the brawn-
   buttock, or any buttock.

208.1 *Exeunt*] F (*Exit*)

2.2.1–2 **put you . . . breeding** i.e. test the
   social skills that your upbringing has
   inculcated
   3 **highly fed and lowly taught** Plays on
   the proverb 'Better fed than taught'
   (Tilley F174), often applied to the
   spoilt children of the upper classes;
   the Clown implies that with such
   appropriate *breeding* he will fit in well
   at the court, which values superficial
   graces of behaviour but not the manners and morals of the truly educated
   (hence the dismissive attitude of *but to
   the court* (l. 4)). Or, as Delius suggests,
   he may twist *breeding* into its cattle-
   raising sense, which involves feeding,
   to get from *the height of your breeding*
   to *highly fed*.

9 **put it off** carry it off (Onions), picking
   up on the Countess's *put off* (l. 6) =
   'dismiss'
9–14 **He . . . men** Any fool can get by at
   court through physical courtesies,
   without giving himself away in speech,
   and the Clown improves on this by
   having an all-purpose response to any
   question or comment.
17 **barber's . . . buttocks** 'As common as
   a barber's chair' was a current proverb
   (Tilley B73); the variant recorded
   later, 'Like a barber's chair, fit for
   every buttock' (B74) was perhaps
   influenced by this play.
18 **pin** narrow or sharp
   quatch Meaning unknown, probably
   related to 'quat', *v.*[1] 1 'to squash' or

COUNTESS Will your answer serve fit to all questions?   20

CLOWN As fit as ten groats is for the hand of an
attorney, as your French crown for your taffeta
punk, as Tib's rush for Tom's forefinger, as a pancake
for Shrove Tuesday, a Morris for May Day, as the
nail to his hole, the cuckold to his horn, as a scolding   25
quean to a wrangling knave, as the nun's lip to the
friar's mouth; nay, as the pudding to his skin.

COUNTESS Have you, I say, an answer of such fitness
for all questions?

CLOWN From below your duke to beneath your con-   30
stable, it will fit any question.

COUNTESS It must be an answer of most monstrous size
that must fit all demands.

CLOWN But a trifle neither, in good faith, if the learned
should speak truth of it. Here it is, and all that   35
belongs to't. Ask me if I am a courtier; it shall do
you no harm to learn.

COUNTESS To be young again, if we could. I will be a
fool in question, hoping to be the wiser by your
answer. I pray you, sir, are you a courtier?   40

2.2.40 I pray] F (*La⟨dy⟩*. I pray)

2, 'to squat'; Hanmer's 'squat or flat'
is a good guess.
brawn fleshy

21–7 **As fit ... skin** Besides the two holi-
days, other threads of association run
through the Clown's catalogue of 'fit'
things: the attorney's fee of ten groats
calls up the prostitute's French crown,
both the coin that pays her and the
bald head caused by the 'French disease' contracted from her; sexual
anatomy connects Tib's rush-ring and
Tom's forefinger back to the prostitute
and forward to nail and hole and to
pudding and skin. On taffeta as the
dress of whores, see *1 Henry IV* 1.2.10
and Middleton's *Spanish Gypsy* (1623)
4.3.70–1. For the rush-ring as rustic
love-gift, see *Kinsmen* 4.1.88–91 and
Spenser, *Shepheardes Calender*, 'Novem-
ber', 116. The last two items in the
Clown's list vary the proverb 'as fit as
a pudding for a friar's mouth' (Tilley
P620), presumably increasing the

'fitness' by reassigning the friar's
mouth to a nun's and the sausage-like
pudding to its tightly enclosing skin.

30 **below ... beneath** Taylor's emendation of *below* to *beyond* makes better
sense of the class difference, but the
clown is still thinking of his answer as
a barber's chair, applicable to—and
under—all ranks alike.

34 **neither** on the contrary (*OED, adv.* A.
3, intensifying negative)

38 **To be ... could** The Clown's invitation
to learn prompts the Countess's *To be
young again*, followed by the wry qualification *if* [only] *we could*. Learning
and youth are associated in proverbs—
Tilley L152 and L153 (Dent cites
16th-century uses of the latter); see
also *Merchant* 3.2.160–1.

40 F's repeated speech prefix begins a new
page, but the catchword *Lady* ending
the previous page rules out simple
error. Taylor guesses that a speech of
the Clown's has dropped out, but Bowers suspects that it rather marks mar-

CLOWN O Lord, sir!—There's a simple putting off.
More, more, a hundred of them.

COUNTESS Sir, I am a poor friend of yours that loves
you.

CLOWN O Lord, sir!—Thick, thick, spare not me.   45

COUNTESS I think, sir, you can eat none of this homely
meat.

CLOWN O Lord, sir!—Nay, put me to't, I warrant you.

COUNTESS You were lately whipped, sir, as I think.

CLOWN O Lord, sir!—Spare not me.   50

COUNTESS Do you cry 'O Lord, sir!' at your whipping,
and 'spare not me'? Indeed your 'O Lord, sir!' is
very sequent to your whipping. You would answer
very well to a whipping, if you were but bound to't.

CLOWN I ne'er had worse luck in my life in my 'O Lord,   55
sir!' I see things may serve long, but not serve ever.

COUNTESS I play the noble housewife with the time, to
entertain it so merrily with a fool.

CLOWN O Lord, sir!—Why, there't serves well again.

COUNTESS

An end, sir. To your business. (*Giving him a letter*)
Give Helen this   60

60 An end, sir. To] ROWE 1714 (Sir;); And end sir to F; An end, Sir, to ROWE   *Giving him a letter*] not in F

ginal addition to the Countess's original speech ('Speech Prefixes', p. 69n).

41 **O Lord, sir** An empty phrase fashionable with courtiers, mocked also by
Jonson (*Every Man Out* 3.1.22, Asotus
in *Cynthia's Revels* 1.4); as an answer
it was noncommittal, evasive (*putting
off*). Steevens credits Farmer with citation of Cleveland's 'How the Commencement Grows New' (1636) in
which gentlemen come to show off
their clothes and 'to answer O Lord sir
and talk play-book oaths.'

45 **Thick** in rapid succession

52–3 **is very sequent to** properly follows,
i.e. as pleading for mercy, rather than
the unfortunate (in this context of
whipping) *spare not me*

53–4 **answer . . . to** (a) repay (b) reply
(with *O Lord, sir!*)

54 **bound to't** (a) legally obligated to
answer (b) tied to the whipping post

57–8 **I play . . . fool** A fine household
manager I am, wasting time joking
with a fool. For 'noble' in such an
ironic sense, see *Dream* 5.1.216, *As
You Like It* 2.7.33 and 3.4.40, *Much
Ado* 5.4.50, etc. *Housewife* may itself
carry its later pejorative meaning (=
'hussy'); the term is specifically connected with time-wasting by Beaumont and Fletcher, *The Maid's Tragedy*
2.2.84–5.

60 **To your business** The reading suggested by F, 'an end to your business'
(= 'commotion', *OED* 7b), is possible,
but the F text of this play frequently omits necessary punctuation, and
the ongoing sentence undercuts the
Countess's mocking echo of 'O Lord,
sir!' as well as the allusion to the
Clown's *business* from line 4, picking
up with her mission after the paren-
thesis of foolery.

And urge her to a present answer back.
Commend me to my kinsmen and my son.
This is not much.

CLOWN Not much commendation to them.

COUNTESS

Not much employment for you. You understand me.   65

CLOWN Most fruitfully. I am there before my legs.

COUNTESS Haste you again.   *Exeunt severally*

2.3   *Enter Bertram, Lafeu, and Paroles*

LAFEU They say miracles are past, and we have our
philosophical persons to make modern and familiar
things supernatural and causeless. Hence is it that
we make trifles of terrors, ensconcing ourselves into
seeming knowledge when we should submit our-   5
selves to an unknown fear.

PAROLES Why, 'tis the rarest argument of wonder that
hath shot out in our latter times.

BERTRAM And so 'tis.

LAFEU To be relinquished of the artists—   10

PAROLES So I say, both of Galen and Paracelsus.

LAFEU Of all the learned and authentic fellows—

PAROLES Right, so I say.

---

67 *Exeunt severally*] CAPELL; *Exeunt* F
   2.3.0.1 *Bertram*] F (*Count*)   13 Right,] F3; Right‸ FI

---

61 **present** immediate
66 **Most . . . legs** The Clown picks up the
   meaning of 'erection' in *understand*
   and carries it on in *fruitfully* ('abundantly', 'productive of children');
   because of that erection he is *there*—at
   her meaning as so conceived—before
   his legs.
2.3.0.1 Rolfe and Sisson omit Bertram
   from the initial entrance; but, although on the page his almost silent
   presence looks superfluous, theatric-
   ally he is necessary as the intended
   recipient of Lafeu's serious comments
   (unlikely to be aimed at the hanger-on
   Paroles), who is forestalled in his
   attempted responses by the intrusions
   of his pushy companion (see 2.1.25
   and note).
 I **miracles are past** According to Protes-
   tant doctrine, miracles ceased after

New Testament times. See *Henry V*
1.1.68.
 2 **modern** everyday
 3 **things** i.e. things that are
   causeless without natural cause
 4 **ensconcing** securing
 6 **unknown fear** fear of the unknown.
   See Abbott §374 and Sonnet 124, line
   7, where 'thrallèd discontent' apparently means 'discontent caused by
   enslavement'.
 7 **argument** theme
 8 **latter times** 'times since the end of
   miracles', or perhaps just 'recently'
10 **artists** medical practitioners
11 **Galen and Paracelsus** the two schools
   of medicine
12 **authentic fellows** licensed members,
   i.e. of the *congregated college* (2.1.115)
   of physicians

LAFEU That gave him out incurable—

PAROLES Why, there 'tis. So say I too.   15

LAFEU Not to be helped.

PAROLES Right, as 'twere a man assured of a—

LAFEU Uncertain life and sure death.

PAROLES Just, you say well. So would I have said.

LAFEU I may truly say it is a novelty to the world.   20

PAROLES It is indeed. If you will have it in showing, you shall read it in what-do-ye-call there.

LAFEU ⌈*reads*⌉ *A Showing of a Heavenly Effect in an Earthly Actor.*

PAROLES That's it. I would have said the very same.   25

LAFEU Why, your dolphin is not lustier. Fore me, I speak in respect—

PAROLES Nay, 'tis strange, 'tis very strange; that is the brief and the tedious of it; and he's of a most facinorous spirit that will not acknowledge it to be   30 the—

LAFEU Very hand of heaven.

PAROLES Ay, so I say.

LAFEU In a most weak—

PAROLES And debile minister, great power, great tran-   35 scendence, which should indeed give us a further use to be made than alone the recov'ry of the King, as to be—

LAFEU Generally thankful.

Enter King, Helen, and Attendants

21 indeed.] CAPELL (~:); indeed∧ F; indeed, ROWE   22 what-do-ye-call there] CASE (*conj.* Glover); what do ye call there F   23 reads] *after* ALEXANDER; *not in* F   A . . . Actor] WARBURTON; A . . . actor F   25 it. I would have said∧] F4 (it,); it, I would haue said, F1

16 **helped** cured
21 **in showing** visible, in print
22 **what-do-ye-call** Other examples of such a phrase without an object are 'Whatshicall Court' in Brome, *The Northern Lass* 5.5.18, and 'Scotch what d'ye call' in Milton's sonnet 'On the New Forcers of Conscience'.
23–4 *A Showing . . . Actor* Lafeu fills in the gap in Paroles' memory by reading the title, presumably of a topical broadside ballad.
26 **dolphin** Primarily the sportive fish, with a play on the English form of

'Dauphin'—the young heir of France, as opposed to his old father.
Fore me before me, a mild oath, like *Fore God* (l. 46)
28–9 **the brief and the tedious** Paroles' elegant variation on 'the short and the long' (Tilley L419)
30 **facinorous** flagrantly wicked. F's *facinerious* is listed by *OED* as a variant form.
35 **debile minister** weak agent
35–6 **transcendence** rising above the ordinary
36 **use** (moral) application

PAROLES I would have said it; you say well. Here comes   40
  the King.   .
LAFEU *Lustig*, as the Dutchman says. I'll like a maid
  the better whilst I have a tooth in my head. Why,
  he's able to lead her a coranto.
PAROLES *Mort du vinaigre!* Is not this Helen?   45
LAFEU Fore God, I think so.
KING

Go call before me all the lords in court.

                                    Exit Attendant
Sit, my preserver, by thy patient's side,
And with this healthful hand, whose banished sense
Thou hast repealed, a second time receive   50
The confirmation of my promised gift,
Which but attends thy naming.

        Enter four lords

47.1 *Exit Attendant*] *after* CAPELL; *not in* F   52.1 *four*] *after* SISSON; *3 or 4* F; *several*
CAPELL

42 *Lustig* frolicsome
   Dutchman German
43 **tooth** sweet tooth (Tilley T420), i.e.
   appetite for sensual pleasures
44 **coranto** a lively, springing dance (Bris-
   senden, p. 52). Lafeu's comment may
   be hypothetical, but several modern
   directors have effectively displayed the
   change in the King, and in the mood
   of the court, by having a dance here.
45 *Mort du vinaigre* (F *Mor du vinager*)
   feels in context like a fashionable oath
   but makes no sense, whether one
   assumes a reference in 'vinegar' to the
   Crucifixion or plays up the connection
   with venereal disease, for which vinegar was part of the cure (Nashe, *Pierce
   Penniless*, and *Christ's Tears over Jeru-
   salem*, *Works*, ed. R. B. McKerrow (Oxford, 1958), i. 182, and ii. 185).
46 **Fore . . . so** Editors have difficulty with
   Lafeu's surprise at seeing Helen
   because he himself introduced her at
   court in 2.1. The Clarkes take Lafeu's
   line as affirming his own statement
   about the King's ability to dance a
   coranto, and not as responding to Paroles, whom he ignores; Hunter and
   others take it as irony or emphasis;
   Wilson inclines toward giving the
   speech to Bertram, a solution carried
   out in the Moshinsky production. If in

preference to these strained readings
we take Lafeu's surprise as his own
and as genuine, its most plausible
occasion is recognition of Helen without her earlier protective disguise. See
2.1.91.1 and note.
48 **Sit . . . side** Helen presumably sits at
   the King's invitation, but probably
   rises when going through the choosing
   ritual, moving from one lord to another rather than reviewing them in a
   stationary position (thus allowing
   Lafeu not to hear the actual conversa-
   tions and to conclude as she moves on
   that they are refusing her); certainly
   her humble offering of herself to Bertram implies standing before him
   rather than sitting while he stands.
50 **repealed** recalled, as from exile
52.1 *Enter four lords* Wilson directs that
   Bertram join the four royal wards;
   Sisson, who omitted him from the
   opening entrance, brings him on with
   the other lords here. Bertram may indeed take part in the ritual, watching
   with growing anxiety as others are
   eliminated; or he may stay close to
   Lafeu and Paroles, looking but not
   hearing, until Helen moves beyond the
   group of lords to select him. His surprise at line 107 supports the latter.

Fair maid, send forth thine eye. This youthful parcel
Of noble bachelors stand at my bestowing,
O'er whom both sovereign power and father's voice   55
I have to use. Thy frank election make.
Thou hast power to choose, and they none to forsake.
HELEN
To each of you, one fair and virtuous mistress
Fall when love please; marry, to each but one.
LAFEU *(aside)*
I'd give bay Curtal and his furniture   60
My mouth no more were broken than these boys'
And writ as little beard.
KING   Peruse them well.
Not one of those but had a noble father.
          She addresses her to a lord
HELEN
  Gentlemen,
Heaven hath through me restored the King to health.   65
COURT LORDS
We understand it, and thank heaven for you.
HELEN
I am a simple maid, and therein wealthiest
That I protest I simply am a maid.
—Please it your majesty, I have done already.
The blushes in my cheeks thus whisper me: 70
'We blush that thou shouldst choose; but, be
          refused,

58 mistress∧] ROWE; Mistris; F   63.1 *She … lord*] *as* F; *at l.* 77 *after* stream WILSON
66 COURT LORDS] F (*All.*)   71 choose; but, be refused,] RANN (*conj.* Malone); choose,
but be refused∧ F

54 **stand at my bestowing** are in my
  power (as royal wards) to give in marriage
56 **frank election** free choice
57 **forsake** refuse
59 **but one** (a) only one, or (b) except one
  (to whom I will fall)
60–1 **I'd give … boys'** Lafeu's wager of
  the bay horse, named Curtal for his
  docked tail, and trappings suggests the
  metaphor for youth in his following
  wish, the horse's mouth not yet tamed
  to the bridle-bit.
62 **writ** acknowledged
63.1 ***She addresses her to a lord*** Since

Helen does not in fact address a lord
singly until line 77, this stage direction looks misplaced (suggesting to
Bowers, 'Foul Papers', p. 58, that lines
64–77a were an addition to the manuscript, intended to precede the stage
direction). Wilson so replaces it. But
it would accord with Helen's shyness
and hesitation in this sequence to have
her make a false start at the choosing,
only to retreat into general address
and an attempt to justify her boldness;
lines 67–9 mark an initiative similarly
broken off in confusion.
68 **simply** without qualification

Let the white death sit on thy cheek for ever,
We'll ne'er come there again.'
KING   Make choice, and see.
Who shuns thy love shuns all his love in me.
HELEN
Now, Dian, from thy altar do I fly,   75
And to imperial Love, that god most high,
Do my sighs stream. (*To one lord*) Sir, will you hear
   my suit?
FIRST COURT LORD
And grant it.
HELEN   Thanks, sir. All the rest is mute.
LAFEU (*aside*) I had rather be in this choice than throw
ambs-ace for my life.   80
HELEN (*to another lord*)
The honour, sir, that flames in your fair eyes
Before I speak too threat'ningly replies.
Love make your fortunes twenty times above
Her that so wishes, and her humble love.
SECOND COURT LORD
No better, if you please.
HELEN   My wish receive,   85
Which great Love grant. And so I take my leave.

---

72 **the white death** Johnson identified this with green-sickness, an anaemic condition associated with virgins; *Etmullerus Abridg'd*, 2nd edn. (1703), condensed and translated from the German professor of physic Michael Ettmueller, gives as an alternative name for green-sickness 'White Virgin Fever' (fol. 586). While green-sickness would be appropriate to Helen's continued unmarried state if she were refused, the perpetual pallor she anticipates seems more emotional than physical.

74 **his love** love of him, as at 1.1.73.

78 **All the rest is mute** I have nothing further to say; Helen retreats from the unanticipated acceptance of a suit not seriously intended, like Beatrice in *Much Ado* 2.1.303–4.

80 **ambs-ace** two aces, the lowest dice throw; to Lafeu's comparison, seemingly ironic, P. A. Daniel compares 'I would rather have it than a poke in the eye with a birch-rod' (Hunter). Perhaps instead of seeing Lafeu's life at stake with a low throw at dice, we should read *for my life* as an intensifier: 'as sure as I'm alive', as frequently in Shakespeare.

81–2 **The honour ... replies** Hunter follows Wilson in reading *honour* as 'admiration', i.e. willingness to marry her, which is 'threatening' because this is not the husband she wants. But this stretches the usual senses of 'honour', and public intimation of Helen's private desires in the choosing seems less likely than *honour* as high rank and its imputed threat as disdain of her humble birth. In these latter encounters she takes care to write in advance for the lords the script of rejection.

LAFEU (*aside*) Do all they deny her? An they were sons
   of mine, I'd have them whipped, or I would send
   them to th' Turk to make eunuchs of.
HELEN (*to another lord*)
   Be not afraid that I your hand should take.   90
   I'll never do you wrong, for your own sake.
   Blessing upon your vows, and in your bed
   Find fairer fortune if you ever wed.
LAFEU (*aside*) These boys are boys of ice, they'll none
   have her. Sure, they are bastards to the English; the   95
   French ne'er got 'em.
HELEN (*to another lord*)
   You are too young, too happy, and too good
   To make yourself a son out of my blood.
FOURTH COURT LORD Fair one, I think not so.
LAFEU (*aside*) There's one grape yet. I am sure thy father   100
   drunk wine. But if thou be'st not an ass, I am a
   youth of fourteen. I have known thee already.
HELEN (*to Bertram*)
   I dare not say I take you, but I give
   Me and my service, ever whilst I live
   Into your guiding power.—This is the man.   105
KING
   Why, then, young Bertram, take her. She's thy wife.
BERTRAM
   My wife, my liege! I shall beseech your highness
   In such a business give me leave to use
   The help of mine own eyes.
KING   Know'st thou not, Bertram,
   What she has done for me?
BERTRAM   Yes, my good lord,   110
   But never hope to know why I should marry her.

---

95 her] F2; heere F1

87–9 **Do . . . of** Most commentators think
   that here and at ll. 94–6 Lafeu is taken
   in by Helen's play (see preceding note).
   Price, however (pp. 155–6), argues
   that we should trust Lafeu's comments
   as we do elsewhere: comments that
   here may indicate a stage demeanour
   for the lords of reluctant, formal
   acquiescence.
100–1 **There's . . . wine** By a rather up-
   side-down association with 'good
   wine, good blood' (Tilley W461) Lafeu
   attributes good blood through his
   father to Bertram, the *grape* or fruit of
   noble lineage.
102 **known** seen through

KING

Thou know'st she has raised me from my sickly bed.

BERTRAM

But follows it, my lord, to bring me down
Must answer for your raising? I know her well.
She had her breeding at my father's charge.   115
A poor physician's daughter my wife! Disdain
Rather corrupt me ever.

KING

'Tis only title thou disdain'st in her, the which
I can build up. Strange is it that our bloods,
Of colour, weight, and heat, poured all together,   120
Would quite confound distinction, yet stands off
In differences so mighty. If she be
All that is virtuous—save what thou dislik'st,
'A poor physician's daughter'—thou dislik'st
Of virtue for the name. But do not so.   125
From lowest place when virtuous things proceed,
The place is dignified by th' doer's deed.
Where great additions swell 's, and virtue none,
It is a dropsied honour. Good alone
Is good, without a name! Vileness is so.   130
The property by what it is should go,
Not by the title. She is young, wise, fair;

126 when] THEOBALD (*conj.* Thirlby); whence F   130 name!] F1 (~?); ~. F4
131 it] F2; is F1

113 **bring me down** abase me (by marriage to one beneath me)
116–17 **Disdain . . . ever** The *disdain* is
either Bertram's for Helen or the
King's (= 'anger') for Bertram. Either
way it will *corrupt* or spoil his fortunes.
With the first sense, more likely in
view of the King's *thou disdain'st*
(l. 118), the implied comparison is
'better tainted fortunes than tainted
blood'.
118 **title** Usually glossed 'lack of title'
(Brigstocke cites *food* = 'lack of food',
As You Like It 2.7.104), but as the
Clarkes observe Bertram has just given
Helen the dismissive 'title' of *poor
physician's daughter* (l. 116); and *name*
(l. 125), often educed as parallel to
title, points specifically to the same
phrase, repeated at line 124.

119–22 **Strange . . . mighty** The King
invokes the proverb 'There is no
difference of bloods in a basin' (Tilley
D335), setting types of physical blood
which become one in mixing against
bloods = 'lineages', which *stands off |
In differences*, keep separate and distinct in quality.
125 **name** i.e. of *poor physician's daughter*.
In the following corrective, the *name*
becomes an originating *place* which
Bertram should see as dignified by the
virtuous deed rather than the deed
discounted by its humble origin.
128 **additions swell 's** titles make us great
129 **alone** of itself
130 **so** i.e. vile of itself, regardless of title
131 **The property . . . go** the quality of
character should be known by what it
is intrinsically

In these to nature she's immediate heir,
And these breed honour. That is honour's scorn
Which challenges itself as honour's born   135
And is not like the sire. Honours thrive
When rather from our acts we them derive
Than our foregoers. The mere word's a slave,
Debauched on every tomb, on every grave
A lying trophy; and as oft is dumb   140
Where dust and damned oblivion is the tomb
Of honoured bones indeed. What should be said?
If thou canst like this creature as a maid,
I can create the rest. Virtue and she
Is her own dower; honour and wealth from me.   145

BERTRAM

I cannot love her, nor will strive to do't.

KING

Thou wrong'st thyself. If thou shouldst strive to
      choose . . .

HELEN

That you are well restored, my lord, I'm glad.
Let the rest go.

KING

My honour's at the stake, which to defeat   150
I must produce my power. Here, take her hand,

---

138 word's] F2; words, F1   139 grave∧] grave, STEEVENS; graue: F   141–2 tomb∧
. . . indeed.] THEOBALD (*conj.* Thirlby); Tombe. . . . indeed, F   147 thyself. If . . . choose
. . .] *after* OXFORD (choose—); thy selfe, if . . . choose. F

133 **In these . . . heir** she derives these directly from nature, without intermediate transmission, as of honour through ancestors (Johnson)
135 **challenges itself as** claims to be
139 **Debauched** led astray from honest service
140 **trophy** memorial
142 **honoured** honourable, as *Coriolanus* 3.1.76 and *Antony* 4.9.11
143–4 **creature . . . create** Repeating the root, the King again pays tribute to Helen's innate qualities, nature's creation, to put in perspective his own gifts (of *honour and wealth*, l. 145) as only supplementary.
147 **Thou . . . choose . . .** With F's punctuation, the King's line means something like 'You wrong yourself (by

losing an excellent bride, or by losing my favour) if you should strive to choose for yourself' (picking up on Bertram's refusal to *strive* to love Helen). But the conditional *shouldst*, implying future rebellion, is at odds with the present of the actual rebellion and *wrong'st thyself*. Taylor's repointing so that *Thou wrong'st thyself* is complete and *If thou shouldst strive to choose* begins a new sentence is attractive for that reason, but an ominous pause succeeding seems preferable to Helen's interrupting the King in this formal scene, no matter how uncomfortable she may be.

150 **which** refers to the threat to his honour, baited at the stake like a bull or bear (Abbott §271)

Proud, scornful boy, unworthy this good gift,
That dost in vile misprision shackle up
My love and her desert; that canst not dream
We, poising us in her defective scale,   155
Shall weigh thee to the beam; that wilt not know
It is in us to plant thine honour where
We please to have it grow. Check thy contempt.
Obey our will, which travails in thy good.
Believe not thy disdain, but presently   160
Do thine own fortunes that obedient right
Which both thy duty owes and our power claims;
Or I will throw thee from my care for ever
Into the staggers and the careless lapse
Of youth and ignorance, both my revenge and hate   165
Loosing upon thee in the name of justice,
Without all terms of pity. Speak, thine answer.

BERTRAM

Pardon, my gracious lord; for I submit
My fancy to your eyes. When I consider
What great creation and what dole of honour   170

169 eyes.] ROWE; eies, F

153 **misprision shackle** 'The similitude of misprision and prison begot shackle instantaneously' (Thirlby).

155–62 Having vowed to produce his power, the King abandons the avuncular *I* for the royal *we* in commanding Bertram; F capitalizes the plural pronouns at ll. 157, 159 and 162, presumably following Shakespeare's own emphasis in the manuscript. In returning to the singular at l. 163, the King moves from political threats of royal disfavour to the withdrawal of personal care from his ward.

155–6 **We ... beam** The King, adding his weight (*poising*) to Helen's otherwise lighter side of the scale will so outweigh Bertram's side as to send it up to the crossbar.

160 **presently** at once

161 **obedient right** right claimed by obedience

164 **staggers** A disease of horses characterized by a staggering gait, called a 'coltish disease' in the subtitle of *Hic Mulier* (1620).

164 **careless** W. W. Williams (*Parthenon*, 1 November 1862) supports his proposed emendation to *cureless*, adopted by Dyce, by the awkwardness of repeating *care* from the previous line, the ease of *a/u* misprints, and the parallel of *lapse* for 'youthful fall' with 'ruin' in *Merchant* 4.1.140–1: 'Repair thy wit, good youth, or it will fall | To cureless ruin'. But, as Hunter says, *careless* (= 'reckless, irresponsible') is more consonant with the giddiness of *staggers* and with youth and ignorance; these in any case have a cure in time.

167 **terms** conditions

168–9 **I submit ... eyes** Bertram follows, at least outwardly, a version of Theseus' advice to Hermia, 'Rather your eyes must with his [her father's] judgement look' (*Dream* 1.1.57).

170 **great creation** creation of greatness through titles and wealth (ll. 144–5)
dole portion

Flies where you bid it, I find that she which late
Was in my nobler thoughts most base is now
The praisèd of the King; who so ennobled
Is as 'twere born so.

KING   Take her by the hand,
And tell her she is thine; to whom I promise   175
A counterpoise, if not to thy estate
A balance more replete.

BERTRAM   I take her hand.

KING
Good fortune and the favour of the King
Smile upon this contract, whose ceremony
Shall seem expedient on the now-born brief   180
And be performed tonight. The solemn feast
Shall more attend upon the coming space,
Expecting absent friends. As thou lov'st her
Thy love's to me religious; else, does err.

> *Exeunt all but Paroles and Lafeu, who stay*
> *behind commenting of this wedding*

LAFEU Do you hear, monsieur? A word with you.   185
PAROLES Your pleasure, sir.
LAFEU Your lord and master did well to make his
recantation.
PAROLES Recantation? My lord? My master?
LAFEU Ay. Is it not a language I speak?   190
PAROLES A most harsh one, and not to be understood
without bloody succeeding. My master!

171 it,] CAPELL; it: F   184.1–2 *all but . . . behind*] F (*Parolles and Lafeu stay behind,*)

176–7 **A counterpoise . . . replete** Returning to his metaphor of the scale,
Helen's side as a poor commoner
defective against Bertram's weightier
one (ll. 155–6), the King defines how
with honour and wealth he will mend
the balance—either by making her estate to equal or even outweigh Bertram's or by improving it to a better
balance even if not the match of his
(*if not* and *more replete* can support
either construction).
179–80 **this contract . . . brief** Probably
'this agreement, the religious rites per-
taining to which shall be fitting [*seem*]
soon after [*expedient on*] the just-con-

cluded contract', or perhaps 'the just-
issued royal mandate' [*brief*].
182–3 **Shall . . . friends** shall wait a longer
time, allowing relatives not now here
to arrive
184 **religious** dutiful, devoted
184.1–2 *Exeunt . . . wedding* Bowers sees
in this unusual stage direction a note
made by Shakespeare when writing
was interrupted, to remind himself
how the scene was to go on; but he
observes that on resuming the scene
what Shakespeare elected to develop
was not comment on the wedding but
comic abuse of Paroles ('Foul Papers',
p. 59).

LAFEU Are you companion to the Count Roussillon?

PAROLES To any count. To all counts. To what is man.

LAFEU To what is count's man. Count's master is of   195
another style.

PAROLES You are too old, sir. Let it satisfy you, you are
too old.

LAFEU I must tell thee, sirrah, I write man; to which
title age cannot bring thee.   200

PAROLES What I dare too well do, I dare not do.

LAFEU I did think thee for two ordinaries to be a pretty
wise fellow; thou didst make tolerable vent of thy
travel, it might pass. Yet the scarves and the bannerets about thee did manifoldly dissuade me from   205
believing thee a vessel of too great a burden. I have
now found thee. When I lose thee again, I care not.
Yet art thou good for nothing but taking up, and
that thou'rt scarce worth.

PAROLES Hadst thou not the privilege of antiquity upon   210
thee—

211 thee—] ROWE 1714; ~. F

192 **bloody succeeding** bloodshed following

193 **companion** Lafeu's insults continue
with the term *companion*, which often
implied contempt, as in *Caesar* 4.2.190
and *Bussy D'Ambois* 1.2.92 (Brook, p.
58). The term is applied to Paroles
twice later in disreputable circumstances, at 3.5.15 and 5.3.250.

195 **man** Lafeu twists Paroles' grand *man*
= 'mankind' into *man* = 'servant', to
say that Paroles may be fit comrade
for a count's servant but not for his
master (perhaps alluding to Lafeu's
own familar relations with the King).

199 **write man** assert manhood

202 **ordinaries** meals

203 **vent** (a) expression (b) marketing.
Compare Jonson's *Epigram* 107, 'To
Captain Hungry', for a sketch of a
needy adventurer earning his suppers
by retailing travellers' tales and diplomatic gossip.

204–5 **scarves . . . bannerets** The first of
several references (2.3.226–8, 3.5.85,
4.3.144–5 and 326–7) to Paroles'
exaggerated display of the military
officer's scarf or sash, which here reminds Lafeu of a ship (*vessel*) decked

in pennants: compare *Merchant*
2.6.15, 'scarfèd barque'.

205 **manifoldly** in many ways, punning on
the multitude of *scarves* and *bannerets*
through the cloth suggestion of *fold*.

206–7 **I have . . . care not** Having *found*
Paroles, i.e. found him out, Lafeu will
part with him willingly, playing on the
proverb 'Better lost than found' (Tilley
L454).

208 **taking up** Continuing Lafeu's play on
finding and losing, this seems to
require one negative meaning (what
Paroles is fit for) and one positive meaning (what he is not worthy of), but it
is not clear which is meant of several
that *OED* offers in each category: on
the one hand bringing (a falcon) under
restraint, arresting or being arrested,
rebuking or being rebuked, and on the
other hand picking up from a prone
position, bringing (a horse) to stable,
enlisting, purchasing wholesale, adopting as a protégé. Wilson may be right
to have good and bad meanings conjoin
in 'enlisting as a common soldier'—with
an insult to Paroles' officer-pretensions
in 'common' but a remaining dignity in
'soldier' that he hardly merits.

LAFEU Do not plunge thyself too far in anger, lest thou
hasten thy trial; which if, Lord have mercy on thee
for a hen. So, my good window of lattice, fare thee
well. Thy casement I need not open, for I look   215
through thee. Give me thy hand.

PAROLES My lord, you give me most egregious indig-
nity.

LAFEU Ay, with all my heart, and thou art worthy of
it.   220

PAROLES I have not, my lord, deserved it.

LAFEU Yes, good faith, ev'ry dram of it, and I will not
bate thee a scruple.

PAROLES Well, I shall be wiser.

LAFEU Ev'n as soon as thou canst, for thou hast to pull   225
at a smack o'th' contrary. If ever thou beest bound
in thy scarf and beaten, thou shall find what it is to
be proud of thy bondage. I have a desire to hold my
acquaintance with thee, or rather my knowledge,
that I may say in the default, 'He is a man I know'.   230

PAROLES My lord, you do me most insupportable vexa-
tion.

214 **hen** i.e. as opposed to a cock, lacking
in masculine courage
window of lattice The image offers a
double insult, associating Paroles with
the taverns that often had signs of red
lattice, and implying as well that he is
easy to see through; if *lattice* could
also refer to openwork in clothes,
Lafeu is also anticipating his sneer at
Paroles as a 'snipped-taffeta fellow'
(4.5.1–2).

217 **egregious** Pistol's use of this uncommon term in rant (*Henry V* 2.1.44 and
4.4.11) renders it suspect as an affectation, and the suggestion is supported
by other examples from Jonson, Marston, etc., listed by A. H. King, *The
Language of the Satirized Characters in
'Poetaster'*, Lund Studies in English, 10
(Lund, 1941).

224 **I shall be wiser** Has the air of a stock
phrase, like so many of Paroles' lines
in this scene. Whether his phrasing is
hackneyed or not, his meaning of 'I
won't make the mistake again of talking to you' is wilfully misunderstood
by Lafeu (ll. 225–6) as an actual

resolve to seek wisdom.

225–6 **pull at a smack o'th' contrary** Perhaps 'swallow a fair taste of your own
folly' (Hunter), picking up the drinking
metaphor from *dram* and *scruple* (l.
222–3); but if *at* retains its older
meaning of 'against', as after other
verbs (*OED* 3c, 17), perhaps 'strive
against a tendency to the opposite', i.e.
folly, accords better with Lafeu's advice to start soon, which implies the
task will be long and difficult.

228 **thy bondage** what binds you, i.e. the
scarf of which Paroles is indeed proud
and *in* which he is proud = 'splendid,
magnificent'; compare for *proud* in a
context of fine clothing Marston, *Antonio's Revenge* 3.2.2–6.

230 **In the default** when you fail (see the
parallel construction in *The Revenger's
Tragedy* 2.3.129–30: 'Many a beauty
have I turned to poison | In the
denial'); or possibly 'in my inability'
(to say anything better), as in Capell's
paraphrase, 'since I cannot say—I
know he is a man, I may say—he is
a man that I know' (*Notes*, p. 12).

LAFEU I would it were hell-pains for thy sake, and my
poor doing eternal. For doing I am past, as I will by
thee in what motion age will give me leave.   *Exit*   235
PAROLES Well, thou hast a son shall take this disgrace
off me. Scurvy, old, filthy, scurvy lord! Well, I must
be patient, there is no fettering of authority. I'll beat
him, by my life, if I can meet him with any convenience, an he were double and double a lord. I'll have   240
no more pity of his age than I would have of—I'll
beat him, an if I could but meet him again.
       Enter Lafeu
LAFEU Sirrah, your lord and master's married. There's
news for you. You have a new mistress.
PAROLES I most unfeignedly beseech your lordship to   245
make some reservation of your wrongs. He is my
good lord; whom I serve above is my master.
LAFEU Who? God?
PAROLES Ay, sir.
LAFEU The devil it is that's thy master. Why dost thou   250
garter up thy arms o' this fashion? Dost make hose
of thy sleeves? Do other servants so? Thou wert best
set thy lower part where thy nose stands. By mine
honour, if I were but two hours younger I'd beat
thee. Methink'st thou art a general offence, and every   255
man should beat thee. I think thou wast created for
men to breathe themselves upon thee.

234–5 **For doing I am past, as I will by
thee** Most editors take *doing* in the
sense of 'sexual activity', but as Lafeu
is probably recalling Paroles' 'You are
too old' (l. 197), which dismissed his
fighting rather than his sexual ability,
perhaps it has a more general import
of 'manly performance'. Lafeu then
plays on the action in *past* to *pass* by
Paroles on his way out.

236–42 Paroles vents his outrage in a
combination of learned court phrases
and his own vocabulary, the deficien-
cies of which show up in ineffective
repetition and incomplete compari-
sons; the allusion to a son of Lafeu on
whom he may avenge his honour presumably belongs to the first category,
as we hear nothing elsewhere of such

a son, and indeed in later offering his
daughter as Bertram's second wife
Lafeu says the marriage will swallow
up his house's name (5.3.73–4).
246 **make some reservation of** keep back
somewhat
247 **good lord** patron (*OED, good, adj.* 2b
and *goodlordship*)
252–3 **Thou ... stands** If Paroles is going
to make his arms into legs by gartering
them, he might do even better to put
what is between his legs in place of his
nose.
255 **Methink'st** F *mee-|think'st*, the im-
personal verb influenced toward the
second-person form by the separation
of *mee* and the proximity of *thou*
257 **breathe** exercise

PAROLES This is hard and undeserved measure, my
lord.

LAFEU Go to, sir, you were beaten in Italy for picking   260
a kernel out of a pomegranate. You are a vagabond,
and no true traveller. You are more saucy with lords
and honourable personages than the commission of
your birth and virtue gives you heraldry. You are
not worth another word, else I'd call you knave. I   265
leave you.   *Exit*

PAROLES Good, very good. It is so, then. Good, very
good. Let it be concealed awhile.
     Enter Bertram

BERTRAM Undone, and forfeited to cares for ever!

PAROLES What's the matter, sweet heart?   270

BERTRAM

Although before the solemn priest I have sworn,
I will not bed her.

PAROLES   What? What, sweet heart?

BERTRAM

O my Paroles, they have married me!
I'll to the Tuscan wars, and never bed her.

PAROLES

France is a dog-hole, and it no more merits   275
The tread of a man's foot. To th' wars!

263–4 commission . . . heraldry] F; heraldry . . . commission HANMER (*conj*. Thirlby)
268.1 Enter Bertram] *after l*. 266 F (*Enter Count Rossillion*.)

260–1 you . . . pomegranate If there is no
   specific reference here, the import is
   probably 'you were so despised that
   men beat you on the smallest excuse'
   (Harrison); Italy as location perhaps
   increases the emphasis, since the English thought of theft as commonplace
   there.
261–2 vagabond, and no true traveller
   'not one who travels (as Elizabethans
   were required to) with official licence,
   but a mere tramp' (Hunter)
263–4 commission . . . heraldry Thirlby's
   emendation gives an easier reading,
   but F's order does make sense, with
   commission of as 'authority derived
   from' and *heraldry* as 'social position,
   rank'.
270, 272 Since Paroles knows very well

that Bertram has just been married
against his will, his repeated questions
as to what ails him may be a sign of
incomplete revision here (a view further supported by Bertram's dramatic
announcement at l. 273, as if his marriage would be news to his friend);
alternatively, the questions may suggest a stage direction, Paroles trying
in vain to get the attention of a distracted Bertram.
   sweet heart I retain Paroles' address
   for Bertram from F instead of the usual
   modernization *sweetheart*, because the
   separated form allows the meaning
   heart = 'bold fellow', which gets lost
   in the romantic emphasis of the com-
   bined form.

BERTRAM

There's letters from my mother. What th'import is
I know not yet.

PAROLES

Ay, that would be known. To th' wars, my boy,
    to th' wars!
He wears his honour in a box unseen   280
That hugs his kicky-wicky here at home,
Spending his manly marrow in her arms
Which should sustain the bound and high curvet
Of Mars's fiery steed. To other regions!
France is a stable, we that dwell in't jades.   285
Therefore, to th' war!

BERTRAM

It shall be so. I'll send her to my house,
Acquaint my mother with my hate to her
And wherefore I am fled, write to the King
That which I durst not speak. His present gift   290
Shall furnish me to those Italian fields
Where noble fellows strike. Wars is no strife
To the dark house and the detested wife.

PAROLES

Will this *capriccio* hold in thee, art sure?

284 regions!] CAPELL; ~, F   293 detested] ROWE (detefted); detected F

280–2 **He . . . arms** *Honour* and *marrow*
  are more or less equivalent terms for
  manly energy and the capacity to do
  great things. The husband wastes and
  uses up this capacity (*wears*, *Spending*)
  in private lovemaking (for *box* as
  female genitals, compare *case* at 1.3.23).
  Idea and image are similar to Massinger, *The Picture* 3.4.7–10: 'there is
  no such soaker | As a young spongy
  wife; she keeps a thousand | Horse-
  leeches in her box, and the thieves will
  suck out | Both blood, and marrow.'
  kicky-wicky The term, probably related to *kicksey-winsey* = 'whim', 'er-
  ratic fancy' and to *kickshaw* = 'quelque
  chose', downgrades even a loved
  woman as an irrelevant trifle.
283 **curvet** leap
284 **regions!** F's punctuation offers the
  possible reading 'Compared to other
  regions' (as 'Compared to the dark
  house' at l. 293); but there is a term
  of comparison only for *France*, not for
  we that dwell in't. In Capell's punctuation the speech accords with Paroles'
  speech modes in this passage, of assertion without comparison (*France is a
  dog-hole*) and exhortation (*To th' wars!*).
293 **dark house** Some editors have
  invoked the practice of locking up
  madmen in a dark house (Malvolio in
  Twelfth Night, Ephesian Antipholus in
  Errors) to gloss *dark house* here, but the
  proverbial smoky house and scolding
  wife that drive a man out of doors
  (Tilley H781, S574) provide a better
  direction, with an appropriate double
  image of strife that makes war look
  peaceful by contrast.
294 The term *capriccio* (whim), whether
  in foreign or anglicized form, was
  new; its use is a mark of Paroles'
  fashionable language.

BERTRAM

Go with me to my chamber, and advise me.   295
I'll send her straight away. Tomorrow
I'll to the wars, she to her single sorrow.

PAROLES

Why, these balls bound, there's noise in it. 'Tis hard:
A young man married is a man that's marred.
Therefore, away, and leave her bravely. Go.   300
The King has done you wrong. But hush 'tis so.

Exeunt

2.4   *Enter Helen, reading a letter, and Clown*

HELEN My mother greets me kindly. Is she well?

CLOWN She is not well, but yet she has her health.
She's very merry, but yet she is not well. But, thanks
be given, she's very well, and wants nothing i'th'
world. But yet she is not well.   5

HELEN If she be very well, what does she ail that she's
not very well?

CLOWN Truly, she's very well indeed, but for two
things.

HELEN What two things?   10

CLOWN One, that she's not in heaven, whither God
send her quickly. The other, that she's in earth, from
whence God send her quickly.

Enter Paroles

PAROLES Bless you, my fortunate lady.

HELEN I hope, sir, I have your good will to have mine   15
own good fortunes.

301 hush∧] F; hush, ROWE   301.1 *Exeunt*] F (*Exit*)
2.4.0.1 *reading a letter*] *not in* F   16 fortunes] CAPELL (*conj.* Thirlby); fortune F

298 **these balls bound** you are playing
your game with proper force; perhaps,
in view of Paroles' earlier denigration
of sexual for martial performance, the
balls = testicles equation is in play
here—i.e. *this* is the proper manly
spirit.
   noise in it Perhaps idiomatic, but in
any case Shakespeare frequently associates *noise* with war.
299 **A young . . . marred** Proverbial (Tilley
M701).

301 **hush 'tis so** don't say so aloud
2.4.2–5 The Clown plays on *well* = 'in
physical health' and *well* in the spiritual sense = 'delivered from this
world's evils by death': an ambiguity
Shakespeare also exploits at *Macbeth*
4.3.178–80, *Antony* 2.5.30–2, *2
Henry IV* 5.2.3–5, etc.
16 **fortunes** Capell's emendation is supported by the repeated *them* in Paroles'
answering speech and by Compositor
B's tendency to drop or add final *s*.

PAROLES You had my prayers to lead them on, and to
keep them on have them still. O my knave, how does
my old lady?

CLOWN So that you had her wrinkles and I her money,   20
I would she did as you say.

PAROLES Why, I say nothing.

CLOWN Marry, you are the wiser man; for many a
man's tongue shakes out his master's undoing. To
say nothing, to do nothing, to know nothing, and to   25
have nothing, is to be a great part of your title,
which is within a very little of nothing.

PAROLES Away, thou'rt a knave.

CLOWN You should have said, sir, 'before a knave,
thou'rt a knave'; that's 'before me, thou'rt a knave'.   30
This had been truth, sir.

PAROLES Go to, thou art a witty fool. I have found thee.

CLOWN Did you find me in yourself, sir, or were you
taught to find me?

PAROLES In myself.   35

CLOWN The search, sir, was profitable; and much fool
may you find in you, even to the world's pleasure
and the increase of laughter.

33–6 sir, . . . me? PAROLES In myself. CLOWN] WILSON (*after* Thirlby *conj.*); sir, . . . me?
Clo. F; sir [*Parolles nods*] . . . me? [*Parolles shakes his head*] SISSON

20–1 **So . . . say** Editors guess that the
Clown picks up on Paroles' *does* and
puns on *did/died* (though they show
some unease about how close the
words were in sound), i.e. if I had
the best of the inheritance, I would
she died as you say. But he may instead be picking up on Paroles' con-
descending *my old lady*, saying 'I
would she was as you say, yours and
old, if it meant you would own her
wrinkles and her money would be left
for me.'

24 **shakes out** brings about by wagging;
behind this may be the sense of 'rob-
bing' (property), *OED*, *v.* 16a. For *man*
(servant) and *master*, see 2.3.195–6.

26 **your title** what you are entitled to,
'you' being either any 'man', or servant, or the worthless Paroles specifically; in the latter case, Wilson's
hypothesis of a pun on Paroles' name
is possible: empty words (*nothing*, l.

27) as opposed to substantial posses-
sions.

27 **little** Possibly quibbling on *title* (l. 26)
as 'tittle' (Hunter).

29–30 **You . . . knave** The Clown's
answer rejects Paroles' dismissal of
knavery, turning the attempted distance of his *away* into the close
proximity of *before* and then, by con-
version to Lafeu's favourite oath, into
identification: *before a knave* = 'before
me'.

35 The Clown's question (ll. 33–4) and
the new speech heading for l. 36 in F
indicate that an answer by Paroles has
dropped out here, and the follow-up
much fool may you find in you (ll. 36–7)
suggests with some precision the substance if not the form of the missing
reply: *in myself*, meant by Paroles as
'by my own wits, not taught by
others', is taken otherwise by the
Clown.

PAROLES A good knave, i'faith, and well fed.
Madam, my lord will go away tonight.   40
A very serious business calls on him.
The great prerogative and right of love
Which as your due time claims, he does acknow-
      ledge,
But puts it off to a compelled restraint;
Whose want and whose delay is strewed with sweets,   45
Which they distil now in the curbèd time
To make the coming hour o'erflow with joy
And pleasure drown the brim.
HELEN   What's his will else?
PAROLES
That you will take your instant leave o'th' King,
And make this haste as your own good proceeding,   50
Strengthened with what apology you think
May make it probable need.
HELEN   What more commands he?
PAROLES
That, having this obtained, you presently
Attend his further pleasure.
HELEN
In every thing I wait upon his will.   55
PAROLES
I shall report it so.   *Exit*
HELEN   I pray you.—Come, sirrah.
                        Exeunt Helen and Clown

---

56 *Exit*] F (*Exit Par.*)   you.—Come] THEOBALD; you‿ come F   56.1 *Exeunt . . . Clown*]
F (*Exit*)

---

39 **well fed** Usually connected by editors
with 'Better fed than taught' at 2.2.3,
though the application here is less
clear. Perhaps it is equivalent to 'full
of beans', i.e. high-spirited.

42 **right** F *rite*: the words were not ortho-
graphically distinguished, and Paroles'
use here probably gathers in both
meanings, but the underlying legal
metaphor (*prerogative, due, claims*, etc.)
supports *right* as the dominant sense.

44 **to** in accordance with, in obedience to
(*Shrew* 4.3.97)

45 **Whose want and whose delay** i.e. the
(temporary) lack and postponement of
marital consummation

48 **What's . . . else** Here, as in the next
scene with Bertram, Helen shows up
with her simple responses the elaborate convoluted language in which the
men dress up Bertram's graceless conduct.

50 **make** represent

51 **apology** excuse

52 **make it probable need** make the
necessity seem plausible

2.5   *Enter Lafeu and Bertram*

LAFEU   But I hope your lordship thinks not him a soldier.

BERTRAM   Yes, my lord, and of very valiant approof.

LAFEU   You have it from his own deliverance.

BERTRAM   And by other warranted testimony.   5

LAFEU   Then my dial goes not true. I took this lark for a bunting.

BERTRAM   I do assure you, my lord, he is very great in knowledge, and accordingly valiant.

LAFEU   I have then sinned against his experience, and   10
transgressed against his valour; and my state that
way is dangerous, since I cannot yet find in my heart
to repent. Here he comes. I pray you make us friends.
I will pursue the amity.

     Enter Paroles

PAROLES   (*to Bertram*) These things shall be done, sir.   15

LAFEU   Pray you, sir, who's his tailor?

PAROLES   Sir!

LAFEU   O, I know him well, ay, 'Sir'. He, sir, 's a good
workman, a very good tailor.

BERTRAM   (*aside to Paroles*) Is she gone to the King?   20

PAROLES   She is.

BERTRAM   Will she away tonight?

PAROLES   As you'll have her.

2.5.18 ay, 'Sir'] OXFORD, *after* Hunter; I sir F

2.5.3 **very valiant approof** (a) proved to
be very valiant, or (b) much approved
for his valour (Clarkes)

6–7 **Then ... bunting** Lafeu's *dial* could
be either a timepiece, as elsewhere in
Shakespeare, or a mariner's compass;
if it *goes not true* it gives him inaccur-
ate bearings in time or space. In taking
the lark, or better thing, for a bunting,
or worse thing, he reverses the proverbial 'take a bunting for a lark' (Tilley
B722). J. Johnson (Reed 1803) points
out that the two are similar in appearance but the bunting makes an unat-
tractive sound.

16 **Pray . . . tailor** As Capell observes
(*Notes*, p. 13) Lafeu's new intentions
to treat Paroles better do not survive

the sight of him, still dressed in the
scarves, bannerets, and gartered
sleeves that so irritated the old lord in
2.3.

who's his tailor? Addressed to Bertram, implies Paroles is the proverbial
man made by a tailor (Tilley T17). The
thought is repeated more clearly below
with *The soul of this man is his clothes*
(ll. 44–5).

18 **'Sir'** In Hunter's punctuation, Lafeu
clearly picks up on Paroles' protesting
Sir!, pretending to take it as the
tailor's name he has requested; 'Sir',
the title alone with no nominal substance, is an apt label for a tailor who
makes gentlemen of nobodies.

BERTRAM
  I have writ my letters, casketed my treasure,
  Given order for our horses, and tonight,   25
  When I should take possession of the bride,
  End ere I do begin.
LAFEU A good traveller is something at the latter end
  of a dinner, but one that lies three-thirds and uses a
  known truth to pass a thousand nothings with   30
  should be once heard and thrice beaten.—God save
  you, captain.
BERTRAM Is there any unkindness between my lord and
  you, monsieur?
PAROLES I know not how I have deserved to run into   35
  my lord's displeasure.
LAFEU You have made shift to run into't, boots and
  spurs and all, like him that leaped into the custard;
  and out of it you'll run again rather than suffer
  question for your residence.   40
BERTRAM It may be you have mistaken him, my lord.
LAFEU And shall do so ever, though I took him at 's
  prayers. Fare you well, my lord, and believe this of
  me: there can be no kernel in this light nut. The
  soul of this man is his clothes. Trust him not in   45
  matter of heavy consequence. I have kept of them
  tame, and know their natures.—Farewell, monsieur.
  I have spoken better of you than you have or will
  to deserve at my hand, but we must do good against
  evil.   *Exit*   50

27 End] COLLIER; And F   48 or] F; wit or OXFORD (*conj.* Singer)   50 *Exit*] *not in* F

28–31 **A good ... beaten** While Bertram
  has been talking in private to Paroles,
  Lafeu has presumably continued his
  contemptuous musings on Paroles, of
  which we now hear the latter end. For
  travellers telling tales over dinner, see
  2.3.202–4 and note; their lies were
  proverbial (Tilley T476; Marlowe, *Edward II* 1.1.28–31).
37–8 **You ... custard** Theobald notes the
  custom at City entertainments of having the fool or zany jump into a large
  custard, citing Jonson, *The Devil is an
  Ass*, 1.1.97.
39–40 **suffer question for your residence**
  be interrogated about why you are

there
42–3 **And ... prayers** Lafeu agrees with
  Bertram by twisting his *mistaken* from
  'misunderstood' to 'taken in bad part,
  objected to'. *OED*'s first citation for this
  use is 1725, but it seems clearly the
  one intended: earlier senses centre on
  error, which is no part of Lafeu's intention here.
46–7 **kept of them tame** had some of
  these creatures, domesticated, in my
  household; *of them* is the partitive
  genitive (Abbott §177), parallel to Fr.
  des.
48–9 **have or will to deserve** have (deserved) or intend to deserve. This is not

PAROLES An idle lord, I swear.

BERTRAM I think not so.

PAROLES Why, do you not know him?

BERTRAM

Yes, I do know him well, and common speech

Gives him a worthy pass. Here comes my clog.   55

    Enter Helen

HELEN

I have, sir, as I was commanded from you,

Spoke with the King, and have procured his leave

For present parting; only he desires

Some private speech with you.

BERTRAM   I shall obey his will.

You must not marvel, Helen, at my course,   60

Which holds not colour with the time nor does

The ministration and requirèd office

On my particular. Prepared I was not

For such a business, therefore am I found

So much unsettled. This drives me to entreat you   65

That presently you take your way for home,

And rather muse than ask why I entreat you;

For my respects are better than they seem,

52 not] SINGER 1856 (*conj.* Walker); *not in* F   53 you not] F; you SINGER (*conj.* Walker)   55.1 *Enter Helen*] F (*Helena*); *Enter Helen* ⌐ *attended* ⌐ OXFORD

an entirely satisfactory paraphrase, creating, as Taylor says, 'an awkward ellipsis involving a retrospective past tense inferred from the infinitive, while ignoring an alternative construction ("have to deserve")'. Singer's hypothesis that neither *have* nor *will* are auxiliaries but the second is a noun, one object of the first, is attractive, presupposing a first object before *or* that was omitted in printing; but there is not enough support for the insertion of *wit* in the blank thus created, notwithstanding Taylor's citation of other Shakespearian passages coupling *wit* and *will*.

51 **idle** trifling, foolish

52 **I think not so** Bertram cannot be agreeing with Paroles, since he is about to contradict him in lines 54–5. It seems appropriate to follow Singer in supplying a *not* here for one that presumably dropped out. His hypo-

thesis that it was misplaced to the next line, which should therefore read *do you know him?*, is more problematic: having travelled with them to Paris and been in their company since, Paroles must be aware that Bertram knows Lafeu, while the negative form of his query can question not actual acquaintance but penetration to essential character (as at 2.3.102)—in Hunter's paraphrase, 'Haven't you seen through him yet?' Memory error is as likely to drop one word as to misplace it.

55 **worthy pass** approval, reputation of worthiness

clog block impeding action, the proverbial 'clog at one's heel' (Dent C426.1)

61–3 **Which ... particular** which does not match the (bridal) occasion and fails in performance of the duty required of me personally (as bridegroom)

68 **respects** motivating considerations

And my appointments have in them a need
Greater than shows itself at the first view   70
To you that know them not. (*Giving her a letter*) This
    to my mother.
'Twill be two days ere I shall see you, so
I leave you to your wisdom.
HELEN   Sir, I can nothing say
But that I am your most obedient servant—
BERTRAM
Come, come, no more of that.
HELEN   —And ever shall   75
With true observance seek to eke out that
Wherein toward me my homely stars have failed
To equal my great fortune.
BERTRAM   Let that go.
My haste is very great. Farewell. Hie home.
HELEN
Pray, sir, your pardon.
BERTRAM   Well, what would you say?   80
HELEN
I am not worthy of the wealth I owe,
Nor dare I say 'tis mine, and yet it is;
But, like a timorous thief, most fain would steal
What law does vouch mine own.
BERTRAM   What would you have?
HELEN
Something, and scarce so much. Nothing, indeed.   85
I would not tell you what I would, my lord.
Faith, yes:
Strangers and foes do sunder and not kiss.
BERTRAM
I pray you stay not, but in haste to horse.
HELEN
I shall not break your bidding, good my lord.   90

71 *Giving her a letter*] not in F

74–5 **servant—** . . . **—** **And** I alter F's
    punctuation to bring out what seems
    implicit in the text, Bertram's breaking
    in to cut off Helen's first speech to her
    new husband, in his haste to be rid of
    her, and Helen's persistence neverthe-

less in her act of formal submission.
75–8 **And . . . fortune** Helen will try to
    make up in *observance*, dutiful service,
    the gap between her *homely stars*,
    humble origins, and her elevated posi-
    tion as Bertram's wife.

—Where are my other men? (*To Paroles*) Monsieur,
  farewell.   *Exit*

BERTRAM

Go thou toward home, where I will never come
Whilst I can shake my sword or hear the drum.
Away, and for our flight.

PAROLES   Bravely. *Coraggio!* *Exeunt*

3.1   *Flourish. Enter the Duke of Florence and the two*
    French Lords, with a troop of soldiers

DUKE

So that from point to point now have you heard
The fundamental reasons of this war,
Whose great decision hath much blood let forth
And more thirsts after.

FIRST LORD   Holy seems the quarrel
Upon your grace's part, black and fearful   5
On the opposer.

---

91 Where...men? Monsieur, farewell. *Exit*] F; *Exit Helena* [*after l.* 90] *Ber.*
Where . . . men, Monsieur?—farewell THEOBALD 1740; *Ber.* Where ... men? *Hel.* Monsieur, farewell KEIGHTLEY   *Exit*] F; *Exeunt Helen and attendants* OXFORD   94 *Exeunt*] not
in F

   3.1.0.1–2 *Florence and the two French Lords*] F (*Florence, the two Frenchmen*)

91 **Where . . . farewell** Theobald's emendation reassigns the line from Helen,
who has no 'man' on hand to make
sense of the *other*, to Bertram, who has
Paroles. Continuing speeches under
one speech prefix that should switch
to another is characteristic of this text,
yet the need for reassignment is not
clear here. As Keightley's later emendation suggests, Helen is the logical
speaker of the second part, since she
is leaving while the other two are not
separating; she can speak the first part
naturally enough, too, talking of the
attendants who came with her to Paris
(promised by the Countess, 1.3.253),
as distinguished from the Clown, with
whom we have recently seen her. Taylor addresses the problem by bringing
on Helen at 55.1 '*attended*'.

3.1 The first Italian scene begins a
counterpoint in this middle phase of
the play between military bustle in
Florence (scenes 1, 3, 5) and con-

straint and grief at Roussillon (2, 4);
most productions turn to light and colour here after the sombreness of the
French settings.

1 **from point to point** in every particular;
Shakespeare repeats the idiom at
4.3.61–2 (*point from point*) and
5.3.325, but uses it nowhere else in
his works.

3–4 **Whose . . . after** The process of decid-
ing the issues of the war has produced
much bloodshed and calls for more.

4 FIRST LORD The F speech prefix *1. Lord*,
which distinguishes this speech from
those below headed *French E* and *Fren.
G*, is perhaps a trace of a character
later revised out of this scene. Collier
observed that the extreme endorse-
ment of Florence and condemnation of
Siena would come more plausibly from
a Florentine than from the Frenchmen; and otherwise their mode in this
scene is careful diplomacy rather than
partisan fervour.

DUKE

Therefore we marvel much our cousin France
Would in so just a business shut his bosom
Against our borrowing prayers.

SECOND LORD   Good my lord,

The reasons of our state I cannot yield   10
But like a common and an outward man
That the great figure of a council frames
By self-unable motion; therefore dare not
Say what I think of it, since I have found
Myself in my uncertain grounds to fail   15
As often as I guessed.

DUKE   Be it his pleasure.

FIRST LORD

But I am sure the younger of our nation,
That surfeit on their ease, will day by day
Come here for physic.

DUKE   Welcome shall they be,

And all the honours that can fly from us   20
Shall on them settle. You know your places well.
When better fall, for your avails they fell.
Tomorrow to th' field.   *Flourish. Exeunt*

3.2   *Enter Countess, with a letter, and Clown*

COUNTESS It hath happened all as I would have had it,
  save that he comes not along with her.

CLOWN By my troth, I take my young lord to be a very
  melancholy man.

COUNTESS By what observance, I pray you?   5

17 nation] ROWE; nature F   23 to th'] F2; to'th the F1   *Exeunt] not in* F
3.2.0.1 *with a letter] not in* F

11–13 **like ... motion** i.e. like an ordinary man not privy to state secrets (*outward*) who makes a guessing version
  of the council's deliberations using his
  own feeble mental powers (*self-unable
  motion*); for *motion* in this sense, see
  Othello 1.2.76.
17 **younger of our nation** In the F reading, restored by Steevens, *the younger
  of our nature* means 'young men like
  us'; but the talk specifically of *French*
  participation makes preferable Rowe's
  emendation, which as Taylor points

out 'assumes an easy misreading, here
  assisted by assimilation (*young*er, *sure*,
  *plea*sure)'.
18 **surfeit on their ease** are made ill by
  their excess of leisure and lack of activity
22 **When . . . fell** when better places
  become available, it will be for your
  advantage
3.2.3–9 The connection between melancholy and singing implied here is not
  obvious, music being more usually advanced as a cure than as a symptom;

145

CLOWN Why, he will look upon his boot and sing, mend
the ruff and sing, ask questions and sing, pick his
teeth and sing. I know a man that had this trick of
melancholy sold a goodly manor for a song.

COUNTESS Let me see what he writes, and when he   10
means to come.

She reads the letter

CLOWN I have no mind to Isbel since I was at court.
Our old ling and our Isbels o'th' country are nothing
like your old ling and your Isbels o'th' court. The
brains of my Cupid's knocked out, and I begin to love   15
as an old man loves money, with no stomach.

COUNTESS What have we here?

CLOWN E'en that you have there.   *Exit*

COUNTESS (*reads*) 'I have sent you a daughter-in-law.
She hath recovered the King and undone me. I have   20
wedded her, not bedded her, and sworn to make the
"not" eternal. You shall hear I am run away. Know
it before the report come. If there be breadth enough
in the world, I will hold a long distance. My duty to
you.   25

> Your unfortunate son,
> Bertram.'

---

9 sold] F3; hold F1   11.1 *She reads the letter*] *not in* F   13 ling] F2; Lings F1   19
COUNTESS (*reads*)] *A Letter.* F

but Parson Evans in *Merry Wives* sings
when 'melancholies' (3.1.11 ff.), as
does the mad Ophelia, and Burton lists
among the signs of love-melancholy a
disposition to sing (*Anatomy of Melancholy* 3.2.3.)

7 **ruff** May be, as modern editors
assume, connected with *boot* in the
preceding phrase as a variant or misprint of *ruffle*, the turned-over flap of
a top-boot (*OED, sb.* II. 6). The only
support for such a connection is *the
ruff* where *his ruff* would be more
usual. On the other hand, the subsequent phrases ending *and sing* are
not so connected, and the intended
image may be rather of a courtier
adjusting his fashionable neckwear.

8–9 **I know . . . song** The F line calls for
some emendation on grammatical
grounds alone. Assuming that *know* is
an error for *knew* harmonizes the verb

tenses but yields a puzzling sense—
why should a song entitle this man to
possession of a manor? Taking instead
hold as an error for *sold* has been the
popular course, given the current proverbial phrase 'sold for a song' (Tilley S636), and seems the best one
available.

13–14 **old ling** *Ling* is a fish related to cod,
which if *old* would be salted; the
Clown is drawing on obscene meanings of 'fish' (a woman viewed sexually: Partridge) and 'salt', lecherous.

14–16 **The brains . . . stomach** The *brains*
and *stomach* which the Clown's love
now lacks may have the same
meaning. Florio lists as a sense of *teste*
'certain eminent parts . . . of the brain,
which the anatomists called so,
because they are like and somewhat
resemble the stones of a man'. If that
connection is invoked here, *brains* are

This is not well, rash and unbridled boy:
To fly the favours of so good a king,
To pluck his indignation on thy head   30
By the misprizing of a maid too virtuous
For the contempt of empire.
    Enter Clown

CLOWN O madam, yonder is heavy news within, between two soldiers and my young lady.

COUNTESS What is the matter?   35

CLOWN Nay, there is some comfort in the news, some
comfort: your son will not be killed so soon as I
thought he would.

COUNTESS Why should he be killed?

CLOWN So say I, madam, if he run away, as I hear he   40
does. The danger is in standing to't; that's the loss
of men, though it be the getting of children. Here
they come will tell you more. For my part, I only
hear your son was run away.   ⌜*Exit*⌝
    Enter Helen with a letter, and the two French Lords

SECOND LORD Save you, good madam.   45

HELEN Madam, my lord is gone, for ever gone.

FIRST LORD Do not say so.

COUNTESS

Think upon patience, pray you.—Gentlemen,
I have felt so many quirks of joy and grief

---

44 *Exit*] not in F   44.1 *with a letter*] not in F   48 you.—Gentlemen] HANMER (you:);
you‸ Gentlemen F

parallel to *stomach* as sexual appetite.

18 **E'en** Theobald's 'emendation' of F's *In*,
which is in fact a variant spelling of
it: *Errors* 2.2.103, *Antony* 4.16.75.

22 **not** A quibble on 'knot' (marriage):
Bertram has had to accept the everlasting tie of marriage, but his rejection of true marital relations will be
equally eternal.

32 **for the contempt of empire** for an
emperor to hold in contempt

41–2 **The danger . . . children** The
Clown's paradox plays on an apparent
escape from danger in *run away*, even
though to a war, as the safer course
than facing the danger, *standing to't*,
i.e. tumescence in the marital bed,

which is the *loss of men* because it
brings about both the immediate sexual 'death' and the cumulative deple-
tion of life and hastening of death that
in popular belief resulted from many
orgasms.

44 *Exit* F does not provide an exit for the
Clown, who might stay on stage until
the Countess and French lords exit
after l. 98; but since this would leave
him uncharacteristically silent for an
extended period, and since 1.3 has
indicated that the Countess does not
tolerate his presence when serious
family matters are discussed, an exit
here seems preferable.

49 **quirks** sudden strokes

147

That the first face of neither on the start   50
Can woman me unto't. Where is my son, I pray you?

FIRST LORD

Madam, he's gone to serve the Duke of Florence.
We met him thitherward, for thence we came,
And, after some dispatch in hand at court,
Thither we bend again.   55

HELEN

Look on his letter, madam; here's my passport.
    She reads the letter
'When thou canst get the ring upon my finger, which
never shall come off, and show me a child begotten
of thy body that I am father to, then call me husband. But in such a "then", I write a "never".' This   60
is a dreadful sentence.

COUNTESS

Brought you this letter, gentlemen?

FIRST LORD   Ay, madam;
And for the contents' sake are sorry for our pains.

COUNTESS

I prithee, lady, have a better cheer.
If thou engrossest all the griefs are thine,   65
Thou robb'st me of a moiety. He was my son,
But I do wash his name out of my blood,
And thou art all my child. Towards Florence, is he?

FIRST LORD

Ay, madam.

COUNTESS   And to be a soldier?

FIRST LORD

Such is his noble purpose, and, believe't,   70
The Duke will lay upon him all the honour

56.1 *She reads the letter*] *not in* F   65 engrossest‿] F4; engrossest, F1

50 **on the start** on their sudden onset
51 **woman me unto't** make me break
   down under it in tears, like the stereo-
   typical woman
56 **passport** dismissal, walking papers
61 **sentence** Sometimes understood as
   'imposition of tasks', but Shakespeare
   never uses the word in this sense; on
   first reading Bertram's letter, Helen
   understands not a list of requirements

difficult to fulfil but a judgement
against her, an absolute casting-off.
65 **If . . . thine** i.e. if you take into exclu-
   sive possession all the griefs that
   (indeed) touch you most immediately;
   in the elliptic phrasing *griefs* = 'griefs
   that'.
66 **moiety** share
68 **all my** my only

That good convenience claims.

COUNTESS   Return you thither?

SECOND LORD

Ay, madam, with the swiftest wing of speed.

HELEN

'Till I have no wife I have nothing in France.'
'Tis bitter.

COUNTESS   Find you that there?

HELEN   Ay, madam.   75

SECOND LORD

'Tis but the boldness of his hand, haply,
Which his heart was not consenting to.

COUNTESS

Nothing in France until he have no wife!
There's nothing here that is too good for him
But only she; and she deserves a lord   80
That twenty such rude boys might tend upon
And call her, hourly, mistress. Who was with him?

SECOND LORD

A servant only, and a gentleman
Which I have sometime known.

COUNTESS Paroles, was it not?   85

SECOND LORD Ay, my good lady, he.

COUNTESS

A very tainted fellow, and full of wickedness.
My son corrupts a well-derivèd nature
With his inducement.

SECOND LORD   Indeed, good lady,
The fellow has a deal of that too much   90
Which holds him much to have.

COUNTESS   You're welcome, gentlemen.
I will entreat you, when you see my son,
To tell him that his sword can never win
The honour that he loses. More I'll entreat you
Written to bear along.

90 that∧] ROWE 1714; ~, F

72 **good convenience claims** is suitable
90–1 **that . . . have** *That* could be either
    an adjective, modifying *too much* taken
    as a noun (as in *Hamlet* Add. Pass.
    M.5/4.7.118), or a pronoun. The

meanings that result are not dissimi-
lar: Paroles has a large share of that
excess, or a large, indeed excessive,
share of that facility of inducement,
that has served to his advantage.

FIRST LORD   We serve you, madam,   95
  In that and all your worthiest affairs.
COUNTESS
  Not so, but as we change our courtesies.
  Will you draw near?   *Exeunt Countess and Lords*
HELEN
  'Till I have no wife I have nothing in France.'
  Nothing in France until he has no wife.   100
  Thou shalt have none, Roussillon, none in France;
  Then hast thou all again. Poor lord, is't I
  That chase thee from thy country and expose
  Those tender limbs of thine to the event
  Of the none-sparing war? And is it I   105
  That drive thee from the sportive court, where thou
  Wast shot at with fair eyes, to be the mark
  Of smoky muskets? O you leaden messengers
  That ride upon the violent speed of fire,
  Fly with false aim, cleave the still-piecing air   110
  That sings with piercing; do not touch my lord.
  Whoever shoots at him, I set him there.
  Whoever charges on his forward breast,
  I am the caitiff that do hold him to't,
  And though I kill him not I am the cause   115
  His death was so effected. Better 'twere
  I met the ravin lion when he roared

98 *Exeunt Countess and Lords*] Exit. F   110 cleave] OXFORD; moue F; wound COLLIER
1858   still-piecing] STEEVENS 1778 (*conj.* Thirlby); still-peering F

96 **worthiest** most deserving of respect
97–8 **Not . . . near** The Countess rejects
   one-sided service (l. 95) for the mutual
   exchange of courtesies, inviting them
   presumably to take some refreshment.
104 **event** outcome
110 **cleave the still-piecing air** In F's *moue
   the still-peering aire*, two words have
   given trouble: the meanings of 'peer-
   ing', or the variant 'pearing' (=
   appearing), have no natural relevance
   to Helen's wish that the air rather
   than Bertram be penetrated by musket
   shot, while 'move' seems too mild and
   diffuse to match *piercing* in the next
   line. Thirlby proposed 'still-peecing',
   i.e. piecing, continually putting itself
   back together, which involves an easy
   single-letter error. Taylor notes that

the widely accepted emendation to
piecing highlights the difficulties of
moue, which lacks both the forceful
wounding effect that necessitates self-
repair and the explicitness of the verbs
in parallel passages (Q2 *Hamlet* Add.
Pass. I.5/4.1.44, *Tempest* 3.3.63–4,
Catiline 3.522). Collier's *wound* meets
these criteria, but as Taylor says, *cleue*
is more easily misread as *moue*.
111 **sings** Conveys both the sound of a
   bullet in flight and the air's un-
   wounded well-being.
113 **forward** i.e. in the front lines
114 **caitiff** wretch
117 **ravin** ravenous, with a suggestion of
   the standard phrase *beast of ravin*,
   beast of prey

With sharp constraint of hunger; better 'twere
That all the miseries which nature owes
Were mine at once. No, come thou home, Roussillon,   120
Whence honour but of danger wins a scar,
As oft it loses all. I will be gone.
My being here it is that holds thee hence.
Shall I stay here to do't? No, no, although
The air of paradise did fan the house   125
And angels officed all. I will be gone,
That pitiful rumour may report my flight
To consolate thine ear. Come, night; end, day;
For with the dark, poor thief, I'll steal away.   *Exit*

3.3   *Flourish. Enter the Duke of Florence, Bertram, a*
       drummer and trumpeter, soldiers, and Paroles

DUKE (*to Bertram*)
    The general of our horse thou art, and we,
    Great in our hope, lay our best love and credence
    Upon thy promising fortune.

BERTRAM   Sir, it is
    A charge too heavy for my strength, but yet
    We'll strive to bear it for your worthy sake   5
    To th' extreme edge of hazard.

DUKE   Then go thou forth;
    And fortune play upon thy prosperous helm
    As thy auspicious mistress.

BERTRAM   This very day,
    Great Mars, I put myself into thy file.
    Make me but like my thoughts, and I shall prove   10
    A lover of thy drum, hater of love.   *Exeunt*

3.3.0.1–2 *Bertram, a drummer and trumpeter, soldiers, and*] F (*Rossillion, drum and trumpets, soldiers,*)   11 *Exeunt*] F (*Exeunt omnes*)

121–2 **Whence . . . all** from the place
    where honour wins (at best) only a
    scar by undergoing danger, and where
    it often loses life itself
126 **officed all** performed all services
127 **pitiful** i.e. taking pity on Bertram
128 **consolate** console
3.3.2 **lay** wager
  7 **play** dance, glitter
11 Hunter notes that Mars's attribute is
    a drum rather than the usual trumpet.

Significantly, the parallel instances he
cites in Shakespeare's other work,
Venus 107 and *Kinsmen* 1.1.181, both
portray Mars's drum as abandoned
because of the more powerful force of
love; Bertram's vow not only to follow
war but to hate love, its opposite,
which feels out of place in this conversation, gains point in this context as a
deliberate reversal of priorities.

3.4   *Enter Countess and Steward with a letter*
COUNTESS

Alas! And would you take the letter of her?
Might you not know she would do as she has done
By sending me a letter? Read it again.
STEWARD (*reads the letter*)

'I am Saint Jacques' pilgrim, thither gone.
    Ambitious love hath so in me offended   5
That barefoot plod I the cold ground upon,
    With sainted vow my faults to have amended.
Write, write, that from the bloody course of war
    My dearest master, your dear son, may hie.
Bless him at home in peace, whilst I from far   10
    His name with zealous fervour sanctify.
His taken labours bid him me forgive;
    I, his despiteful Juno, sent him forth
From courtly friends, with camping foes to live,
    Where death and danger dogs the heels of worth.   15
He is too good and fair for death, and me,
    Whom I myself embrace to set him free.'

3.4.0.1 *with a letter*] not in F   4 STEWARD (*reads the letter*)] *Letter.* F   9 hie.] F3; ~,
F1   10 peace,] F3; ~. F1

3.4.4–17 By adopting the sonnet form for
her letter, Helen links her situation
with two prominent 'motives' of the
English sonnet, adoring love and religious soul-searching; the highly wrought
form, already in the writer's absence
one step from her actual voice, further
distances the audience from Helen's
true feelings and intentions—perhaps
through this mystification helping us
to accept her appearance in Florence
(see next note).

4 **Saint Jacques** Probably Saint James the
Great, whose shrine at Compostela was
the most famous pilgrimage destina-
tion in Europe. The lesser shrines that
have been proposed were not likely to
be familiar to Shakespeare or his audience. Since Florence is, as Johnson
observed, 'somewhat out of the road'
from Roussillon in southern France to
Compostela in north-western Spain,
the geography here represents either
error or deliberate mystification by
Shakespeare; a third hypothesis, that
Helen uses the pilgrimage only as a

cover for her pursuit of Bertram to a
different place, must account for other
pilgrims to St Jacques who pass
through Florence (3.5.26–8).

7 **sainted** holy
my faults to have amended to cause
my misdeeds to be rectified

10–11 **Bless . . . sanctify** The Countess
may with a mother's familiarity and
sanctioned nearness *bless* Bertram *at
home*, while Helen will from a respectful distance *sanctify* his name, render
it holy, by praying for—or even to—
him.

12 **taken labours** exertions undergone by
outside infliction, like the labours
imposed on Hercules by *despiteful Juno*
(l. 13)

14 **Camping** Sets up a double contrast,
not only between friendly and hostile
associates but between comfortable living at court and harsh accommoda-
tions in a battle camp.

17 **Whom . . . free** Helen corrects the mis-
matches of Bertram in line 16, with
herself and possibly with death, by

COUNTESS
    Ah, what sharp stings are in her mildest words!
    Rinaldo, you did never lack advice so much
    As letting her pass so. Had I spoke with her,   20
    I could have well diverted her intents,
    Which thus she hath prevented.
STEWARD   Pardon me, madam.
    If I had given you this at overnight,
    She might have been o'erta'en. And yet she writes
    Pursuit would be but vain.
COUNTESS   What angel shall   25
    Bless this unworthy husband? He cannot thrive
    Unless her prayers, whom heaven delights to hear
    And loves to grant, reprieve him from the wrath
    Of greatest justice. Write, write, Rinaldo,
    To this unworthy husband of his wife.   30
    Let every word weigh heavy of her worth
    That he does weigh too light. My greatest grief,
    Though little he do feel it, set down sharply.
    Dispatch the most convenient messenger.
    When, haply, he shall hear that she is gone,   35
    He will return; and hope I may that she,
    Hearing so much, will speed her foot again,
    Led hither by pure love. Which of them both
    Is dearest to me, I have no skill in sense
    To make distinction. Provide this messenger.   40
    My heart is heavy, and mine age is weak;
    Grief would have tears, and sorrow bids me speak.
                                                        Exeunt

18 COUNTESS] CAPELL; *not in* F

vowing to set him free by marrying
death herself.

19 **advice** prudence, discretion
23 **at overnight** on the preceding evening
27–8 **her . . . grant** From *her prayers* the
    relative *whom* first takes its antecedent
    in *her* (Helen) and acts as the object
    of *hear*, and then without changing
    form takes a second antecedent in

prayers as the object of *grant*.
30 **unworthy husband** husband unworthy
32–3 **My . . . it** It is unclear what the sub-
    ordinate clause is qualifying: the sense
    may be either 'this, the greatest sor-
    row *I* have felt, though *he* feel it so
    little' or 'though he may have little
    feeling for my sorrow, let it be set out
    unsparingly'.

3.5   *A tucket afar off. Enter an old Widow of*
       Florence, her daughter ⌈Diana⌉, and Mariana,
       with other citizens

WIDOW Nay, come, for if they do approach the city we
    shall lose all the sight.

DIANA They say the French count has done most hon-
    ourable service.

WIDOW It is reported that he has taken their great'st   5
    commander, and that with his own hand he slew the
    Duke's brother.
       ⌈*Tucket*⌉
    We have lost our labour. They are gone a contrary
    way. Hark, you may know by their trumpets.

MARIANA Come, let's return again, and suffice our-   10
    selves with the report of it. Well, Diana, take heed
    of this French earl. The honour of a maid is her
    name, and no legacy is so rich as honesty.

WIDOW (*to Diana*) I have told my neighbour how you
    have been solicited by a gentleman, his companion.   15

MARIANA I know that knave, hang him! One Paroles:
    a filthy officer he is in those suggestions for the
    young earl. Beware of them, Diana. Their promises,
    enticements, oaths, tokens, and all these engines of
    lust are not the things they go under. Many a maid   20

3.5.0.1 *an*] not in F   **0.2** *her daughter ⌈Diana⌉*] *her daughter, Violenta* F ; *Diana, Violenta*
ROWE   **7.1** *Tucket*] CAPELL ; *not in* F

3.5.0.1–2 The F entry direction suggests
either that Shakespeare originally
planned a character named Violenta
but later dropped her from the action,
or that Violenta was Shakespeare's
first thought for the name of the
Widow's daughter, which he later
changed to Diana elsewhere but by
oversight did not alter here. Since
ll. 93–5 below indicate only Helen, the
Widow, Diana, and Mariana on-stage,
and since Diana's name receives
unusual emphasis in both the stage
direction beginning her next scene and
the opening lines (4.2.0–2), the second
theory seems more likely. For Mariana's name, see note on 1.3.19.

0.1 *tucket* series of notes on the trumpet.
As the tucket was a cavalry marching

signal, Capell added another after line
7 to account for the Widow's conclusion in line 8 that the troops have
gone in another direction.

1–15 See Appendix D. F prints these lines,
which end the second column of X1ᵛ,
in brief, uneven verse lines; this
device, which fills twenty lines rather
than the twelve or so required for the
same in prose, is explained by B's need
to fill out the page, X2 being already
composed. The widely spaced entrance
direction serves the same end.

13 **honesty** chastity

17 **filthy officer** one who does a filthy
office, i.e. as pander
    suggestions promptings to evil

20 **go under** masquerade as

hath been seduced by them; and the misery is
example that so terrible shows in the wreck of
maidenhood cannot for all that dissuade succession,
but that they are limed with the twigs that threatens
them. I hope I need not to advise you further; but   25
I hope your own grace will keep you where you are,
though there were no further danger known but the
modesty which is so lost.

DIANA You shall not need to fear me.

Enter Helen, dressed as a pilgrim

WIDOW I hope so. Look, here comes a pilgrim. I know   30
she will lie at my house, thither they send one
another. I'll question her.

God save you, pilgrim, whither are you bound?

HELEN To Saint Jacques le Grand.

Where do the palmers lodge, I do beseech you?   35

WIDOW

At the Saint Francis here beside the port.

HELEN Is this the way?

A march afar

WIDOW

Ay, marry, is't. Hark you, they come this way.
If you will tarry, holy pilgrim,
But till the troops come by,   40

---

21 the misery] F; their misery *conj.* This edition   is example] F; is, Example, ROWE
1714   29.1 *dressed as a pilgrim] not in* F   33 are you] F2; are FI   34 le] F3; *la* FI

21–3 **the misery . . . succession** Rowe's
emendation is widely accepted, making *example* either parenthetical—'for
example', 'according to past prece-
dent'—so that the long noun clause
tells what the misery is, or the subject
of the main verb: 'the misery is (that)
example, which shows so terribly in
the wrack of maidenhead, cannot dissuade . . .'. But F yields a straightforward reading with the noun clause
completing *example*: the misery of the
maids or their situation *is example* (the
word without an article was common
in Shakespeare and Jonson), i.e. demonstrates, that even the sight of so
many maids ruined cannot persuade
others not to follow the same course.
Though this reading can accommodate
the misery, the text should perhaps

read *their misery*: the error of *y^e* for *y^r*
is an easy one.
24–5 **limed with the twigs that threatens
them** caught like birds with lime by
what they should fear and avoid
27 **further danger** i.e. of pregnancy
33 **are you** If F's *are* were a misprint
for *art*, the omitted pronoun would
be quite usual (Abbott §241); but as
the Widow elsewhere uses the second person plural to address this
stranger, it is likely that *you* was
omitted in error, as F2's alteration
indicates.
36 **port** city gate
37.1 *march* i.e. march-like music
37–40 F frames 38–9, two regular lines
(with *pilgrim* as trisyllabic, as Abbott
§477), with 37 and 40, two short
ones. Editors have variously adjusted

I will conduct you where you shall be lodged,
The rather for I think I know your hostess
As ample as myself.
HELEN   Is it yourself?
WIDOW
If you shall please so, pilgrim.
HELEN
I thank you and will stay upon your leisure.   45
WIDOW
You came, I think, from France?
HELEN   I did so.
WIDOW
Here you shall see a countryman of yours
That has done worthy service.
HELEN   His name, I pray you?
DIANA
The Count Roussillon. Know you such a one?
HELEN
But by the ear, that hears most nobly of him.   50
His face I know not.
DIANA   Whatsome'er he is,
He's bravely taken here. He stole from France,
As 'tis reported, for the King had married him
Against his liking. Think you it is so?
HELEN
Ay, surely, mere the truth. I know his lady.   55
DIANA
There is a gentleman that serves the Count
Reports but coarsely of her.
HELEN   What's his name?
DIANA
Monsieur Paroles.
HELEN   O, I believe with him.
In argument of praise, or to the worth

the lineation without achieving complete regularity, which perhaps was
not the intention: Hunter notes that
the line-division may have been meant
to allow for 'pauses and noises off'.

42 **The rather for** all the sooner because
51 **Whatsome'er** Shakespearian variant of

whatever (*Antony* 2.6.99, Q2 *Hamlet*
1.2.248)
52 **He's bravely taken** he has made a
splendid impression
55 **mere the truth** absolutely true
57 **coarsely** slightingly
59 **In . . . worth** if the question is of praise
or of comparison with the worth

Of the great Count himself, she is too mean   60
To have her name repeated. All her deserving
Is a reservèd honesty, and that
I have not heard examined.
DIANA   Alas, poor lady.
'Tis a hard bondage to become the wife
Of a detesting lord.   65
WIDOW
I warrant, good creature, wheresoe'er she is,
Her heart weighs sadly. This young maid might
      do her
A shrewd turn if she pleased.
HELEN   How do you mean?
Maybe the amorous Count solicits her
In the unlawful purpose?
WIDOW   He does indeed,   70
And brokes with all that can in such a suit
Corrupt the tender honour of a maid.
But she is armed for him, and keeps her guard
In honestest defence.
      Enter, with drummer and colours, Bertram,
      Paroles, and the whole army
MARIANA
The gods forbid else!
WIDOW   So, now they come.   75
That is Antonio, the Duke's eldest son.
That, Escalus.
HELEN   Which is the Frenchman?
DIANA   He,

66 warrant] GLOBE (*conj.* Thirlby); write F   74.1 *Enter, with drummer and colours,*
Bertram] F (*Drumme and Colours.* | *Enter Count Rossillion*)

61 **repeated** mentioned
62 **reservèd honesty** carefully guarded
      chastity
63 **examined** called into question
66 **I warrant** F's *I write* is almost certainly
      an error, since Shakespeare's other
      uses of the construction are all reflex-
      ive (e.g. Lafeu's 'I write man',
      2.3.199). The F reading also, like some
      emendations, leaves *her heart weighs*
      sadly hanging, grammatically; and
      almost all have the Widow asserting a
      sure knowledge that Helen's account

has not given her. Thirlby's conjecture
that *write* was an error for *warrant*
(*war*') makes a grammatical whole and
frames the Widow's words more appropriately as a sympathetic guess rather
than an independent proclamation.
68 **shrewd** injurious, i.e. the opposite of a
      good turn
71 **brokes** trades, i.e. in sexual entice-
      ments: *broker* in Shakespeare is almost
      always the equivalent of bawd or pan-
      der.
77 **Escalus** See note on 1.3.19

That with the plume. 'Tis a most gallant fellow.
I would he loved his wife. If he were honester,
He were much goodlier.   80
Is't not a handsome gentleman?
HELEN   I like him well.
DIANA
'Tis pity he is not honest. Yond's that same knave
That leads him to these places. Were I his lady,
I would poison that vile rascal.
HELEN   Which is he?
DIANA
That jackanapes with scarves. Why is he melan-
        choly?   85
HELEN
Perchance he's hurt i'th' battle.
PAROLES   Lose our drum! Well!
MARIANA
He's shrewdly vexed at something.
        ⌈*Paroles bows to them*⌉

                              Look, he has spied us.
WIDOW (*to Paroles*)
Marry, hang you.
MARIANA (*to Paroles*)
                    And your curtsy, for a ring-carrier.
                    Exeunt Bertram, Paroles, and the army
WIDOW
The troop is passed. Come, pilgrim, I will bring you
Where you shall host. Of enjoined penitents   90
There's four or five, to Great Saint Jacques bound,
Already at my house.
HELEN   I humbly thank you.
Please it this matron and this gentle maid

---

87 *Paroles bows to them*] *not in* F   88.1 *Exeunt Bertram, Paroles, and the army*] *Exit* F

83 **places** situations (?)
86 **Lose our drum!** According to a memorandum from F. W. Fairholt quoted by Halliwell, regimental drums of the day were decorated with the colours of the battalion, so that losing the drum was like losing the regiment's flag.
87.1 ***Paroles bows to them*** Presumably some motion of Paroles generates Mar-

iana's *Look, he has spied us* immediately following, and her scorn for his *curtsy* in the next line suggests it was a bow.
88 **ring-carrier** go-between
90 **host** lodge
   enjoined obligated by oath
93–5 **Please . . . me** Some commentators have thought it strange for Helen to invite Diana to dinner in her own

To eat with us tonight, the charge and thanking
Shall be for me. And, to requite you further,   95
I will bestow some precepts of this virgin
Worthy the note.
⌜DIANA *and* MARIANA⌝ We'll take your offer kindly.

Exeunt

3.6   *Enter Bertram and the French* ⌜*Lords*⌝, *as at first*
SECOND LORD Nay, good my lord, put him to't. Let him
    have his way.
FIRST LORD If your lordship find him not a hilding, hold
    me no more in your respect.
SECOND LORD On my life, my lord, a bubble.   5
BERTRAM Do you think I am so far deceived in him?
SECOND LORD Believe it, my lord. In mine own direct
    knowledge, without any malice, but to speak of him
    as my kinsman, he's a most notable coward, an
    infinite and endless liar, an hourly promise-breaker,   10
    the owner of no one good quality worthy your lord-
    ship's entertainment.
FIRST LORD It were fit you knew him, lest, reposing too
    far in his virtue, which he hath not, he might at
    some great and trusty business in a main danger fail   15
    you.
BERTRAM I would I knew in what particular action to
    try him.
FIRST LORD None better than to let him fetch off his

98 DIANA *and* MARIANA] CAPELL; *Both.* F; OXFORD *reads* WIDOW *and* MARIANA
    3.6.0.1 *Bertram* . . . ⌜*Lords*⌝] F (*Count Rossillion and the Frenchmen*)

house, but so far there has been nothing in the dialogue to let her know
that Diana is the Widow's daughter.

96 **of** on
97 The F speech prefix *Both* seems most
    naturally to refer to *this matron and*
    this gentle maid, grouped together in
    l. 93; but Helen makes her offer to the
    Widow as well, and the latter might
    well take the lead in accepting rather
    than her young daughter.
3.6.0.1 *as at first* See Introduction, p. 63.
    3 **hilding** good-for-nothing
    5 **bubble** something showy that is easily
    destroyed: applied to reputation in *As*

You Like It (2.7.152) and high position
in *Richard III* (4.4.90), it suits Paroles'
external glitter as well as his lack of
substance.
    9 **as my kinsman** i.e. making allow-
    ances, as I would for a relative
    12 **entertainment** retaining in service
    14 **virtue** courage, manly excellence
    14–16 **at some . . . you** on some import-
    ant occasion requiring trust fail you
    when danger is strong
    19 **fetch off** rescue, as at l. 42. The first
    OED listing for this meaning is 1648,
    but Edwards and Gibson note its
    appearance in Massinger's *Renegado*
    2.5.39, dated 1624 or earlier.

drum, which you hear him so confidently undertake   20
to do.

SECOND LORD I, with a troop of Florentines, will suddenly surprise him. Such I will have whom I am sure
he knows not from the enemy. We will bind and
hoodwink him so that he shall suppose no other but   25
that he is carried into the leaguer of the adversary's
when we bring him to our own tents. Be but your
lordship present at his examination. If he do not for
the promise of his life, and in the highest compulsion
of base fear, offer to betray you and deliver all the   30
intelligence in his power against you, and that with
the divine forfeit of his soul upon oath, never trust
my judgement in anything.

FIRST LORD O, for the love of laughter, let him fetch his
drum. He says he has a stratagem for't. When your   35
lordship sees the bottom of his success in't, and to
what metal this counterfeit lump of ore will be
melted, if you give him not John Drum's entertainment your inclining cannot be removed. Here he
comes.   40

    Enter Paroles

SECOND LORD (*aside*) O, for the love of laughter, hinder
not the honour of his design. Let him fetch off his
drum in any hand.

BERTRAM How now, monsieur! This drum sticks sorely
in your disposition.   45

36 his] ROWE; this F   37 ore] THEOBALD (oure); ours F

26 **leaguer** military camp
  adversary's F's *aduersaries* might be
modernized to either a singular possessive (the redundancy is still standard in constructions like 'a friend of
mine') or a plural; but the modifying
the suggests a singular, as also at
4.1.15 (F *aduersaries*), 62, and 65 (F
enemies).
31 **intelligence** secret information
36 **bottom of his success** The metaphor
includes both the end or outcome and
the essential reality.
37 **ore** F's *ours* gives a possible reading,
but it leaves the key term *counterfeit
lump* without clear participation in the
metaphor running from *metal* to

melted, which is supplied by Theobald's
emendation. The copy probably read
oure, listed by *OED* as a variant spelling of *ore*.
38–9 **give . . . entertainment** To receive
John (or Jack, or Tom) Drum's entertainment is to be thrust out (see Tilley
J12); Rolfe thought the saying was
based on a personification of the drum,
its 'entertainment' being to be beaten.
First Lord's locution may be a play on
words here, harking back to the drum
whose attempted recovery is to lure
Paroles to his undoing.
43 **in any hand** apparently equivalent to
at any hand, 'in any case' (*Shrew*
1.2.144, 226)

FIRST LORD A pox on't! Let it go, 'tis but a drum.

PAROLES But a drum. Is't but a drum? A drum so lost! There was excellent command, to charge in with our horse upon our own wings and to rend our own soldiers! 50

FIRST LORD That was not to be blamed in the command of the service. It was a disaster of war that Caesar himself could not have prevented if he had been there to command.

BERTRAM Well, we cannot greatly condemn our success. Some dishonour we had in the loss of that drum, but it is not to be recovered. 55

PAROLES It might have been recovered.

BERTRAM It might, but it is not now.

PAROLES It is to be recovered. But that the merit of service is seldom attributed to the true and exact performer, I would have that drum or another, or *hic iacet*. 60

BERTRAM Why, if you have a stomach, to't, monsieur! If you think your mystery in stratagem can bring this instrument of honour again into his native quarter, be magnanimous in the enterprise and go on. I will grace the attempt for a worthy exploit. If you speed well in it, the Duke shall both speak of it and extend to you what further becomes his greatness, even to the utmost syllable of your worthiness. 65 70

PAROLES By the hand of a soldier, I will undertake it.

BERTRAM But you must not now slumber in it.

PAROLES I'll about it this evening; and I will presently pen down my dilemmas, encourage myself in my certainty, put myself into my mortal preparation; and by midnight look to hear further from me. 75

51–2 **command of the service** orders given for the military operation
55–6 **success** outcome
62–3 **or *hic iacet*** or die in the attempt (*hic iacet*, 'here lies . . .')
64 **stomach** appetite, inclination
65 **mystery** art, skill
66 **his** its
69 **speed** succeed
73 **slumber in** neglect, be slothful about
75–6 **pen . . . certainty** Perhaps Paroles'

means that by writing out his alternative courses of action he will conclude which is best to follow and then fortify his spirit by faith in that choice.

76 **put . . . mortal preparation** Paroles' words can mean preparing to inflict death on others, but also making ready for his own death. Riverside links this latter possibility to the preceding *dilemmas* and contrasting *certainty*, speculating that the whole

BERTRAM May I be bold to acquaint his grace you are
    gone about it?

PAROLES I know not what the success will be, my lord,   80
    but the attempt I vow.

BERTRAM I know thou'rt valiant, and to the possibility
    of thy soldiership will subscribe for thee. Farewell.

PAROLES I love not many words.   *Exit*

SECOND LORD No more than a fish loves water. Is not   85
    this a strange fellow, my lord, that so confidently
    seems to undertake this business which he knows is
    not to be done; damns himself to do, and dares better
    be damned than to do't?

FIRST LORD You do not know him, my lord, as we do.   90
    Certain it is that he will steal himself into a man's
    favour and for a week escape a great deal of dis-
    coveries; but when you find him out, you have him
    ever after.

BERTRAM Why, do you think he will make no deed at   95
    all of this that so seriously he does address himself
    unto?

SECOND LORD None in the world but return with an
    invention and clap upon you two or three probable
    lies. But we have almost embossed him. You shall   100
    see his fall tonight. For, indeed, he is not for your
    lordship's respect.

FIRST LORD We'll make you some sport with the fox ere
    we case him. He was first smoked by the old Lord
    Lafeu. When his disguise and he is parted, tell me   105
    what a sprat you shall find him, which you shall see
    this very night.

SECOND LORD I must go look my twigs. He shall be
    caught.

BERTRAM (*to First Lord*) Your brother he shall go along   110
    with me.

---

passage addresses not military strategy
but self-dramatizing preparation for
death; but the military theme is more
in line with Paroles' habitual mode of
posturing.

82 **possibility** capacity, power

100 **embossed** run down, like a deer;
related to *ambushed*

104 **case** skin, strip off his *disguise* (l. 105)
    smoked forced out of protective cover,
    like a fox

108 **twigs** i.e. twigs smeared with bird-
    lime, to catch birds. For the transitive
    look, see *OED* 6d ('seek, search out')
    or 6f ('provide').

FIRST LORD As't please your lordship. I'll leave you.

Exit

BERTRAM

Now will I lead you to the house and show you

The lass I spoke of.

SECOND LORD   But you say she's honest.

BERTRAM

That's all the fault. I spoke with her but once   115

And found her wondrous cold. But I sent to her

By this same coxcomb that we have i'th' wind

Tokens and letters, which she did re-send.

And this is all I have done. She's a fair creature.

Will you go see her?

SECOND LORD   With all my heart, my lord.   120

Exeunt

3.7   *Enter Helen and the Widow*

HELEN

If you misdoubt me that I am not she,

I know not how I shall assure you further

But I shall lose the grounds I work upon.

WIDOW

Though my estate be fall'n, I was well born,

Nothing acquainted with these businesses,   5

And would not put my reputation now

In any staining act.

HELEN   Nor would I wish you.

First give me trust the Count he is my husband,

And what to your sworn counsel I have spoken

Is so from word to word. And then you cannot,   10

By the good aid that I of you shall borrow,

Err in bestowing it.

112.1 *Exit*] *not in* F
3.7.0.1 *the*] *not in* F

112 On the confusion of functions for the
two French lords that begins at this
point or in 4.1, see Introduction,
pp. 59–60.

117 **have i'th' wind** have caught the
scent of, continuing the hunt imagery
from *fox, case, smoked,* and *twigs*

3.7.3 **But...upon** without forfeiting the

basis of my stratagem, i.e. by revealing
myself to my husband

9 **to your sworn counsel** privately to
you, who are sworn to secrecy

10 **so from word to word** true in every
word

11 **By** with respect to

WIDOW   I should believe you,
  For you have showed me that which well approves
  You're great in fortune.
HELEN   Take this purse of gold,
  And let me buy your friendly help thus far,   15
  Which I will over-pay and pay again
  When I have found it. The Count he woos your
        daughter,
  Lays down his wanton siege before her beauty,
  Resolved to carry her. Let her in fine consent
  As we'll direct her how 'tis best to bear it.   20
  Now his important blood will naught deny
  That she'll demand. A ring the County wears
  That downward hath succeeded in his house
  From son to son some four or five descents
  Since the first father wore it. This ring he holds   25
  In most rich choice. Yet, in his idle fire,
  To buy his will it would not seem too dear,
  Howe'er repented after.
WIDOW   Now I see
  The bottom of your purpose.
HELEN
  You see it lawful, then: it is no more   30
  But that your daughter, ere she seems as won,
  Desires this ring; appoints him an encounter;
  In fine, delivers me to fill the time,
  Herself most chastely absent. After,

19 Resolved] COLLIER; Resolue F   34 After] F1 (after); after this F2

14 **fortune** (a) social position, but the
Widow perhaps glances also at (b)
wealth, inviting the offer of money
that follows immediately
14–17 **Take ... it** Helen pays for help in
prospect and promises to pay a greater
sum and yet more (*over-pay and pay
again*) when she has actually received
this assistance (*found it*).
19 **Resolved** F's *Resolue* could result from
B's habit of dropping or adding final *s*,
or from the easy *e/d* error; in the
choice between *Resolues* of the later
Folios and Collier's *Resolvd*, the parti-
cipial form is marginally preferable to
the indicative, since the decision to

woo should logically precede the courtship.
in fine finally
20 **bear it** carry off her part
21 **important blood** importunate passion
22 **County** Count
24 **descents** transmissions by inheritance
26 **choice** estimation
idle delirious, mad
32 **encounter** sexual assignation, as often
in Shakespeare
34 If the somewhat short line is inten-
tional, the pause would naturally
come after *absent*, as Helen passes over
the actual *encounter* in agitated silence.

To marry her I'll add three thousand crowns   35
To what is passed already.
WIDOW   I have yielded.
Instruct my daughter how she shall persever
That time and place with this deceit so lawful
May prove coherent. Every night he comes
With musics of all sorts, and songs composed   40
To her unworthiness. It nothing steads us
To chide him from our eaves, for he persists
As if his life lay on't.
HELEN   Why then tonight
Let us assay our plot; which, if it speed,
Is wicked meaning in a lawful deed,   45
And lawful meaning in a wicked act,
Where both not sin, and yet a sinful fact.
But let's about it.   *Exeunt*

4.1   *Enter ⌈First Lord⌉ with five or six other soldiers
in ambush*

FIRST LORD He can come no other way but this hedge-
corner. When you sally upon him, speak what terrible language you will. Though you understand it

46 wicked] WARBURTON; lawfull F   48 *Exeunt*] *not in* F
4.1.0.1 First Lord] *one of the Frenchmen* F

36 **passed** conveyed, or agreed to, in a
legal sense; as in *Shrew* (4.2.119,
4.4.44), in the context of dowry
arrangements.
40 **musics** Shakespeare's only other use of
musics, *Cymbeline* 2.3.37, also designates wooing serenades, which may be
a particular meaning of the plural
form; or it may more generally mean
musical compositions, instruments, or
bands of musicians.
41 **To her unworthiness** to her, even
though she (as his social inferior) is
unworthy (of such tributes)
45–7 **Is . . . fact** Malone's justification of
line 46 as in F—both Helen's intention
and her action are lawful—makes logical sense but ignores the clearly meant
rhetorical pattern of these three lines,
which rather than such separation of
Helen from Bertram points to symmetry between them. *His* paradox of
wicked (adulterous) intention and lawful cohabitation with his wife is

matched by *her* paradox of achieving
such lawful cohabitation by deceiving
him and involving Diana in the deceit:
in effect she is glossing the Widow's
oxymoron *this deceit so lawful* (l. 38),
showing how her position matches
and answers her husband's. Diana's
final lines in her scene with Bertram
(4.2.75–6) also posit *this disguise* as
sinful if not justified by the aim of
defeating Bertram's illicit intentions.
Warburton's emendation to *wicked* in
line 46 also removes the rhetorical
lopsidedness of line 47 in Malone's
reading, with the first clause referring
to both partners but the second only
to Bertram; here both *not sin* indeed,
but both also have their versions of
sinful fact, i.e. crime. Taylor's hypothesis of a dittography error is probably right.
4.1.0.1 For the emendation of F's *Lord. E.*
to First Lord in this scene, see Introduction, pp. 63–4.

not yourselves, no matter. For we must not seem to
understand him, unless some one among us, whom   5
we must produce for an interpreter.

FIRST SOLDIER Good captain, let me be th'interpreter.

FIRST LORD Art not acquainted with him? Knows he
not thy voice?

FIRST SOLDIER No, sir, I warrant you.   10

FIRST LORD But what linsey-woolsey hast thou to speak
to us again?

FIRST SOLDIER E'en such as you speak to me.

FIRST LORD He must think us some band of strangers
i'th' adversary's entertainment. Now, he hath a   15
smack of all neighbouring languages. Therefore we
must every one be a man of his own fancy, not to
know what we speak one to another. So we seem to
know is to know straight our purpose. Choughs'
language, gabble enough and good enough. As for   20
you, interpreter, you must seem very politic. But
couch, ho! Here he comes, to beguile two hours in
a sleep and then to return and swear the lies he
forges.

⌜*They stand aside.*⌝ *Enter Paroles*

PAROLES Ten o'clock. Within these three hours 'twill   25
be time enough to go home. What shall I say I have
done? It must be a very plausive invention that
carries it. They begin to smoke me, and disgraces
have of late knocked too often at my door. I find my
tongue is too foolhardy, but my heart hath the fear   30

17–18 fancy, . . . another.] F (another:); fancy; . . . another, NEILSON (*conj.* Perring)
24.1 *They stand aside.*] *after* COLLIER 1858; *not in* F

5 **unless** except for
11 **linsey-woolsey** medley of sounds, nonsense (literally, fabric of mixed wool and flax)
15 **entertainment** service
16–19 **we must . . . purpose** i.e. each man must talk an imaginary language rather than try to be understood; as long as we seem to understand, we achieve our aim.
not to know not knowing (Abbott § 356)
to know straight perhaps 'experience directly' (*OED* II. 5. c), though it

should mean something like 'see achieved'
19–20 **Choughs' language** jackdaws' babble
20 **gabble . . . enough** The formula 'x enough and y enough' is proverbial (Dent E157.1), sometimes, as here, with the implication that x causes y: the gabble makes it good. Compare Jonson, *Poetaster* 4.1.27 and Marston, *Malcontent* 3.1.108.
22 **couch** crouch, lie low
27 **plausive** plausible

of Mars before it, and of his creatures, not daring the reports of my tongue.

FIRST LORD (*aside*) This is the first truth that e'er thine own tongue was guilty of.

PAROLES What the devil should move me to undertake   35
the recovery of this drum, being not ignorant of the impossibility and knowing I had no such purpose? I must give myself some hurts and say I got them in exploit. Yet slight ones will not carry it. They will say, 'Came you off with so little?' And great ones I   40
dare not give. Wherefore, what's the instance? Tongue, I must put you into a butter-woman's mouth, and buy myself another of Bajazet's mute if you prattle me into these perils.

FIRST LORD (*aside*) Is it possible he should know what   45
he is, and be that he is?

PAROLES I would the cutting of my garments would serve the turn, or the breaking of my Spanish sword.

FIRST LORD (*aside*) We cannot afford you so.

PAROLES Or the baring of my beard, and to say it was   50
in stratagem.

FIRST LORD (*aside*) 'Twould not do.

PAROLES Or to drown my clothes and say I was stripped.

FIRST LORD (*aside*) Hardly serve.   55

---

43 mute] HANMER (*conj.* Theobald and Warburton); Mule F

32 **reports** statements or accounts, but with a play on the noise of firearms discharging: Paroles' craven heart fears the warlike noises of his boasting tongue. It is in this discounting of his previous loud lies that First Lord hears Paroles' first truth.

41 **instance** proof, as in Heywood, *A Woman Killed with Kindness* 8.80: 'What instance hast thou of this strange report?'

42–3 **Tongue . . . mute** i.e. he must give away his too-talkative tongue to a proverbial scold (Dent B781) and procure another one. For the location of that more discreet tongue, diligent scholarship has cast no light on F's *Baiazeths Mule*. Only a well-known anecdote would give the allusion point in the theatre, but no such story has come to light. On the other hand, Bajazet was a generic Turkish name, and *Henry V* 1.2.231–2 demonstrates an association between Turks and enforced silence: 'or else our grave, | Like Turkish mute, shall have a tongueless mouth'. Hunter objects to Hanmer's emendation on just this basis, that the mute in fact has no tongue, but a non-tongue is the only thing that would ensure Paroles' prudence.

49 **afford you so** allow you that

50 **baring** shaving, an unusual sense found also in *Measure* 4.2.177

PAROLES Though I swore I leaped from the window of
the citadel—

FIRST LORD (*aside*) How deep?

PAROLES Thirty fathom.

FIRST LORD (*aside*) Three great oaths would scarce make   60
that be believed.

PAROLES I would I had any drum of the enemy's, I
would swear I recovered it.

FIRST LORD (*aside*) You shall hear one anon.

PAROLES A drum, now, of the enemy's—   65
    Alarum within

FIRST LORD *Throca movousus, cargo, cargo, cargo.*

SOLDIERS *Cargo, cargo, cargo, villianda par corbo, cargo.*
    They seize and blindfold Paroles

PAROLES O, ransom, ransom! Do not hide mine eyes.

FIRST SOLDIER *Boskos thromuldo boskos.*

PAROLES

I know you are the Muscos' regiment,   70
And I shall lose my life for want of language.
If there be here German or Dane, Low Dutch,
Italian, or French, let him speak to me,
I'll discover that which shall undo the Florentine.

FIRST SOLDIER *Boskos vauvado.* I understand thee and   75
can speak thy tongue. *Kerelybonto.* Sir, betake thee
to thy faith, for seventeen poniards are at thy bosom.

PAROLES O!

FIRST SOLDIER O, pray, pray, pray! *Manka revania dul-*
che?   80

67 SOLDIERS] F (*All.*)   67.1 *They seize and blindfold Paroles*] *after* CAPELL; *not in* F; *after*
l. 68 ROWE

57 **citadel** Presumably the enemy's,
although the Sienese and their allies,
encamped near Florence, would not
have a standing fortress in which to
hold Paroles: either Shakespeare's
memory lapse or Paroles' exaggeration.

59 **Thirty fathom** The direction of Paroles'
musing intersects with one of the
eavesdroppers' scoffs, so that he appears to answer First Lord's question:
a brief comic breakdown of the barrier
maintained by stage convention between onlookers speaking 'aside' and
the one they overhear, who is not

supposed to hear them.

65.1 ***Alarum*** The general term for noises
offstage during stage battles probably
indicated specifically those of drum
and trumpet, according to Taylor
(Oxford *Henry V*, note on 3.0.33.1)
used both to rally troops and to communicate commands. The situation
here seems clearly to call for a drum-
beat in comic response to Paroles' just-
expressed wish.

70 **Muscos'** Muscovites' (?)

73 **let him speak** if he will speak

74 **discover** reveal

FIRST LORD *Oscorbidulchos volivorco.*

FIRST SOLDIER
The general is content to spare thee yet,
And, hoodwinked as thou art, will lead thee on
To gather from thee. Haply thou mayst inform
Something to save thy life.

PAROLES   O, let me live,   85
And all the secrets of our camp I'll show,
Their force, their purposes. Nay, I'll speak that
Which you will wonder at.

FIRST SOLDIER   But wilt thou faithfully?

PAROLES
If I do not, damn me.

FIRST SOLDIER   *Accordo linta.*
Come on, thou art granted space.   90
                    Exit with Paroles guarded

        A short alarum within

FIRST LORD
Go tell the Count Roussillon and my brother
We have caught the woodcock, and will keep him
      muffled
Till we do hear from them.

SECOND SOLDIER   Captain, I will.

FIRST LORD
A will betray us all unto ourselves.
Inform on that.

SECOND SOLDIER   So I will, sir.   95

FIRST LORD
Till then I'll keep him dark and safely locked.
                    Exeunt severally

4.2   *Enter Bertram and the maid called Diana*

BERTRAM
They told me that your name was Fontybell.

DIANA
No, my good lord, Diana.

90 art] F3; are FI   90.1 *with Paroles guarded* | *not in* F   96.1 *Exeunt severally*] F (*Exit*)

83 **lead thee on** direct your conversation   and hence a type of stupidity.
92 **woodcock** The bird is easily caught   4.2.0.1, 4.2.1–2 For the emphasis in the

BERTRAM   Titled goddess,
And worth it with addition. But, fair soul,
In your fine frame hath love no quality?
If the quick fire of youth light not your mind   5
You are no maiden but a monument.
When you are dead you should be such a one
As you are now; for you are cold and stern,
And now you should be as your mother was
When your sweet self was got.   10

DIANA
She then was honest.

BERTRAM   So should you be.

DIANA   No.
My mother did but duty: such, my lord,
As you owe to your wife.

BERTRAM   No more o' that!
I prithee do not strive against my vows.
I was compelled to her, but I love thee   15
By love's own sweet constraint, and will for ever
Do thee all rights of service.

DIANA   Ay, so you serve us
Till we serve you. But when you have our roses,
You barely leave our thorns to prick ourselves,
And mock us with our bareness.

BERTRAM   How have I sworn!   20

entrance direction on Diana's name,
repeated in the opening exchange between Diana and Bertram, see Introduction, pp. 56–7. Thiselton, following
a suggestion by Dowden, saw in *Fontybell* (l. 1) a reference to a fountain
adorned with a statue of Diana, to
which Rosalind may be alluding in *As
You Like It* 4.1.145–6. But the connections seem tenuous, and the conjunction of unmoved sculpture with
flowing water in the notion of a fountain Diana blurs the symbolic opposition that seems required here between
Bertram's desired *Fontybel*, liquid and
yielding, and Diana's 'cold and stern'
chastity.

3 **worth it with addition** deserving of the
name of goddess with further marks of
distinction (playing on *addition* as both

'more' and 'title')

4 **hath love no quality** is love absent as
an element or attribute

14 **vows** Probably vows not to consummate his marriage to Helen (see
2.3.272 and 274, 3.2.20–2) but possibly his vows of love to Diana (see l.
20 below).

17 **rights** Primarily duties to her imposed
by love's *sweet constraint*, but the word
also includes *rites* (of love) in the sense
frequent in Shakespeare.

18 **roses** maidenheads, perhaps with a
visual image of female genitals (see *As
You Like It* 3.2.109)

19 **barely** (a) only just, (b) in a poor,
naked condition

20 **bareness** The condition implied is
defenceless and destitute, but also
'deflowered'. The image of the stripped
flower for the seduced woman resem-

DIANA

'Tis not the many oaths that makes the truth,
But the plain single vow that is vowed true.
What is not holy, that we swear not by,
But take the high'st to witness. Then, pray you
     tell me,
If I should swear by Jove's great attributes   25
I loved you dearly, would you believe my oaths
When I did love you ill? This has no holding,
To swear by him whom I protest to love
That I will work against him. Therefore your oaths
Are words, and poor conditions but unsealed,   30
At least in my opinion.

BERTRAM   Change it, change it.

Be not so holy-cruel. Love is holy,
And my integrity ne'er knew the crafts
That you do charge men with. Stand no more off,
But give thyself unto my sick desires,   35
Who then recovers. Say thou art mine, and ever
My love as it begins shall so persever.

DIANA

I see that men make rope's in such a scarre,
That we'll forsake ourselves. Give me that ring.

4.2.25 Jove's] F (Ioues); God's GLOBE *(conj.* Cambridge); Love's RANN *(conj.* Johnson)
30 words, and poor conditions₍] THEOBALD; words and poor conditions, F 38 make
rope's in such a scarre] F; *often emended: see note.*

bles *Complaint* 146–7: 'Threw my
affections in his charmèd power, |
Reserved the stalk and gave him all
my flower.'

22 **single** (a) one, as opposed to many
(l. 21), but also (b) unmixed with contrary elements, unduplicitous
    true rightly, properly

23–30 **What . . . unsealed** Diana deconstructs Bertram's protestations to show
they are not *vowed true.* She notes first
that in order to be credited we swear
by the holiest divinity, and then puts
in her own person Bertram's case: he
swears by the powers of the holiest,
Jove, that he loves her dearly but
undercuts this appeal for credit by loving her *ill,* in a way repugnant to
Jove's holiness. This swearing by a
deity an action contrary to the deity's

essence *has no holding:* 'is not valid or
binding', or possibly 'lacks consistency' (although *OED* gives only this
example). The implied legal figure continues in Diana's conclusion that Bertram's oaths are merely words, inferior
covenants that are not legally ratified
(*unsealed*).

35 **sick** (a) longing (*OED* II. 4a) in Bertram's intention, but conveying also
(b) corrupted (III. 7)

36 **Who** Abbott (§264) lists examples of
who referring to things or feelings
when they are personified, e.g. *Venus*
1040–4, *Titus* 3.2.8–9: Bertram's
desires, like a person, are sick but may
recover.

38 **make . . . scarre** In this line, a celebrated crux, *make rope's* and *scarre* are
probably both corrupt. Since none of the
proposed emendations is convincing,

BERTRAM

  I'll lend it thee, my dear, but have no power   40
  To give it from me.

DIANA   Will you not, my lord?

BERTRAM

  It is an honour 'longing to our house,
  Bequeathèd down from many ancestors,
  Which were the greatest obloquy i'th' world
  In me to lose.

DIANA   Mine honour's such a ring.   45
  My chastity's the jewel of our house,
  Bequeathèd down from many ancestors,
  Which were the greatest obloquy i'th' world
  In me to lose. Thus your own proper wisdom
  Brings in the champion honour on my part   50
  Against your vain assault.

BERTRAM   Here, take my ring.
  My house, mine honour, yea, my life be thine,
  And I'll be bid by thee.

DIANA

  When midnight comes, knock at my chamber
      window.
  I'll order take my mother shall not hear.   55
  Now will I charge you in the band of truth,
  When you have conquered my yet-maiden bed,
  Remain there but an hour, nor speak to me.
  My reasons are most strong, and you shall know
      them

I leave it unaltered. Taylor sets out categories of possibility and works through the problems carefully in 'Textual Double Knots: "make rope's in such a scarre" ' (in *Shakespeare: Text, Subtext, and Context*, ed. Ronald Dotterer (London and Toronto, 1989), pp. 163–85). Rather than list the scores of proposed emendations, I refer the reader to his study, which provides a useful kit for do-it-yourself emendation.

42 **honour** token of distinction, as in *Henry V* 4.8.60
45 **honour** chastity; perhaps more concretely the virgin hymen, predating

OED's first entry for this sense (*sb.* 3b, 1688). This would support Diana's equation of Bertram's ring with her virginity, through application of the image of an uncurrent coin, 'cracked in the ring', to lost maidenhead (see Middleton, *Your Five Gallants* 2.3.120–1: 'Here's mistress rose-noble | Has lost her maidenhead, crack'd in the ring'). Lost virginity is a strong subtext to the action of *Complaint*'s seduced and abandoned woman who 'Cracked many a ring of posied gold and bone' (l. 45).

55 **order take** make arrangements
56 **band** bond

When back again this ring shall be delivered.   60
And on your finger in the night I'll put
Another ring, that what in time proceeds
May token to the future our past deeds.
Adieu till then, then fail not. You have won
A wife of me, though there my hope be done.   65

BERTRAM

A heaven on earth I have won by wooing thee.
        ⌈*Exit*⌉

DIANA

For which, live long to thank both heaven and me.
You may so in the end.
My mother told me just how he would woo,
As if she sat in 's heart. She says all men   70
Have the like oaths. He has sworn to marry me
When his wife's dead. Therefore I'll lie with him
When I am buried. Since Frenchmen are so braid,
Marry that will, I live and die a maid.
Only, in this disguise I think't no sin   75
To cozen him that would unjustly win.   *Exit*

66.1 *Exit*] F2; *not in* F; *at l.* 68 HARRISON   71 has] GRANT WHITE; had F

62 **what in time proceeds** whatever happens afterwards

65 **though there my hope be done** though my own prospects of being your wife are destroyed (by this yielding). By hinting that she will present him with a wife even while denying the position for herself, Diana speaks for the audience's appreciation rather than Bertram's.

66. The exit F2 supplies for Bertram is probably in the right place, but Harrison's placement of it after line 68 is supported by the shortness of that line and Diana's subsequent change of subject. If the exit is thus delayed, lines 67–8 are addressed to Bertram and like lines 64–5 offer a surface meaning to him while Diana shares a deeper one with the audience.

71 **has sworn** Diana's verb form in F indicates 'he would have sworn', i.e. he was ready to though he did not actually do so, which agrees with the lack of such a promise in the interchange just enacted. But she and Paroles both attest later that Bertram did promise her marriage (5.3.140, 263–4), and the vow must have been part of the courting process if Paroles knew of it. The final scene has some loose ends and discrepancies, but this confirmation of the promise as having occurred before Diana's yielding supports the indicative *has* here, as does the expectation of grammatical symmetry between this premise and the following *therefore* conclusion.

73 **braid** probably related to *OED*, *sb.* II. 3, 'an adroit turn; a trick or subtilty'. Steevens cites *Greene's Never Too Late*: 'Dian rose with all her maids, | Blushing thus at love's braids' (*Works*, ed. A. B. Grosart, 15 vols. (1881–6), viii. 214). Probably both adjective and noun derive from OE breȝden, 'deceitful'.

4.3   *Enter the two French ⌈Lords⌉ and some two or three soldiers*

FIRST LORD You have not given him his mother's letter?

SECOND LORD I have delivered it an hour since. There is something in't that stings his nature, for on the reading it he changed almost into another man.   5

FIRST LORD He has much worthy blame laid upon him for shaking off so good a wife and so sweet a lady.

SECOND LORD Especially he hath incurred the everlasting displeasure of the King, who had even tuned his bounty to sing happiness to him.˙I will tell you   10 a thing, but you shall let it dwell darkly with you.

FIRST LORD When you have spoken it 'tis dead, and I am the grave of it.

SECOND LORD He hath perverted a young gentlewoman here in Florence of a most chaste renown, and this   15 night he fleshes his will in the spoil of her honour. He hath given her his monumental ring, and thinks himself made in the unchaste composition.

FIRST LORD Now, God delay our rebellion! As we are ourselves, what things are we!   20

4.3.0.1 Lords] F (*Captaines*)   19 rebellion!] ROWE (~;); rebellion‸ F

4.3.1–2 An audience would assume that *his mother's letter* is the rebuking one that it heard the Countess ask the two Lords to carry to Bertram (3.2.92–5), even though in terms of events considerable time has passed, and no reason is evident why Second Lord should not have given Bertram the letter as soon as he returned from France. Presumably we are not to scrutinize very closely the time sequence, which leaves too much time for delivery of this letter and too little for Helen to broadcast the news of her death through the rector of St Jacques (ll. 47–59). This news, received by Bertram before his mother's letter, perhaps accounts for his strong reaction to her rebukes (ll. 3–5).

6 **worthy** deserved

9 **even** fully (*OED, adv.* 7)

11 **darkly** secretly

16 **fleshes ... honour** One fleshes a hound by giving it a taste of the spoil, the

hunted animal's flesh. There is a comparable physical meaning here, by which Bertram gorges his *will* (carnal appetite) in the flesh of his prey Diana. Figuratively, the phrase connotes initiation (Hanmer notes that 'a soldier is said to *flesh his sword* when he first wounds an enemy'), which is also relevant to Bertram's first sexual conquest, as he feeds his desire (*will*) through the despoiling (*spoil*) of her honour.

17 **monumental** In Shakespeare's use, *monument* usually means a tomb, often as in *Much Ado*, *Titus*, and *Romeo* a family tomb; Bertram's ring is *monumental* in that it pertains to his dead ancestors.

18 **composition** contract

19 **delay** hinder

rebellion i.e. of the flesh. Wilson notes the flesh/rebel association also in *Measure* 3.1.378–9 and *2 Henry IV* 2.4.354.

SECOND LORD Merely our own traitors. And, as in the common course of all treasons we still see them reveal themselves till they attain to their abhorred ends, so he that in this action contrives against his own nobility, in his proper stream o'erflows himself.   25

FIRST LORD Is it not meant damnable in us to be trumpeters of our unlawful intents? We shall not, then, have his company tonight?

SECOND LORD Not till after midnight, for he is dieted to his hour.   30

FIRST LORD That approaches apace. I would gladly have him see his company anatomized, that he might take a measure of his own judgements wherein so curiously he had set this counterfeit.

SECOND LORD We will not meddle with him till he come,   35
for his presence must be the whip of the other.

FIRST LORD In the meantime, what hear you of these wars?

SECOND LORD I hear there is an overture of peace.

25 nobility, . . . stream‸] THEOBALD; Nobillity‸ . . . streame, F

21 **Merely** absolutely
traitors (a) as self-corrupters through giving in to the rebellion of the flesh, referring to what has preceded, but also (b) as self-revealers who boast about our own misdoing, referring to what follows
21–5 **as . . . himself** i.e. as traitors commonly talk of their intended treasonable doings until they achieve their bad intentions, so Bertram—who in this behaviour is a traitor to his own noble heritage—caught up in his own current of desire, cannot contain his **secret. Hunter** objects that such a **paraphrase (based** partly on Steevens and Johnson) **violates the rhetorical structure, which requires that** *reveal themselves* be parallel to *contrives*; but *contrives* (i.e. 'plots', in its usual **Shake**spearian meaning) *against his own nobility* operates rather to justify **the analogy of Bertram** as traitor. Taking *ends* as **'deaths'** rather than 'aims' yields the alternative **reading** 'As traitors commonly **show their true natures, so that** they arrive **at their dreadful deaths (by execution)'; but this reading goes** against the parallel

with Bertram, whose treason as Hunter says has at this point attained success rather than punishment.
26 **Is it not meant damnable** Perhaps 'does it not show a damnable *meaning* or disposition' (Rolfe).
29–30 **dieted to his hour** restricted to his appointed time—which is in fact an hour (4.2.58)
32 **company** habitual associate
anatomized exposed to full view, as for dissection
33–4 **so curiously he had set this counterfeit** such an elaborate setting he had given this spurious gem
36 **his . . . other** In the most straightforward reading, *his* = Bertram's and *the other* = Paroles, but the non-specific references allow Delius's interpretation that the presence of each one must be the whip of the other. Paroles will suffer exposure before Bertram, but Bertram will have to hear himself denigrated by Paroles and bear the consequence of his faulty judgement as First Lord has just said. For *his* and *the other* as 'this one' and 'that one', see *Macbeth* 4.3.81.

FIRST LORD Nay, I assure you, a peace concluded.   40

SECOND LORD What will Count Roussillon do then? Will
    he travel higher, or return again into France?

FIRST LORD I perceive by this demand you are not
    altogether of his counsel.

SECOND LORD Let it be forbid, sir. So should I be a great   45
    deal of his act.

FIRST LORD Sir, his wife some two months since fled
    from his house. Her pretence is a pilgrimage to Saint
    Jacques le Grand, which holy undertaking with most
    austere sanctimony she accomplished. And, there   50
    residing, the tenderness of her nature became as a
    prey to her grief; in fine, made a groan of her last
    breath; and now she sings in heaven.

SECOND LORD How is this justified?

FIRST LORD The stronger part of it by her own letters,   55
    which makes her story true even to the point of her
    death. Her death itself, which could not be her office
    to say is come, was faithfully confirmed by the rector
    of the place.

SECOND LORD Hath the Count all this intelligence?   60

FIRST LORD Ay, and the particular confirmations, point
    from point, to the full arming of the verity.

SECOND LORD I am heartily sorry that he'll be glad of
    this.

FIRST LORD How mightily sometimes we make us com-   65
    forts of our losses!

SECOND LORD And how mightily some other times we
    drown our gain in tears! The great dignity that his
    valour hath here acquired for him shall at home be
    encountered with a shame as ample.   70

FIRST LORD The web of our life is of a mingled yarn,
    good and ill together. Our virtues would be proud if

---

42 **higher** farther (?); compare *Merry
    Wives* 5.5.104, and 2.1.208 above.
46 **act** Second Lord's *act* shifts the
    meaning of First Lord's *counsel* to *coun-
    cil*, as in 'Acts of the Council'. The F
    spelling *councell* does not discriminate
    between them.
48 **pretence** purpose

50 **sanctimony** personal holiness
54 **justified** verified
58 **rector** Used generally for 'governor',
    specifically for the head of a religious
    or educational institution.
61–2 **point from point** See 3.1.1 and note.
62 **to the full arming of the verity** render-
    ing its truth unassailable

our faults whipped them not, and our crimes would
despair if they were not cherished by our virtues.

    Enter ⌈a Servant⌉

How now? Where's your master?   75

SERVANT He met the Duke in the street, sir, of whom
he hath taken a solemn leave. His lordship will next
morning for France. The Duke hath offered him letters of commendations to the King.

SECOND LORD They shall be no more than needful there,   80
if they were more than they can commend.

    Enter Bertram

FIRST LORD They cannot be too sweet for the King's
tartness. Here's his lordship now. How now, my lord,
is't not after midnight?

BERTRAM I have tonight dispatched sixteen businesses   85
a month's length apiece. By an abstract of success:
I have congeed with the Duke, done my adieu with
his nearest, buried a wife, mourned for her, writ to
my lady mother I am returning, entertained my
convoy, and between these main parcels of dispatch   90
effected many nicer needs. The last was the greatest,
but that I have not ended yet.

SECOND LORD If the business be of any difficulty, and
this morning your departure hence, it requires haste
of your lordship.   95

BERTRAM I mean the business is not ended as fearing
to hear of it hereafter. But shall we have this dialogue

74.1 *Servant*] ROWE; *Messenger* F   81.1 *Bertram*] F (*Count Rossillion*)   82 FIRST LORD]
F3 (*Cap.G.*); *Ber.* F1   86 apiece. By] *after* ALEXANDER (apiece;); apiece, by F
91 effected] F3; affected F1

74.1 **Enter a Servant** F's *Enter a Messenger*
   contradicts the speech prefix *Ser.* at l.
   76, and in any case the man has not
   been charged with any message.
   Bowers, noting that this seems to be
   the servant who came with Bertram to
   Florence (3.2.83), hypothesizes either
   a change of plan or incomplete later
   revision ('Foul Papers', p. 65).
80–1 **They . . . commend** i.e. the commendations will be no more powerful than
   what is needed (for Bertram to regain
   the King's favour), even if they were
   more glowing than the facts warrant.
86 **By . . . success** 'by way of a summary

of the several businesses I have dispatched in succession' (Thiselton), or
   'successfully'
87 **congeed with** paid farewell respects to
89–90 **entertained my convoy** hired my
   means of transport, or my travel party.
   The two meanings are apparently
   fused below at 4.4.10 and in *Troilus*
   1.1.104, and perhaps here as well.
90 **parcels of dispatch** items of business to
   be settled
91 **nicer needs** more delicate errands
96–7 **I mean . . . hereafter** Bertram may
   hear more of his seduction if Diana
   becomes pregnant or presses him to

between the fool and the soldier? Come, bring forth
this counterfeit model has deceived me like a double-
meaning prophesier.   100

SECOND LORD Bring him forth.   *Exeunt soldiers*
Has sat i'th' stocks all night, poor gallant knave.

BERTRAM No matter, his heels have deserved it in usurping his spurs so long. How does he carry himself?

SECOND LORD I have told your lordship already: the   105
stocks carry him. But to answer you as you would
be understood: he weeps like a wench that had shed
her milk; he hath confessed himself to Morgan,
whom he supposes to be a friar, from the time of his
remembrance to this very instant disaster of his   110
setting i'th' stocks. And what think you he hath
confessed?

BERTRAM Nothing of me, has a?

SECOND LORD His confession is taken, and it shall be
read to his face. If your lordship be in't, as I believe   115
you are, you must have the patience to hear it.

Enter Paroles, blindfolded and guarded, with First
Soldier as his interpreter

99 has] F (ha s); 'has F3; h'as ROWE 1714   101 *Exeunt soldiers*] CAPELL; *not in* F
102 Has] ha's F1; h'as F4   116.1–2 *Enter ... interpreter*] F (*Enter Parolles with his Interpreter.*)

honour his promise of marriage
(4.2.71–2 and note).

97–8 **this . . . soldier** The phrasing suggests that Bertram sees the imminent
exposure as an entertainment, an
interlude featuring type characters (F
the Foole and the Soldiour). Paroles is
the fool in dialogue with his soldier-
interrogators; or perhaps Delius is
right to see Paroles containing both
in himself, and Bertram inviting the
others to watch his self-serving and his
soldierly pride in conflict under stress.

99 **counterfeit model** false image (of a soldier) who

99–100 **double-meaning prophesier** The
Weird Sisters in *Macbeth* are *double-
meaning prophesiers* (5.10.19–20), and
the *locus classicus* of equivocal prophe-
cy is quoted in *2 Henry VI* (*Contention*)
1.4.59: '*Aio Aeacidam, Romanos vincere
posse.*' The implication that Bertram

is only now realizing Paroles' other
'meaning', as fool, supports Delius's
reading of the dialogue as between two
aspects of one man.

102 **gallant** not 'chivalrously brave'
(*OED, adj.* 5), but 'showy in appearance' (1)

103–4 **his heels . . . spurs** The usual interpretations of usurping spurs in terms
of false claims of knighthood on
Paroles' part leave *heels* unexplained.
As a whole, the phrase suggests rather
the means of flight (*heels*) prevailing
over the impulse to go forward
(*spurs*)—the same craven favouring of
retreat over advance of which Paroles
later accuses Second Lord (ll. 292–4).

107–8 **he weeps . . . milk** 'To cry for spilt
milk' (Tilley M939).

109–10 **time of his remembrance** point at
which his memory begins

110 **instant** present

114 **taken** written down

BERTRAM A plague upon him! Muffled! He can say
nothing of me.

FIRST LORD (*aside to Bertram*) Hush, hush. Hoodman
comes. (*Aloud*) Portotartarossa.   120

FIRST SOLDIER (*to Paroles*) He calls for the tortures. What
will you say without 'em?

PAROLES I will confess what I know without constraint.
If ye pinch me like a pasty, I can say no more.

FIRST SOLDIER *Bosko chimurcho?*   125

FIRST LORD *Boblibindo chicurmurco.*

FIRST SOLDIER You are a merciful general. Our general
bids you answer to what I shall ask you out of a
note.

PAROLES And truly, as I hope to live.   130

FIRST SOLDIER 'First, demand of him how many horse
the Duke is strong.' What say you to that?

PAROLES Five or six thousand, but very weak and
unserviceable. The troops are all scattered and the
commanders very poor rogues, upon my reputation   135
and credit, and as I hope to live.

FIRST SOLDIER Shall I set down your answer so?

PAROLES Do. I'll take the sacrament on't, how and
which way you will.

BERTRAM (*aside*) All's one to him. What a past-saving   140
slave is this!

FIRST LORD (*aside*) You're deceived, my lord. This is
Monsieur Paroles, the gallant militarist—that was his
own phrase—that had the whole theoric of war in

119 Hush, hush] *ascribed to First Lord,* HANMER; *part of previous speech,* F   126 FIRST
LORD] ROWE; *Cap.* F   140 All's one to him] *ascribed to Bertram,* CAPELL; *part of previous
speech,* F; *ascribed to First Lord Dumaine,* OXFORD (*conj.* Ritson)

117 **Muffled** blindfolded
119 In F *hush, hush* continues Bertram's
preceding speech, but it clearly goes
with the following *Hoodman comes,* and
with the Lords' general game-playing
spirit, which makes the occasion into
a game of 'hoodman-blind', rather
than with Bertram's anxiety. For this
misplacement and that at l. 140 below
as indications of Shakespeare's revising hand, marginal additions misread
by Compositor B, see Introduction,
p. 56.

129 **note** memorandum of topics
140 **All's one to him** F assigns these words
to Paroles, but the comment on him
cannot be spoken *by* him, and is rather
a logical preface for Bertram's following exclamation of contempt. See l.
119 above and note.
143 **militarist** This passage is the first *OED*
citation for this word, which may be
intended as a Paroles neologism: *his
own phrase* not only as self-assigned
but also as self-invented.
144–6 **the whole theoric . . . dagger** Both

the knot of his scarf and the practice in the chape   145
of his dagger.

SECOND LORD (*aside*) I will never trust a man again for
keeping his sword clean, nor believe he can have
everything in him by wearing his apparel neatly.

FIRST SOLDIER Well, that's set down.   150

PAROLES Five or six thousand horse, I said. I will say
true—'or thereabouts' set down, for I'll speak truth.

FIRST LORD (*aside*) He's very near the truth in this.

BERTRAM (*aside*) But I con him no thanks for't, in the
nature he delivers it.   155

PAROLES 'Poor rogues', I pray you say.

FIRST SOLDIER Well, that's set down.

PAROLES I humbly thank you, sir. A truth's a truth,
the rogues are marvellous poor.

FIRST SOLDIER 'Demand of him of what strength they   160
are a-foot.' What say you to that?

PAROLES By my troth, sir, if I were to live but this
present hour, I will tell true. Let me see: Spurio a
hundred and fifty, Sebastian so many, Corambus so
many, Jacques so many; Guiltian, Cosmo, Lodowick,   165
and Gratii, two hundred fifty each; mine own company, Chitopher, Vaumond, Bentii, two hundred fifty

147 SECOND LORD] F (*Cap.E.*); BERTRAM Walker *conj.*   162 live but] HANMER; liue F;
die DYCE 1864   165 Guiltian] F; Guillaum OXFORD (*conj.* Wilson)   167 Chitopher] F;
Christopher *conj.* Wilson

theory and practice in Paroles are dec-
orative only: the knot in his sash,
perhaps suggesting a lady's favour
(Hunter), and the metal mounting of
his dagger's sheath (*chape*), significantly the part that covers the point when
it is not in use.

147–9 **I will . . . neatly** Some editors are
attracted by Walker's conjectural reassignment of this speech to Bertram,
since he more than Second Lord has
been taken in by Paroles' dashing ex-
terior, but it is too soon in the dynamic
of the scene for Bertram to see his
naïve misjudgement so clearly. The
speech is not his but, as Taylor observes, *aimed at* him.

154 **con him no thanks** acknowledge no
gratitude due him

154–5 **in the nature** considering the mode
in which

162 **live but** Paroles' protestation that he
tells the truth as *in extremis* apparently
requires a meaning opposite to F's *liue*.
Some editors gloss as 'live only', but
as Taylor says the understood *only* is
not communicable in the theatre. Hanmer's emendation is marginally preferable to Dyce's in assuming a simpler
error, of omission.

163–8 **Spurio . . . each** One oddity in
this list is the inclusion of *Gratii* and
Bentii, which according to Mario Praz
('Shakespeare's Italy', *Shakespeare Survey 7* (Cambridge, 1954), p. 105n)
represent the Florentine *family* names
Grazzi and Benci, among the personal
names. *Guiltian* and *Chitopher* may be
misprints of *Guillaum* and *Christopher*,
as Wilson conjectures, though it does
not seem likely that in this exotic
hodgepodge a familiar French name

each. So that the muster file, rotten and sound, upon
my life, amounts not to fifteen thousand poll, half of
the which dare not shake the snow from off their   170
cassocks lest they shake themselves to pieces.

BERTRAM (*aside*) What shall be done to him?

FIRST LORD (*aside*) Nothing but let him have thanks.
Demand of him my condition, and what credit I have
with the Duke.   175

FIRST SOLDIER Well, that's set down. 'You shall demand
of him whether one Captain Dumaine be i'th' camp,
a Frenchman: what his reputation is with the Duke,
what his valour, honesty, and expertness in wars;
or whether he thinks it were not possible with well-   180
weighing sums of gold to corrupt him to a revolt.'
What say you to this? What do you know of it?

PAROLES I beseech you let me answer to the particular
of the inter'gatories. Demand them singly.

FIRST SOLDIER Do you know this Captain Dumaine?   185

PAROLES I know him. A was a botcher's 'prentice in
Paris, from whence he was whipped for getting the
sheriff's fool with child, a dumb innocent that could
not say him nay.

⌈*First Lord moves to strike Paroles*⌉

BERTRAM (*aside to First Lord*) Nay, by your leave, hold 190
your hands—though I know his brains are forfeit to
the next tile that falls.

188 sheriff's] F (Shrieues)   189.1 *First . . . Paroles*] *not in* F

and an even more familiar English one
should be the ones to give trouble.
Other names look backward in this
and other plays: *Spurio* has already
been named by Paroles as an old
adversary (2.1.41); the disguised
Duke in *Measure* is called Friar Lodowick; the Polonius character in the
Q1 *Hamlet* is named Corambis.

169 **poll** heads, as in a head-count.
Paroles' figures for horse and foot in
fact add up to well below ten thousand, let alone fifteen thousand.

180-1 **well-weighing** Makes an equation
through wordplay: gold that is sufficient in amount to be weighty will
have strong influence.

186 **botcher** patcher of shoes or clothes

188 **sheriff's fool** 'The sheriff had charge
of idiots whose property was not of
sufficient value to make them profitable wards for the Crown' (Wilson).
innocent idiot

190-1 Bertram's line apparently responds
to some threatening movement by
First Lord toward Paroles.

191-2 **brains . . . falls** Being   suddenly
struck by a falling tile was a cliché for
unexpected death (e.g. Plutarch, *Life
of Pyrrhus*, 34; Whitney, *Choice of
Emblems*, 176), which in turn was the
traditional penalty for bearing false
witness: 'A sudden death, with shame,
is due | To him that swears what is
untrue' (Wither, *A Collection of Emblems*, i. 38).

FIRST SOLDIER Well, is this captain in the Duke of
  Florence's camp?

PAROLES Upon my knowledge he is, and lousy.   195

FIRST LORD (*aside*) Nay, look not so upon me. We shall
  hear of your lordship anon.

FIRST SOLDIER What is his reputation with the Duke?

PAROLES The Duke knows him for no other but a poor
  officer of mine, and writ to me this other day to turn   200
  him out o'th' band. I think I have his letter in my
  pocket.

FIRST SOLDIER Marry, we'll search.

PAROLES In good sadness, I do not know. Either it is
  there or it is upon a file with the Duke's other letters   205
  in my tent.

FIRST SOLDIER Here 'tis, here's a paper. Shall I read it
  to you?

PAROLES I do not know if it be it or no.

BERTRAM (*aside*) Our interpreter does it well.   210

FIRST LORD (*aside*) Excellently.

FIRST SOLDIER (*reads*) 'Dian, the Count's a fool, and full
  of gold.'

PAROLES That is not the Duke's letter, sir. That is an
  advertisement to a proper maid in Florence, one   215
  Diana, to take heed of the allurement of one Count
  Roussillon: a foolish, idle boy, but for all that very
  ruttish. I pray you, sir, put it up again.

FIRST SOLDIER Nay, I'll read it first, by your favour.

PAROLES My meaning in't, I protest, was very honest   220
  in the behalf of the maid. For I knew the young
  Count to be a dangerous and lascivious boy, who is
  a whale to virginity and devours up all the fry it
  finds.

197 lordship] POPE; Lord F   212 (*reads*)] *not in* F

195 **lousy** If not just an extra insult
  ('mean, vile'), it perhaps is offered in
  further affirmation that Captain Dumaine lives in the *camp*, where literal
  lousiness is prevalent.
204 **sadness** earnest
215 **advertisement** admonition
  proper respectable
217 **idle** trivial

218 **ruttish** lustful, with an animal con-
  notation
223 **fry** small fish, the virgins helpless
  before the strength of Bertram as de-
  vouring whale; whales were identified
  with the sea-monsters of legend who
  abducted maidens (Roger J. Trienens,
  'The Symbolic Cloud in *Hamlet*', *SQ*, 5
  (1954), 212–13).

BERTRAM (*aside*) Damnable both-sides rogue!   225
FIRST SOLDIER (*reads*)

'When he swears oaths, bid him drop gold, and take it.
    After he scores, he never pays the score.
Half-won is match well made. Match, and well make it.
    He ne'er pays after-debts. Take it before.
And say a soldier, Dian, told thee this: 230
Men are to mell with, boys are not to kiss.
For count of this: the Count's a fool, I know it,
Who pays before, but not when he does owe it.
        Thine, as he vowed to thee in thine ear,
                Paroles.'   235

BERTRAM (*aside*) He shall be whipped through the army
with this rhyme in 's forehead.
SECOND LORD (*aside*) This is your devoted friend, sir, the
manifold linguist and the armipotent soldier.

226 (*reads*)] *Let.* F

225 Paroles as *both-sides rogue* looks back
to *double-meaning prophesier* (above,
ll. 99–100 and note).
227 **After . . . score** After he obtains goods
on credit he never pays the bill. *OED*
cites Heywood, *I Fair Maid of the West*,
1.5.2–4: 'It is the commonest thing
that can be for these captains to score
and to score, but when the scores are
to be paid, *Non est inventus*' (ed. Brow-
nell Salomon, Salzburg Studies in English (Salzburg, 1975)). The first *scores*
in Paroles' poem also plays on 'makes
a hit'.
228 **Half-won . . . make it** The noun *match*
means 'bargain', the verb *match*
means 'be equal': 'being half (but not
completely) won puts you in a position
to make a good bargain; be his equal
in cunning and achieve that advant-
ageous bargain'. Both noun and verb
play on *match* as 'mate, mating'. Some
editors take the first *match* as subject,
with variations on 'a match well-made
is half-won' (Wilson), but *half-won* is
in the subject position and the idea of
Diana as attracted but not yet com-
mitted is central to Paroles' argument
that she take *before* what she will have
no force to command *after*.
229 **after-debts** money owed for goods

already obtained
231 **Men . . . kiss** i.e. mature men, like
Paroles, are the ones with whom to
have sexual relations (*mell*); boys, like
Bertram, are not to embrace sexually.
Capell (*Notes*, p. 19) observes that this
line and the preceding one depart from
what came before; indeed, they contradict it, in that rather than encouraging Diana to get all she can by
selling herself to Bertram he now suggests she should reject Bertram and
mell with himself, presumably without
profit. Given the context, logic is less
important than piling up betrayals of
Bertram.
232 **count of** reckon on
233 **Who pays . . . owe it** In an irony of
which Paroles is unaware, Bertram
has in fact 'paid before' in the scene
just preceding, by giving Diana his
family ring.
237 **in 's** i.e. displayed upon his
239 **armipotent** Shakespeare uses *armipotent* elsewhere in situations of
heightened formality, one of them
comically grandiloquent (*Kinsmen*
5.1.53, *L.L.L.* 5.2.637, 644); Second
Lord's use here is probably meant to
parody Paroles' pretensions.

BERTRAM (*aside*) I could endure anything before but a   240
cat, and now he's a cat to me.

FIRST SOLDIER I perceive, sir, by the General's looks we
shall be fain to hang you.

PAROLES My life, sir, in any case! Not that I am afraid
to die, but that, my offences being many, I would   245
repent out the remainder of nature. Let me live, sir,
in a dungeon, i'th' stocks, or anywhere, so I may
live.

FIRST SOLDIER We'll see what may be done, so you
confess freely. Therefore once more to this Captain   250
Dumaine. You have answered to his reputation with
the Duke and to his valour. What is his honesty?

PAROLES He will steal, sir, an egg out of a cloister. For
rapes and ravishments he parallels Nessus. He professes not keeping of oaths. In breaking 'em he is   255
stronger than Hercules. He will lie, sir, with such
volubility that you would think truth were a fool.
Drunkenness is his best virtue: for he will be swine-
drunk, and in his sleep he does little harm, save to
his bedclothes about him; but they know his condi-   260
tions, and lay him in straw. I have but little more
to say, sir, of his honesty. He has everything that an

242 the] F3; your F1   260 bedclothes about him; but they] F (him:); bedclothes;
but they about him OXFORD (*conj.* Watkiss Lloyd)

241 **cat** For the cat as the object of phobic
dislike, see *Merchant* 4.1.47. A play on
cat as a slang term for 'prostitute' is
conceivable, since the issue here involves changing adherences in each
new situation. Philip Hope-Wallace,
reviewing the 1959 Guthrie production (*Time & Tide*, 2 May 1959, p.
502), says without advancing evidence that *cat* means 'catamite'.

242 **the** F's *your* probably represents y^e
misread as y^r.

253 **He . . . cloister** 'He will steal anything, however trifling, from any
place, however holy' (Johnson). The
minimal value of eggs was the basis of
the stock phrase 'To take eggs for
money' (Tilley E90), used by Shakespeare for a bad bargain in *Winter's
Tale* 1.2.163; see also 'Some trick not
worth an egg', *Coriolanus* 4.4.21. Since
the dominant idea in most Shake-

spearian uses of *cloister* is shutting-
up and difficulty of access, perhaps
Johnson's emphasis in the second part
should be modified to 'any place, however locked up'—i.e. the theft itself is
the point for such a rogue rather than
rich reward or ease of access.

253–4 **For . . . Nessus** Nessus, known in
legend for the attempted ravishment of
Hercules' wife Deianira, is as a centaur
also connected generically with lustful
appetites and habits, as in *Lear* 20.120
(*History*), 4.5.122 (*Tragedy*).

254–5 **professes not** does not make a prin-
ciple of

257 **fool** Perhaps 'gullible, easily taken
in', but more likely 'plaything', as in
Measure 3.1.11.

258–9 **swine-drunk** beastly drunk. For
the association with sleep, see *Shrew*
Ind.1.32 and *Macbeth* 1.7.67.

260 **they** i.e. his companions

honest man should not have; what an honest man
should have, he has nothing.

FIRST LORD (*aside*) I begin to love him for this.   265

BERTRAM (*aside*) For this description of thine honesty?
A pox upon him, for me he's more and more a cat!

FIRST SOLDIER What say you to his expertness in war?

PAROLES Faith, sir, he's led the drum before the English
tragedians. To belie him I will not, and more of his   270
soldiership I know not, except in that country he had
the honour to be the officer at a place there called
Mile End, to instruct for the doubling of files. I would
do the man what honour I can, but of this I am not
certain.   275

FIRST LORD (*aside*) He hath out-villained villainy so far
that the rarity redeems him.

BERTRAM (*aside*) A pox on him, he's a cat still.

FIRST SOLDIER His qualities being at this poor price, I
need not to ask you if gold will corrupt him to revolt.   280

PAROLES Sir, for a *quart d'écu* he will sell the fee-simple
of his salvation, the inheritance of it, and cut th'
entail from all remainders, and a perpetual succession for it perpetually.

269 he's] h'as ROWE; ha's F   281 *quart d'écu*] F2 (Cardecue); Cardceue F1

269–70 **he's ... tragedians** Chambers documents the custom of using drums
and trumpets to advertise performances (*Elizabethan Stage*, ii. 547, note 2).
Paroles thus dismisses First Lord's soldiership, of which the drum is a symbol (see above 3.3.9–11), as mere
play-acting.

273 **Mile End** another local reference,
adding to the charge of fakery one of
ineptness. Mile End Green was the drill
ground of London's citizen militia,
which as a military force was the subject of jokes and disparaging references
(R. P. Cowl, ed., *2 Henry IV*, old Arden
series (1923), note to 3.2.274).
    doubling of files a simple drill man-
oeuvre, converting a square of ten to
five lines of twenty

281–4 **Sir ... perpetually** The nature of
the progression from one clause to another is somewhat unclear (Taylor
conjectures that the clauses beginning
and cut and *and a* were reversed in

printing because of an amgibuously
placed addition) but the general drift
is clear: First Lord would sell the out-
right possession (*fee-simple*) of his salvation and break off the *entail* (his
heirs' right of inheritance) so that not
only his immediate heirs but those succeeding in perpetuity would be cut off.
Since salvation cannot be willed and
inherited, the whole typically elaborate
statement boils down to a simple intensifier: First Lord cares nothing for
his salvation. In that Paroles is better
at fancy words than at sense, the
muddle may be functional.

281 *quart d'écu* F's *cardecue*, like 'kar-de-
kew' in Eliot's *Ortho-epia Gallica* (1593,
p. 58), is a phonetic equivalent of *quart
d'écu*, a French silver coin of small
value; *OED* offers no evidence that the
word had any currency in English
apart from such cross-cultural situations.

FIRST SOLDIER What's his brother, the other Captain   285
  Dumaine?

SECOND LORD (*aside*) Why does he ask him of me?

FIRST SOLDIER What's he?

PAROLES E'en a crow o'th' same nest: not altogether
  so great as the first in goodness, but greater a great   290
  deal in evil. He excels his brother for a coward, yet
  his brother is reputed one of the best that is. In a
  retreat he outruns any lackey. Marry, in coming on
  he has the cramp.

FIRST SOLDIER If your life be saved, will you undertake   295
  to betray the Florentine?

PAROLES Ay, and the captain of his horse, Count Roussillon.

FIRST SOLDIER I'll whisper with the General and know
  his pleasure.   300

PAROLES I'll no more drumming. A plague of all
  drums! Only to seem to deserve well, and to beguile
  the supposition of that lascivious young boy the
  Count, have I run into this danger. Yet who would
  have suspected an ambush where I was taken?   305

FIRST SOLDIER There is no remedy, sir, but you must
  die. The General says you that have so traitorously
  discovered the secrets of your army and made such
  pestiferous reports of men very nobly held, can serve
  the world for no honest use. Therefore you must die.   310
  Come, headsman, off with his head.

PAROLES O Lord, sir, let me live, or let me see my
  death!

FIRST SOLDIER That shall you, and take your leave of
  all your friends.   315

      He removes Paroles' blindfold

315.1 *He removes Paroles' blindfold*] *not in* F

293 **outruns any lackey** a double insult,
  imputing lack of nobility as well as
  shameful speed in running away from
  danger. The allusion is to 'running
  footmen', who when their masters
  travelled by coach or horse ran along-
  side them; for their proverbial speed,
  compare *Jack a' Lent*, 'faster than an

Irish lackey', in *The Works of John Taylor, the Water Poet*, ed. Charles Hindley
  (London and Westminster, 1876),
  p. 5.
  coming on advancing
302–3 **beguile the supposition** make a
  false impression in the mind

So, look about you. Know you any here?

BERTRAM Good morrow, noble captain.

SECOND LORD God bless you, Captain Paroles.

FIRST LORD God save you, noble captain.

SECOND LORD Captain, what greeting will you to my   320
lord Lafeu? I am for France.

FIRST LORD Good captain, will you give me a copy of
the sonnet you writ to Diana in behalf of the Count
Roussillon? An I were not a very coward, I'd compel
it of you. But fare you well.   325

            Exeunt all but Paroles and First Soldier

FIRST SOLDIER You are undone, captain; all but your
scarf, that has a knot on't yet.

PAROLES Who cannot be crushed with a plot?

FIRST SOLDIER If you could find out a country where
but women were that had received so much shame,   330
you might begin an impudent nation. Fare ye well,
sir, I am for France too. We shall speak of you there.

                                Exit

PAROLES

Yet am I thankful. If my heart were great,
'Twould burst at this. Captain I'll be no more,
But I will eat and drink and sleep as soft   335
As captain shall. Simply the thing I am
Shall make me live. Who knows himself a braggart,
Let him fear this; for it will come to pass
That every braggart shall be found an ass.
Rust sword, cool blushes; and Paroles live   340
Safest in shame: being fooled, by fool'ry thrive.
There's place and means for every man alive.
I'll after them.   *Exit*

325.1 *Exeunt all but Paroles and First Soldier*] Exeunt. F   331 begin] F; beget *conj*. This
edition

333 **great** proud, as in *Shrew* 5.2.176;
   compare *big heart* above, 1.3.95
341 **being fooled, by fool'ry thrive** having
   been made a fool of, get my living now
   by being a fool in earnest. When Lafeu

later undertakes to keep him for *sport*
(5.3.322), this resolution is realized,
and perhaps as well the prediction
'Simply the thing I am | Shall make
me live' (above, 336–7).

4.4   *Enter Helen, the Widow, and Diana*

HELEN

That you may well perceive I have not wronged you,
One of the greatest in the Christian world
Shall be my surety, fore whose throne 'tis needful,
Ere I can perfect mine intents, to kneel.
Time was, I did him a desirèd office   5
Dear almost as his life, which gratitude
Through flinty Tartar's bosom would peep forth
And answer thanks. I duly am informed
His grace is at Marseilles, to which place
We have convenient convoy. You must know   10
I am supposèd dead. The army breaking,
My husband hies him home, where, heaven aiding,
And by the leave of my good lord the King,
We'll be before our welcome.

WIDOW   Gentle madam,
You never had a servant to whose trust   15
Your business was more welcome.

HELEN   Nor you, mistress,
Ever a friend whose thoughts more truly labour
To recompense your love. Doubt not but heaven
Hath brought me up to be your daughter's dower,
As it hath fated her to be my motive   20
And helper to a husband. But O, strange men,
That can such sweet use make of what they hate

4.4.0.1 *the*] *not in* F   3 fore] F2; for F1   9 Marseilles] *Marcellæ* F1; *Marsellis* F2
16 you] F4; your F1

4.4.4 **perfect mine intents** fully accomplish my purposes

6 **which gratitude** gratitude for which

7–8 **Through . . . thanks** For Tartars as the people least given to tender emotions, and in their yielding therefore a measure of the occasion's extreme force, compare *Merchant* 4.1.29–32.

9 **Marseilles** The place-name has three syllables, as reflected in F *Marcellæ*, the ending of which is presumably an error for *Marcellus*, as below 4.5.81.

10 **convoy** See note on 4.3.89–90.

15 **trust** probably *OED*, *sb.* 5a, 'the condition of having confidence reposed in one'

19 **brought me up** The usual Shakespearian meaning of *brought up*, i.e. 'reared', is possible here, but Helen's argument that their actions are divinely directed makes more pertinent *brought up* as 'led', a frequent biblical phrase for God's miraculous conducting of Israel out of Egypt; or (Wilson's suggestion) as parallel to 'raised up', also biblical (e.g. Deuteronomy 18: 15: 'The Lord thy God shall raise up unto thee a prophet').

20 **motive** instrument. Compare *Richard II* 1.1.193, where the phrasing—'slavish motive'—shows how the idea of 'means of action' can be separated from those of 'cause' and 'instigation', which are inappropriate here.

When saucy trusting of the cozened thoughts
Defiles the pitchy night! So lust doth play
With what it loathes for that which is away.   25
But more of this hereafter. You, Diana,
Under my poor instructions yet must suffer
Something in my behalf.

DIANA   Let death and honesty
Go with your impositions, I am yours,
Upon your will to suffer.

HELEN   Yet, I pray you.   30
But with the word, 'The time will bring on summer',
When briars shall have leaves as well as thorns,
And be as sweet as sharp. We must away.
Our wagon is prepared, and time revives us.
All's well that ends well; still the fine's the crown.   35
Whate'er the course, the end is the renown.

                                              Exeunt

4.5   *Enter Clown, Countess, and Lafeu*

LAFEU No, no, no, your son was misled with a snipped-
taffeta fellow there, whose villainous saffron would
have made all the unbaked and doughy youth of a

31 the word,] *after* HANMER (word:); the word F; that [y^t] word OXFORD   'The . . .
summer'] HUNTER (*conj.* Perring, 'The . . . sharp.' (l. 33))); the . . . summer, F
4.5.0.1 *Countess*] F (*old Lady*)

22 **use** As often in Shakespeare, *use* has
a sexual sense; but here the usual
allusion to usury is replaced with the
meaning of Bertram's employing what
he has paid for.

23–4 **When . . . night** When lascivious belief in the delusions (of lust) makes the
black night even blacker. The phrasing
of *Defiles the pitchy night* was apparently influenced by the proverb 'Whoso
toucheth pitch shall be defiled withal'
(Ecclesiasticus 13: 1), used as such by
Shakespeare in *Much Ado* 3.3.54–5.

25 **for** taking it for

27 **yet** further

28–30 **Let . . . suffer** I am ready to die
according to your prescriptions, as
long as they allow me to die chaste

30 **Yet** yet further, as at l. 27 above

31 **But . . . summer'** Punctuation and
meaning are governed by what sense

one ascribes to *the word*. Brigstocke
proposes 'promise', but this meaning
usually requires the possessive, i.e. *my
word* (*OED* 8); Everett sees a reference
to the just-spoken word *Yet*, but in this
reading *the word* becomes redundant,
synonymous with *The time*; Perring's
suggestion, incorporated by Hunter,
that *The time* etc. should be enclosed
in quotation marks is the most attractive, rendering *word* as 'watchword' or
'maxim' (*OED* 2e or 10b); Helen's
conclusion of this speech with two
other encouraging proverbs increases
the likelihood of one here.

34 **revives** i.e. will revive, present for
future (Hunter)

35 **All's well . . . crown** Both declarations
are proverbial; the second renders the
Latin *Finis coronat opus*.

36 **course** process, as opposed to outcome
(*end*)

nation in his colour. Your daughter-in-law had been
alive at this hour, and your son here at home, more   5
advanced by the King, than by that red-tailed
humble-bee I speak of.

COUNTESS I would I had not known him. It was the
death of the most virtuous gentlewoman that ever
nature had praise for creating. If she had partaken   10
of my flesh and cost me the dearest groans of a
mother, I could not have owed her a more rooted
love.

LAFEU 'Twas a good lady, 'twas a good lady. We may
pick a thousand salads ere we light on such another   15
herb.

CLOWN Indeed, sir, she was the sweet marjoram of the
salad, or rather the herb of grace.

LAFEU They are not salad-herbs, you knave, they are
nose-herbs.   20

CLOWN I am no great Nebuchadnezzar, sir. I have not
much skill in grass.

---

19 salad-herbs] ROWE; hearbes F; grass OXFORD   22 grass] ROWE; grace F

4.5.1–4 No ... colour Lafeu's vilification
of Paroles starts appropriately with
metaphors from fashion: (a) silk slashed
(*snipped-taffeta*) to show the fabric
underneath, especially of sleeves, as in
Shrew 4.3.89–91—the implication of
show rather than substance is increased by the association of taffeta
with whores (see 2.2.22–3 and note)
and with showy language ('Taffeta
phrases', *L.L.L.* 5.2.406); (b) stiffening
ruffs with yellow starch. As Warburton
remarks, the word *saffron* in this connection apparently led to another,
nonsartorial fashion of colouring
pastry dough, which in turn suggested
unbaked and doughy youth.

5–7 more ... speak of Lafeu's *more ... by
... than by* ... suggests a comparison,
but surely it is pointless to match Paroles' power to advance Bertram
against the King's. Something may
have dropped out here—Taylor notes
that there is no 'if' clause to match
had been—but in the absence of
grounds for reconstruction it may be
better to follow the lead of F's punctuation, which by setting off *more advanced by the King* with commas links

it more firmly with *here at home* and
suggests a comparison of place rather
than person. In this reading, i.e. 'here
at home as opposed to there with Paroles', *than* = 'rather than' (*OED* 3a)
and *by* = 'in the company of' (*OED* I.
3).

6–7 red-tailed humble-bee Compare 'red-
hipped humble-bee', *Dream* 4.1.11–12.
Lafeu returns to the idea of showy
dress, this time including persistent
noise as well.

11 dearest most deeply felt

12 rooted The Countess's plant metaphor
for her firmly fixed love leads Lafeu
and then the Clown into references to
salads, *sweet marjoram*, *herb of grace*,
and *grass*.

19 salad-herbs *OED* offers no support for
the usual editorial assertion that *herbs*
could, by itself, mean 'salad-herbs'.
Since that does indeed seem to be the
distinction at which Lafeu is aiming,
Rowe's emendation seems preferable.

21–2 I am ... grass F's *grace* includes au-
rally the almost homonymic 'grass'.
Both have equal point in the reference
to Nebuchadnezzar, who was driven
out of his kingdom and made to eat

LAFEU Whether dost thou profess thyself, a knave or a
fool?

CLOWN A fool, sir, at a woman's service, and a knave   25
at a man's.

LAFEU Your distinction?

CLOWN I would cozen the man of his wife and do his
service.

LAFEU So you were a knave at his service indeed.   30

CLOWN And I would give his wife my bauble, sir, to do
her service.

LAFEU I will subscribe for thee, thou art both knave
and fool.

CLOWN At your service.   35

LAFEU No, no, no.

CLOWN Why, sir, if I cannot serve you I can serve as
great a prince as you are.

LAFEU Who's that? A Frenchman?

CLOWN Faith, sir, a has an English mien, but his   40
phys'nomy is more hotter in France than there.

LAFEU What prince is that?

CLOWN The black prince, sir, alias the prince of dark-
ness, alias the devil.

---

40 mien] This edition (Anon. *conj.* mein); maine F; name ROWE

grass like a beast, and whose accession
to faith was both sign and cause of his
return to power after this humbling
experience (Daniel 4). No modernization can reproduce the poise
between meanings, but that of 'grass'
has slightly more weight in the dialogue.

28–32 **I would . . . service** The Clown's
operations as both knave and fool
amount to the same sexual *service*,
conceived first as usurping the husband's right, and then as catering to
the wife's appetite with his *bauble* (=
'fool's sceptre', 'penis'): 'They say a
fool's bauble is a lady's playfellow'
(Ford, *'Tis Pity She's a Whore* 1.2.128–
9).

37–8 **Why . . . you are** In the Clown's
comparison of his 'master' with Lafeu
and his subsequent harping on the
devil's association with fire (ll. 40–1,

49–50), Stewart (pp. 93–5) sees a play
on Lafeu's name.

40–1 **Faith . . . there** Rowe's correction of
maine to *name* may be right, as *black
prince* (line 43) was the nickname of
Edward III's son. On the other hand
mien gives a more natural transition to
the facial emphasis of the rest of the
line (I doubt if audiences could hear
the punning connection supposed by
some editors between 'name' and
'fisnamie'). *Maine* for *mien* would be an
easy error if the manuscript read
'mein' or 'meine', as easy as the misreading of minims hypothesized to support *name*. The word is not found
elsewhere in Shakespeare, but then
neither is *fisnomie*. The face of the
Black Prince is hotter in France
because he 'made things hot' for the
French at battlefields like Crécy, but
there is also a play on 'the French
disease'.

LAFEU Hold thee, there's my purse. I give thee not this   45
to suggest thee from thy master thou talk'st of. Serve
him still.

CLOWN I am a woodland fellow, sir, that always loved
a great fire, and the master I speak of ever keeps a
good fire. But sure he is the prince of the world, let   50
his nobility remain in 's court. I am for the house
with the narrow gate, which I take to be too little
for pomp to enter. Some that humble themselves
may, but the many will be too chill and tender, and
they'll be for the flow'ry way that leads to the broad   55
gate and the great fire.

LAFEU Go thy ways, I begin to be aweary of thee. And
I tell thee so before, because I would not fall out with
thee. Go thy ways. Let my horses be well looked to,
without any tricks.   60

CLOWN If I put any tricks upon 'em, sir, they shall be
jades' tricks, which are their own right by the law
of nature.   *Exit*

LAFEU A shrewd knave and an unhappy.

COUNTESS So a is. My lord that's gone made himself   65
much sport out of him. By his authority he remains
here, which he thinks is a patent for his sauciness;
and indeed he has no pace, but runs where he will.

46 **suggest** tempt
48–56 **I am ... great fire** The Clown first
presents himself as serving the devil
and then, on the contrary, as among
the few to be saved. The hinge is *woodland fellow*, which points to enjoyment
of a good fire but also to a rustic simple
life, as distinct from that of the soph-
isticated nobility at the devil's court.
The complete reversal recalls his sexual about-face in 1.3, first driven by
lust and then abruptly tired of his
wife's demands.
50 **the prince of the world** the devil, as in
the Gospel of John (12: 31, 14: 30,
16: 11)
51–3 **house ... enter** The narrow gate to
salvation that keeps out the prideful by
requiring that one stoop to enter, and
the broad, easy way followed by the
many to destruction are based on Mat-
thew 7: 13–14: 'Enter ye in at the
strait gate: for wide is the gate and

broad is the way that leadeth to
destruction: and many there be which
go in thereat. Because strait is the gate
and narrow is the way that leadeth
unto life, and few there be that find
it.'
54 **chill and tender** lacking in zeal and
unable to endure hardship
59–60 **horses ... tricks** The usual ostler's
'trick' is described in Nashe, *A Wonderful Strange ... Prognostication*: 'But
take heed, O you generation of wicked
ostlers, that steal hay in the night from
gentlemen's horses and rub their teeth
with tallow, that they may eat little
when they stand at livery' (*Works*, iii.
391).
62 **jades' tricks** tricks of a fractious horse,
used generally for malicious mischief
64 **shrewd** sharp-tongued
unhappy Perhaps 'unlucky' (in the
tone of his foolery), but in view of the
Clown's glumness, especially in this

LAFEU I like him well, 'tis not amiss. And I was about
to tell you, since I heard of the good lady's death   70
and that my lord your son was upon his return
home, I moved the King my master to speak in the
behalf of my daughter, which in the minority of them
both his majesty out of a self-gracious remembrance
did first propose. His highness hath promised me to   75
do it; and to stop up the displeasure he hath conceived against your son there is no fitter matter. How
does your ladyship like it?

COUNTESS With very much content, my lord, and I wish
it happily effected.   80

LAFEU His highness comes post from Marseilles, of as
able body as when he numbered thirty. A will be
here tomorrow, or I am deceived by him that in such
intelligence hath seldom failed.

COUNTESS It rejoices me that, I hope, I shall see him   85
ere I die. I have letters that my son will be here
tonight. I shall beseech your lordship to remain with
me till they meet together.

LAFEU Madam, I was thinking with what manners I
might safely be admitted.   90

COUNTESS You need but plead your honourable privilege.

LAFEU Lady, of that I have made a bold charter. But,
I thank my God, it holds yet.

Enter Clown

CLOWN O madam, yonder's my lord your son with a   95
patch of velvet on 's face. Whether there be a scar
under't or no, the velvet knows, but 'tis a goodly
patch of velvet. His left cheek is a cheek of two pile
and a half, but his right cheek is worn bare.

scene, the usual modern meaning may
be intended.

68 **has no pace . . . where he will** Picking
up on the equine metaphor, the Countess contrasts the Clown's undisciplined
(verbal) running about with the *pace*
or gait of a trained horse.

74 **self-gracious** i.e. emanating from his
own graciousness, not in response to
a request

91–3 **privilege . . . charter** Shakespeare
joins *charter* and *privilege* in *Richard III*
3.1.54 and Sonnet 58.9–10 as well as
here. Since either word can denote a
document granting rights or a granted
right, they are virtual synonyms.

95–9 **O madam . . . worn bare** The velvet
patch that suggests a scar underneath
was also used to cover lanced syphilitic
chancres. *Two pile and a half* puns on
the thickness of the velvet's nap and

LAFEU A scar nobly got, or a noble scar, is a good liv'ry   100
of honour. So belike is that.

CLOWN But it is your carbonadoed face.

LAFEU Let us go see your son, I pray you. I long to
talk with the young noble soldier.

CLOWN Faith, there's a dozen of 'em, with delicate fine   105
hats, and most courteous feathers which bow the
head and nod at every man.   *Exeunt*

5.1   *Enter Helen, the Widow, and Diana, with two*
        Attendants

HELEN

But this exceeding posting day and night
Must wear your spirits low. We cannot help it.
But since you have made the days and nights as one
To wear your gentle limbs in my affairs,
Be bold you do so grow in my requital   5
As nothing can unroot you.
        Enter a gentleman, ⌈a stranger⌉
                                In happy time!
This man may help me to his majesty's ear,
If he would spend his power.—God save you, sir.

5.1.0.1 *the*] not in F   6.1 *a gentleman, a stranger*] F3 (*after* 'time.'); *a gentle Astringer*
F1 (*after* 'time,'); *a Gentleman Austringer* OXFORD

the piles or haemorrhoids that Elizabethans connected with venereal disease (Colman, p. 207), while Bertram's
other cheek is *worn bare*—without a
patch, and also worn down so as to
lose the pile/piles. J. W. Bennett's suggestion (*SQ*, 18 (1967), 352) that this
cheek is shaven while the other is still
bearded because it has a wound too
fresh to permit shaving leads well into
Lafeu's response, but dictates a rather
ridiculous stage appearance for Bertram.

100–4 **A scar . . . soldier** Printed in F as
short-lined verse (see Appendix D), in
Wilson's theory stretching the text to
fill out the first column so as to begin
the second with the large heading
'Actus Quintus'—though F does contain instances of such a heading a line
or two from the bottom, e.g. T4. The
second column is correspondingly

crowded, with stage directions huddled
against the dialogue.

102 **But . . . face** The Clown qualifies
Lafeu's supposition of Bertram's honour: i.e. unless it is a face in which
incisions (*carbonadoes*) have been made
for syphilis.

5.1.1 **posting** travelling in haste

4 **wear** wear out

5 **Be bold . . . requital** be assured your
claim on compensation from me grows
so strong

6.1 **stranger** F's *Astringer*, or *austringer*,
'keeper of hawks', has its supporters,
but such a specified figure, conceivably
representing an earlier plan not carried out, is not needed for his function
in the drama as we have it. Indeed,
his subsequent speech prefixes are
Gent. and *Gen.*, and when he enters
the court two scenes later F designates
him *Gentleman* (5.3.127.1). It seems
more probable that the copy read 'a

GENTLEMAN And you.

HELEN

Sir, I have seen you in the court of France.   10

GENTLEMAN I have been sometimes there.

HELEN

I do presume, sir, that you are not fall'n
From the report that goes upon your goodness,
And therefore, goaded with most sharp occasions
Which lay nice manners by, I put you to   15
The use of your own virtues, for the which
I shall continue thankful.

GENTLEMAN

What's your will?

HELEN (*offering a paper*) That it will please you
To give this poor petition to the King,
And aid me with that store of power you have   20
To come into his presence.

GENTLEMAN

The King's not here.

HELEN   Not here, sir?

GENTLEMAN   Not indeed.

He hence removed last night, and with more haste
Than is his use.

WIDOW   Lord, how we lose our pains!

HELEN

All's well that ends well yet,   25
Though time seem so adverse, and means unfit.
—I do beseech you, whither is he gone?

GENTLEMAN

Marry, as I take it, to Roussillon,
Whither I am going.

HELEN   I do beseech you, sir,
Since you are like to see the King before me,   30

18 *offering a paper*] *not in* F

gent. a stranger', the latter to indicate
that this was not one of those
gentlemen who entered earlier (F entrance direction at 3.2.44.1, *Enter Hellen and two Gentlemen*), and that the
compositor misread it, accidentally
creating a real word or substituting it
in knowledge. Even the compositor's

familiarity with an elite technical term
is less improbable than Shakespeare's
insertion of such a specialized character for no purpose except local colour.

15 **nice** punctilious
  put you to urge upon you

Commend the paper to his gracious hand,
Which I presume shall render you no blame
But rather make you thank your pains for it.
I will come after you with what good speed
Our means will make us means.

GENTLEMAN ⌈*taking the paper from Helen*⌉ This I'll do for
   you.   35

HELEN

And you shall find yourself to be well thanked,
Whate'er falls more. We must to horse again.
(*To attendants*) Go, go, provide.   *Exeunt severally*

5.2   *Enter Clown and Paroles*

PAROLES Good Monsieur Lavatch, give my lord Lafeu
   this letter. I have ere now, sir, been better known to
   you, when I have held familiarity with fresher
   clothes. But I am now, sir, muddied in Fortune's
   mood, and smell somewhat strong of her strong   5
   displeasure.

CLOWN Truly, Fortune's displeasure is but sluttish if it
   smell so strongly as thou speak'st of. I will henceforth
   eat no fish of Fortune's buttering. Prithee, allow the
   wind.   10

PAROLES Nay, you need not to stop your nose, sir. I
   spake but by a metaphor.

CLOWN Indeed, sir, if your metaphor stink I will stop

---

35 *taking . . . Helen*] *not in* F   38 *Exeunt severally*] *not in* F
   5.2.1 Monsieur] STEEVENS–REED; M^r F; Master NEILSON   5 mood] F; moat THEOBALD

---

35 **Our . . . means** our resources will
   enable us to achieve
5.2.1 Monsieur F's *M^r* may abbreviate
   either 'Monsieur' or 'Master', and
   either would suit Paroles' deference in
   his newly humbled state, to one whom
   he used to patronize. But as 'Monsieur'
   is consistently Paroles' own title,
   exclusively his in this play, *Monsieur
   Lavatch* here more sharply underlines
   his reversal in fortunes by redirecting
   his own honorific to the Clown. Compare his use of *sir* and *you* (in place of
   the former *thou*) below. As for the
   Clown's name, mentioned only here,
   'la vache' (cow) or 'lavage' (slop or

puddle, suggested by the Clarkes) may
figure in its significance, but the particular point is obscure.
5 **mood** anger; it was near enough in
   pronunciation to the first syllable of
   muddied for the quibble proposed by
   Collier. Theobald emended to *moat* as
   a preparation for the Clown's later references to *fish* and *fish-pond*, but the
   basis for his literalizing of Paroles'
   metaphor is already present in ideas of
   mud and bad smells.
9 **buttering** A popular way of preparing
   fish for eating; compare buttered
   shrimps, *Alchemist* 3.4.72.

my nose, or against any man's metaphor. Prithee,
get thee further.   15

PAROLES Pray you, sir, deliver me this paper.

CLOWN Faugh! Prithee, stand away. A paper from Fortune's close-stool, to give to a nobleman! Look, here
he comes himself.

    Enter Lafeu

Here is a pur of Fortune's, sir, or of Fortune's cat,   20
but not a musk-cat, that has fall'n into the unclean
fish-pond of her displeasure, and as he says is muddied withal. Pray you, sir, use the carp as you may,
for he looks like a poor, decayed, ingenious, foolish,
rascally knave. I do pity his distress in my smiles of   25
comfort, and leave him to your lordship.   ⌈*Exit*⌉

PAROLES My lord, I am a man whom Fortune hath
cruelly scratched.

LAFEU And what would you have me to do? 'Tis too
late to pare her nails now. Wherein have you played
the knave with Fortune that she should scratch you,   30

---

25 smiles] F; similes THEOBALD (*conj.* Warburton)   26 *Exit*] CAPELL; *not in* F

17–18 **Fortune's close-stool** Hunter points
out that Theobald's emendation of
mood (see above, l. 5 and note) would
make a better transition not only to
Fortune's fish-pond but to her *close-
stool* or enclosed chamber-pot, since
moats were used as sewers. As the text
stands, the emphasis on unpleasant
smells seems to provide what transition there is.

20 **pur** Hilda Hulme (*RES*, 6 (1955),
130–2) explores several relevant fields
of imagistic meaning, including the
cat-sound (sycophancy), a small fish,
animal dung, and the knave in a card
game.

21 **not a musk-cat** not a source of per-
fume

23 **carp** fish commonly bred in ponds,
with a play on *carp*, *vb.* 4, 'to prate,
chatter'

24 **ingenious** *Ingenuous* and *ingenious*
were more or less interchangeable, but
neither one yields a clear and consistent sense here, except possibly in
hyphenated conjunction with a neighbouring epithet: either *decayed-ingenu-
ous*, declined from former high station,

or *ingenious-foolish*, apparently witty
(with words) but really lacking in
sense. For the comma in place of a
hyphen, see 1.1.174 and note.

25 **smiles** Theobald's emendation to
similes has been widely accepted.
While the error is an easy one, and
occurs elsewhere (*1 Henry IV* 1.2.79),
the reading that results is not very
satisfactory: the Clown's similes (*like
a poor, decayed . . . knave*), or by extension even his earlier animal and dirt
metaphors, have offered the opposite
of comfort. *Smiles* better fits the situation, the tables turned and the Clown
gloating, for Shakespeare very often
uses the word with a negative conno-
tation, to indicate hypocrisy, mockery,
dismissive contempt, and pleasure at
someone else's misfortune. The *smiles*
here reflect the Clown's own comfortable estate and underline the insincer-
ity of his pity for Paroles' contrasting
distress.

26 *Exit* The Clown may stay on till the
end of the scene, but his *leave him to
your lordship* sounds like an exit line.

who of herself is a good lady and would not have
knaves thrive long under her? There's a *quart d'écu*
for you. Let the justices make you and Fortune
friends. I am for other business.   35

PAROLES I beseech your honour to hear me one single
word.

LAFEU You beg a single penny more. Come, you shall
ha't. Save your word.

PAROLES My name, my good lord, is Paroles.   40

LAFEU You beg more than one word, then. Cock's my
passion, give me your hand. How does your drum?

PAROLES O my good lord, you were the first that found
me.

LAFEU Was I, in sooth? And I was the first that lost   45
thee.

PAROLES It lies in you, my lord, to bring me in some
grace, for you did bring me out.

LAFEU Out upon thee, knave! Dost thou put upon me
at once both the office of God and the devil? One   50
brings thee in grace, and the other brings thee out.
    Trumpets sound
The King's coming. I know by his trumpets. Sirrah,
enquire further after me. I had talk of you last night.
Though you are a fool and a knave, you shall eat.
Go to, follow.   ⌜*Exit*⌝   55

PAROLES I praise God for you.   *Exit*

33 her] F2; *not in* F1   41 one word] F3; word F1; a word COLLIER; 'word' CAMBRIDGE
51.1 *Trumpets sound*] *Sound Trumpets* THEOBALD; *not in* F   52 coming.] coming, ROWE;
comming₄ F   55 Exit] *not in* F   56 Exit] *not in* F; *Exeunt* ROWE

34–5 **Let . . . friends** The usual explanation of *the justices* is that it was these magistrates who were to relieve the worthy poor. Or Lafeu may be ironically advising Paroles to bring his complaint against Fortune as a legal action.

41 **more . . . word** There is a choice of emendations of F's *more then word*, but all bring out Lafeu's play on Paroles' (plural) name.

41–2 **Cock's my passion** God's passion

52–5 The address *Sirrah* and the characterization as both *a fool and a knave*, associated hitherto with the Clown, mark Paroles' change in station.

5.3 *Flourish. Enter the King, the Countess, Lafeu,*
⌈*and the two French Lords*⌉, *with attendants*

KING

We lost a jewel of her, and our esteem
Was made much poorer by it. But your son,
As mad in folly, lacked the sense to know
Her estimation home.

COUNTESS   'Tis past, my liege,
And I beseech your majesty to make it   5
Natural rebellion done i'th' blade of youth,
When oil and fire, too strong for reason's force,
O'erbears it and burns on.

KING   My honoured lady,
I have forgiven and forgotten all,
Though my revenges were high bent upon him   10
And watched the time to shoot.

LAFEU   This I must say—
But first I beg my pardon: the young lord
Did to his majesty, his mother, and his lady
Offence of mighty note, but to himself
The greatest wrong of all. He lost a wife   15
Whose beauty did astonish the survey
Of richest eyes; whose words all ears took captive;
Whose dear perfection hearts that scorned to serve
Humbly called mistress.

KING   Praising what is lost
Makes the remembrance dear. Well, call him hither. 20
We are reconciled, and the first view shall kill
All repetition. Let him not ask our pardon.

5.3.0.1–2 *the King . . . Lords*] F (*King, old Lady, Lafew, the two French Lords*)

5.3.0.1–2 **The two French lords** are given
no lines in this scene, and their designation in the entrance direction may
represent an earlier plan not carried
out. Their presence as onlookers is appropriate, however, in that they have
discussed Bertram's defects and begun
the process of educative exposure that
is concluded here.
1 **of** in
  esteem valuation, worth (reduced by
  the loss of the jewel Helen); but leading through the other meaning of 'rec-

ognition of worth' directly into Ber-
tram's failure to *know* | *Her estimation
home* (l. 4)
4 **home** thoroughly
6 **i'th' blade** in the immature time
  (when there is blade or leaf only, before the fruit comes: *OED, blade sb.*
  2b), with *blade* = 'gallant' a possible
  undermeaning
10 **high bent** bent tight, as a bow
17 **richest eyes** eyes that have seen most
22 **repetition** going over what is past

The nature of his great offence is dead,
And deeper than oblivion we do bury
Th'incensing relics of it. Let him approach   25
A stranger, no offender; and inform him
So 'tis our will he should.

ATTENDANT   I shall, my liege.   *Exit*

KING

What says he to your daughter? Have you spoke?

LAFEU

All that he is hath reference to your highness.

KING

Then shall we have a match. I have letters sent me   30
That sets him high in fame.

    Enter Bertram

LAFEU   He looks well on't.

KING

I am not a day of season,
For thou mayst see a sunshine and a hail
In me at once. But to the brightest beams
Distracted clouds give way. So stand thou forth;   35
The time is fair again.

BERTRAM   My high-repented blames,
Dear sovereign, pardon to me.

KING   All is whole.
Not one word more of the consumèd time.
Let's take the instant by the forward top,

---

27 ATTENDANT] F (*Gent.*)   *Exit*] not in F   31 Bertram] F (*Count Bertram*)

---

23 **The nature . . . dead** i.e. the essence of
his offence, disdaining Helen, is now
dead in that she is dead
25 **relics** remains, continuing the metaphor of physical death
26 **A stranger** i.e. as if we were meeting
for the first time
29 **hath reference to your highness** is sub-
mitted to your highness for decision
31 **He looks well on't** It is not clear
whether this refers to the match (he
favours it) or fame (it becomes him).
32 **of season** of normal weather, i.e.
because in evincing both hail and sunshine he mixes the characteristic conditions of different seasons. For the
same metaphor to express mixed emo-

tions, see *History of Lear* 17.19.
35 **Distracted** The word has a literal
meaning for the metaphor's vehicle
clouds, 'parted', and a figurative one
in application to its tenor, 'agitated, in
mental conflict'.
36 **time** present state of affairs, perhaps
incorporating as well the additional
meaning of 'weather', as in Fr. *temps*
39 **forward top** i.e. the lock of hair growing on the front of the head. The
proverb 'to take time by the forelock'
is based on an image of Time, or
Occasion, as bald behind to show that
opportunity cannot be grasped after it
passes (e.g. *Faerie Queene* II. iv. 4). See
fig. 12, p. 67.

For we are old, and on our quick'st decrees   40
Th'inaudible and noiseless foot of time
Steals ere we can effect them. You remember
The daughter of this lord?

BERTRAM

Admiringly, my liege. At first
I stuck my choice upon her, ere my heart   45
Durst make too bold a herald of my tongue;
Where the impression of mine eye infixing,
Contempt his scornful perspective did lend me,
Which warped the line of every other favour,
Scorned a fair colour or expressed it stol'n,   50
Extended or contracted all proportions
To a most hideous object. Thence it came
That she whom all men praised and whom myself,
Since I have lost, have loved, was in mine eye
The dust that did offend it.

KING   Well excused.   55
That thou didst love her strikes some scores away
From the great count. But love that comes too late,
Like a remorseful pardon slowly carried,
To the great sender turns a sour offence,
Crying, 'That's good that's gone.' Our rash faults   60

50 Scorned] F; Stained OXFORD (*conj.* Lambrechts)   58–9 carried, . . . sender∧] THEO-
BALD; carried∧ . . . sender, F

40 **quick'st decrees** edicts most pregnant with consequences

47 *Where* refers to the heart: the visual image of Lafeu's daughter having rooted itself there, the resulting disdain for any other woman in turn distorted his vision of these other women's faces (*warped the line of every other favour*).

48 **perspective** optical glass that makes one see objects differently

50 **Scorned** Taylor's emendation *Stained* indeed goes better with *warped* and *Extended or contracted* as direct action to distort the object of vision; on the other hand, *Scorned* is parallel to *expressed* in the second half of this line, both of them indicating the way the skewed judgement is articulated rather than the mis-seeing on which it is based.

50–1 For colour and proportion as the standard components of beauty, compare Donne, *The First Anniversary*, 250.

54–5 **was . . . offend it** Helen was not only an unpleasant object of sight but an irritation in the very act of seeing.

57 **count** account, reckoning (of Bertram's sins)

58–9 **remorseful pardon . . . sour offence** i.e. a pardon conveyed too slowly to prevent execution becomes an aggravation to the one who sent it—presumably because his struggle to repent of his former harshness and achieve compassion (*remorseful* has both its modern meaning and its older one of 'pitying') has been costly without result. *Sour* plays on the food image, 'spoiled by being kept too long'.

60 **That's . . . gone** Compare *Antony* 1.2.119: 'She's good being gone'.

Make trivial price of serious things we have,
Not knowing them until we know their grave.
Oft our displeasures, to ourselves unjust,
Destroy our friends and after weep their dust.
Our own love, waking, cries to see what's done,   65
While shameful hate sleeps out the afternoon.
Be this sweet Helen's knell, and now forget her.
Send forth your amorous token for fair Maudlin.
The main consents are had, and here we'll stay
To see our widower's second marriage day.   70

COUNTESS

Which better than the first, O dear heaven, bless,
Or, ere they meet, in me, O nature, cesse!

LAFEU

Come on, my son, in whom my house's name
Must be digested: give a favour from you
To sparkle in the spirits of my daughter,   75
That she may quickly come.

    Bertram gives a ring to Lafeu

                  By my old beard
And ev'ry hair that's on't, Helen that's dead
Was a sweet creature. Such a ring as this,
The last that e'er I took her leave at court,
I saw upon her finger.

BERTRAM   Hers it was not.   80

71 COUNTESS] THEOBALD; *not in* F   72 meet,] ROWE; ~⌃ F   76 *Bertram gives a ring to Lafeu*] HANMER (*after* 'beard'); *not in* F

61 **serious** important
65–6 **Our own ... afternoon** Love awakens, after hate has destroyed the friend, to weep at what was done while it was oblivious. Hate now sleeps, either as satiated (*shameful* as 'causing shame') or as now ashamed of itself (*shameful* as 'feeling shame').
67–8 **Be . . . Maudlin** These unrhymed lines interrupt the King's couplets, perhaps to mark the end of his moralizing meditations on Bertram's first marital relationship, as he puts Helen to rest and turns to *our widower's second marriage day.*
71–2 COUNTESS ... **cesse** Although F shows no change of speaker, Theobald observes that these lines, with their wish

not to live to see Bertram in another failed marriage, are clearly more appropriate to the Countess than to the King.
72 **ere they meet** before the past marriage and the projected one merge in similarity, come to follow the same course
cesse I retain F's form rather than modernizing to *cease* because the variant form, unusual even in Shakespeare's time according to Onions, looks like a deliberate choice to set the Countess's prayer as a rhymed couplet.
76 **come** yield, be moved favourably
79 **last** i.e. last time, the phrasing perhaps influenced by the related idiom 'the last I saw of her'
took her leave took leave of her

KING

Now pray you let me see it, for mine eye,
While I was speaking, oft was fastened to't.
⌈*Lafeu gives him the ring*⌉
This ring was mine, and when I gave it Helen
I bade her if her fortunes ever stood
Necessitied to help, that by this token   85
I would relieve her. Had you that craft to reave her
Of what should stead her most?

BERTRAM   My gracious sovereign,
Howe'er it pleases you to take it so,
The ring was never hers.

COUNTESS   Son, on my life,
I have seen her wear it, and she reckoned it   90
At her life's rate.

LAFEU   I am sure I saw her wear it.

BERTRAM

You are deceived, my lord, she never saw it.
In Florence was it from a casement thrown me,
Wrapped in a paper which contained the name
Of her that threw it. Noble she was, and thought   95
I stood ungaged. But when I had subscribed
To mine own fortune, and informed her fully
I could not answer in that course of honour
As she had made the overture, she ceased

82.1 *Lafeu gives him the ring*] *not in* F   96 ungaged] THEOBALD; ingag'd F

---

85 .Necessitied to in need of
   by when in receipt of
86 reave forcibly deprive
87 stead help, avail
96 ungaged F's *ingag'd* is unlikely to be
   variant of *ungag'd*: such use of the *in*
   prefix to denote negation in words
   other than adjectives is very rare. If
   we see this negation as nevertheless
   part of the intended meaning—she
   thought I was unpledged, free to pursue a courtship—we can assume an
   easy minim-error and follow Theobald
   in emending to *ungaged*. The F form
   may alternatively be a variant of
   engag'd. Johnson's paraphrase, 'when
   she saw me pick up the ring, she
   thought me *engaged* to her', begs the

question of why picking up a package
in the street should commit a man to
matrimony; but Thiselton's observation that this word along with *sub-
scrib'd* and *course of honour* constitute
a series of duelling terms, suggests
another possible meaning, of 'com-
mitted to a passage of arms' (*OED*,
engage, 13a), perhaps with some trace
of 'attracted' (*OED* 14)—she thought I
was game for amorous combat. But as
such unconventional behaviour from
a noblewoman makes an unlikely tale
for Bertram to invent, Theobald's
emendation seems preferable.
96-7 subscribed | To mine own fortune
   acknowledged my condition in life

In heavy satisfaction, and would never   100
Receive the ring again.

KING   Plutus himself,
That knows the tinct and multiplying med'cine,
Hath not in nature's mystery more science
Than I have in this ring. 'Twas mine, 'twas Helen's,
Whoever gave it you. Then if you know   105
That you are well acquainted with yourself,
Confess 'twas hers, and by what rough enforcement
You got it from her. She called the saints to surety
That she would never put it from her finger
Unless she gave it to yourself in bed,   110
Where you have never come, or sent it us
Upon her great disaster.

BERTRAM   She never saw it.

KING
Thou speak'st it falsely, as I love mine honour,
And mak'st conjectural fears to come into me
Which I would fain shut out. If it should prove   115
That thou art so inhuman—'twill not prove so.
And yet I know not. Thou didst hate her deadly,
And she is dead, which nothing but to close
Her eyes myself could win me to believe
More than to see this ring.—Take him away.   120
My fore-past proofs, howe'er the matter fall,
Shall tax my fears of little vanity,

---

101 Plutus] F2 *some copies*; *Platus* F1
122 tax] F (taze)

114 conjectural] F2; connecturall F1

100 **heavy satisfaction** 'sorrowful acquiescence' (Rolfe)
101–2 **Plutus . . . med'cine** Plutus, as the god of riches, could be imaged by extension as 'the grand alchimist, who knows the *tincture* which confers the properties of gold upon base metals, and the *matter* by which *gold* is *multiplied*, by which a small quantity of gold is made to communicate its qualities to a large mass of metal' (Johnson).
105–6 **Then if . . . yourself** In its most straightforward reading, the King's clause sounds both redundant—'if you know that you know yourself'—and beside the point, since self-knowledge need not conduce to confession of

crime. Tentative 'paraphrases' like 'if you know what's good for you', or 'if you know anything at all' are not firmly based in the language. Taking *that* as *that which* gives a somewhat more relevant reading: 'if you understand what in fact you yourself must be aware of (that the ring belonged to Helen)'.
121–3 **My . . . little** i.e. however the current question is resolved, the proofs I have already had of Bertram's ill will to Helen (such as his desertion) are such as to show me that present fears are not vain, for at that point I foolishly did not fear enough (and thus did not foresee his desertion). The oblique

Having vainly feared too little. Away with him.
We'll sift this matter further.

BERTRAM   If you shall prove
  This ring was ever hers, you shall as easy   125
  Prove that I husbanded her bed in Florence,
  Where yet she never was.   *Exit guarded*
          Enter the Gentleman with a paper

KING
  I am wrapped in dismal thinkings.

GENTLEMAN   Gracious sovereign,
  Whether I have been to blame or no, I know not.
  Here's a petition from a Florentine   130
  Who hath for four or five removes come short
  To tender it herself. I undertook it,
  Vanquished thereto by the fair grace and speech
  Of the poor suppliant, who, by this, I know
  Is here attending. Her business looks in her   135
  With an importing visage, and she told me,
  In a sweet verbal brief, it did concern
  Your highness with herself.

⌈KING⌉ (*reads the paper*) 'Upon his many protestations
  to marry me when his wife was dead, I blush to say   140
  it, he won me. Now is the Count Roussillon a
  widower. His vows are forfeited to me, and my honour's paid to him. He stole from Florence, taking no
  leave, and I follow him to his country for justice.
  Grant it me, O King. In you it best lies. Otherwise a   145
  seducer flourishes, and a poor maid is undone.
                              Diana Capilet.'

LAFEU I will buy me a son-in-law in a fair, and toll for
  this. I'll none of him.

127 *Exit guarded*] ROWE; *not in* F   127.1 *the Gentleman with a paper*] *a Gentleman* F
129 *to blame*] F (*too blame*)   139 ⌈KING⌉ (*reads the paper*)] *after* ROWE; *A Letter* F

phrasing of line 122 sets up the wordplay of line 123, the charge of *little
vanity* being borne out by his having
vainly feared too *little*.

129 **to blame** F's *too blame* may reflect the
early misapprehension of this phrase,
by which 'the *to* was mistaken as *too*,
and *blame* taken as adj.' (*OED, blame,
vb.* 6).

131 **removes** stopovers on a journey.
Each time she arrived at one, she
found that the King had already
'removed', or departed.
134 **by this** by this time
136 **importing** urgent
137 **verbal brief** spoken summation
148–9 **I will . . . for this** Buying at a fair
may suggest going only by looks, or
running the risk of being cheated or

KING

The heavens have thought well on thee, Lafeu,   150
To bring forth this discov'ry. Seek these suitors.
Go speedily and bring again the Count.
⌈ *Exeunt Gentleman and one or more Attendants* ⌉
I am afeard the life of Helen, lady,
Was foully snatched.

COUNTESS   Now justice on the doers!
    Enter Bertram ⌈*guarded*⌉

KING

I wonder sir, sith wives are monsters to you   155
And that you fly them as you swear them lordship,
Yet you desire to marry.
    Enter the Widow and Diana
                    What woman's that?

DIANA

I am, my lord, a wretched Florentine
Derivèd from the ancient Capilet.
My suit, as I do understand, you know,   160
And therefore know how far I may be pitied.

WIDOW

I am her mother, sir, whose age and honour
Both suffer under this complaint we bring,
And both shall cease without your remedy.

KING

Come hither, Count. Do you know these women?   165

152.1 *Exeunt Gentleman and one or more Attendants*] not in F   154.1 *Enter Bertram*
⌈*guarded*⌉] CAPELL; *Enter Bertram* F (*l.* 152.1)   155 sith‸] DYCE; sir, F; since‸ TYRWHITT
157 *Enter the Widow and Diana*] ROWE (*after* 'that!'); *Enter Widdow, Diana, and Parrolles*
(*after* 'that?') F

of getting stolen goods (Hunter); in
any case Lafeu's point is that even
such a dubious bargain will get him
something better than Bertram. As for
the other side of this transaction, dis-
carding Bertram, he will *toll* for him,
enter him for sale in the market toll-
book as was required when selling a
horse.

151 **suitors** The King knows without
being told that in spite of the single
signature there is more than one in
the petitioning party, as below he
knows that Diana has invoked Paroles

as a witness (ll. 199–200), though we
have not heard her do so. These disparities may point to revision, but may
also be attributed to normal carelessness in the playwright's drive to finish.
156 **as you swear them lordship** as soon
as you vow to be their husband
157 **Enter...Diana** For the inclusion of
Paroles in F's entrance direction as a
sign of interrupted work, with Shakespeare on returning to his work modifying the plan to delay Paroles'
entrance until he is called on to cor-
roborate Diana's story, see Bowers,
'Speech-Prefixes', p. 74.

BERTRAM

My lord, I neither can nor will deny

But that I know them. Do they charge me further?

DIANA

Why do you look so strange upon your wife?

BERTRAM

She's none of mine, my lord.

DIANA   If you shall marry

You give away this hand, and that is mine;   170

You give away heaven's vows, and those are mine;

You give away myself, which is known mine,

For I by vow am so embodied yours

That she which marries you must marry me.

Either both or none.   175

LAFEU (*to Bertram*) Your reputation comes too short for

my daughter. You are no husband for her.

BERTRAM (*to the King*)

My lord, this is a fond and desp'rate creature

Whom sometime I have laughed with. Let your highness

Lay a more noble thought upon mine honour   180

Than for to think that I would sink it here.

KING

Sir, for my thoughts, you have them ill to friend

Till your deeds gain them. Fairer prove your honour

Than in my thought it lies.

DIANA   Good my lord,

Ask him upon his oath if he does think   185

He had not my virginity.

KING

What sayst thou to her?

BERTRAM   She's impudent, my lord,

And was a common gamester to the camp.

DIANA

He does me wrong, my lord. If I were so,

183 them. Fairer] THEOBALD 1740 (them:) (*conj.* Thirlby); them fairer: F

178 **fond** imbecile, but also infatuated
   desp'rate reckless, ready to do anything
183 **gain them** win them over (to your
   side)

187 **impudent** shameless
188 **gamester** The *game* is sexual play, as
   in 'daughters of the game' (*Troilus*
   4.6.64).

He might have bought me at a common price.   190
Do not believe him. O, behold this ring,
Whose high respect and rich validity
Did lack a parallel. Yet, for all that,
He gave it to a commoner o'th' camp,
If I be one.
COUNTESS   He blushes, and 'tis hit.   195
Of six preceding ancestors, that gem,
Conferred by testament to th' sequent issue,
Hath it been owed and worn. This is his wife:
That ring's a thousand proofs.
KING   Methought you said
You saw one here in court could witness it.   200
DIANA
I did, my lord, but loath am to produce
So bad an instrument. His name's Paroles.
LAFEU
I saw the man today, if man he be.
KING
Find him, and bring him hither.   *Exit Attendant*
BERTRAM   What of him?
He's quoted for a most perfidious slave   205
With all the spots o'th' world taxed and debauched,
Whose nature sickens but to speak a truth.
Am I or that or this for what he'll utter
That will speak anything?
KING   She hath that ring of yours.

---

204 *Exit Attendant*] *not in* F   207 sickens$_\wedge$ . . . truth.] HANMER (*conj.* Thirlby); sickens:
. . . truth, F

---

192 **high respect and rich validity** great
    worth in his estimation (as a family
    heirloom) and intrinsic value as an
    object
194 **commoner** prostitute
195 **He . . . hit** In the Countess's tribute to
    Diana's sure aim of her arrow, Shake-
    speare may be playing on the name
    she shares with the hunt-goddess; *'tis
    hit* means 'it is found out', i.e. the
    truth Bertram has been trying to con-
    ceal is discovered, or possibly 'the
    mark of Bertram's conscience is hit'.
197 **sequent issue** next heir

198 **owed** owned
205 **quoted** regarded, spoken of
206 **taxed and debauched** Most commen-
    tators remove the implied parallelism
    by glossing with something like 'cen-
    sured for being corrupt', which may
    be correct; but the parallel with *taxed*
    may stand if *debauched* means 'dis-
    paraged' (*OED, debauch, vb.* 4).
208–9 **Am I . . . anything** i.e. am I to be
    judged one way or the other on the
    testimony of one so unconstrained by
    truthfulness

BERTRAM

I think she has. Certain it is I liked her,   210
And boarded her i'th' wanton way of youth.
She knew her distance, and did angle for me,
Madding my eagerness with her restraint,
As all impediments in fancy's course
Are motives of more fancy; and in fine   215
Her inf'nite cunning with her modern grace
Subdued me to her rate. She got the ring,
And I had that which any inferior might
At market price have bought.

DIANA   I must be patient.
You that have turned off a first so noble wife   220
May justly diet me. I pray you yet—
Since you lack virtue, I will lose a husband—
Send for your ring, I will return it home,
And give me mine again.

BERTRAM   I have it not.

216 inf'nite cunning] SINGER 1856 (*conj.* Walker); infuite comming F; insuite cunning
FRASER (*conj.* Thiselton)

210 Bertram's rather odd *I think she has*
seems to be an attempt to palliate his
shaming admission, like the modern
use of 'I suppose so' for grudging
assent.

211 **boarded** made advances to

212 **She knew ... for me** The *distance*
in fencing is the space between duel-
lists, extended metaphorically to non-
intimacy in social situations ('I pray
you, know your distance', *Alchemist*
4.1.78); Bertram accuses Diana of
resisting close contact while at the
same time luring him with sexual bait.

214 **fancy's** love's

215 **motives** causes

216 **inf'nite cunning ... grace** Most editors emend F's *comming* to *cunning*,
supposing an easy error and restoring
an idea central to Bertram's self-
defence (Hunter notes that Q *Troilus*
misprints 'Comming' for 'conning' at
3.2.129). Of the various explanations
of F's *insuite* the most compelling are
those that support an antithesis with
the following phrase, i.e. suggest that
the wiliness that he has just described
was the unusual thing about her, as
against the ordinary attractions (*mod-*

ern grace) which he states here and
implies in his following remark about
her availability at *market price*. Fraser's
attempt, anticipated by Thiselton, to
achieve the antithesis without emendation by hypothesizing *insuite* as a
Shakespearian coinage from Latin
insuetus ('unusual') is attractive; but
in the absence of any support except
'insuetude', which in any case is not
cited by *OED* until 1824, Walker's proposal of *inf'nite*—which conveys rarity
in a different way—seems preferable.

221 **diet me** Perhaps *diet* means merely
'restrain from full gratification', but
the parallel Diana suggests between
herself and Helen seems to call for a
meaning more like *turn off*. Wilson's
conjecture of 'pay off after a day's
work', based on medieval Latin *dieta*,
is tempting—though unsupported in
contemporary documents.

223 **Send . . . ring** Diana's phrasing
implies that Bertram's ring is not present, although she has just displayed it.
Either *send for* has the sense of 'ask
for', as nowhere else in Shakespeare,
or this is a mark of incomplete revision
(see 157 and note).

KING

What ring was yours, I pray you?

DIANA   Sir, much like   225

The same upon your finger.

KING

Know you this ring? This ring was his of late.

DIANA

And this was it I gave him, being abed.

KING

The story then goes false you threw it him

Out of a casement?

DIANA   I have spoke the truth.   230

Enter Paroles

BERTRAM

My lord, I do confess the ring was hers.

KING

You boggle shrewdly. Every feather starts you.

—Is this the man you speak of?

DIANA   Ay, my lord.

KING

Tell me, sirrah—but tell me true, I charge you,

Not fearing the displeasure of your master,   235

Which on your just proceeding I'll keep off—

By him and by this woman here what know you?

PAROLES So please your majesty, my master hath been

an honourable gentleman. Tricks he hath had in

him, which gentlemen have.   240

KING Come, come, to th' purpose! Did he love this

woman?

PAROLES Faith, sir, he did love her, but how?

KING How, I pray you?

PAROLES He did love her, sir, as a gentleman loves a   245

woman.

245 gentleman] F (Gent.)

223 **home** to its owner

232 **boggle shrewdly . . . starts you** (a) shy
sharply, like a frightened horse (*starts*
= 'startles') and (b) shift your position
cleverly (*starts* = 'causes to move')

234 For *sirrah* in address to Paroles, see
5.2.52–5 and note.

237 **By** about

239 **Tricks** With an amorous connota-
tion, as in 'sportive tricks' (*Richard III*
1.1.14) and 'wanton tricks' (*Lucrece*
320).

245–6 **He . . . a woman** i.e. he loved her
as a man of rank loves a lower-class
woman

KING How is that?

PAROLES He loved her, sir, and loved her not.

KING As thou art a knave and no knave. What an
equivocal companion is this!   250

PAROLES I am a poor man, and at your majesty's
command.

LAFEU He's a good drum, my lord, but a naughty
orator.

DIANA Do you know he promised me marriage?   255

PAROLES Faith, I know more than I'll speak.

KING But wilt thou not speak all thou know'st?

PAROLES Yes, so please your majesty. I did go between
them as I said, but more than that he loved her, for
indeed he was mad for her, and talked of Satan and   260
of limbo and of furies and I know not what. Yet I
was in that credit with them at that time that I knew
of their going to bed and of other motions, as promising her marriage and things which would derive me
ill will to speak of. Therefore I will not speak what   265
I know.

KING Thou hast spoken all already, unless thou canst
say they are married. But thou art too fine in thy
evidence. Therefore, stand aside.
—This ring, you say, was yours?

DIANA   Ay, my good lord.   270

KING
Where did you buy it? Or who gave it you?

DIANA
It was not given me, nor I did not buy it.

KING
Who lent it you?

DIANA   It was not lent me neither.

---

248 **He . . . not** he desired her carnally
but did not wish to marry her
253-4 **He's . . . orator** i.e. he is good at
making noise (*drum* = 'drummer') but
bad at speaking reasonably and coher-
ently. The choice of a noisemaker is
another of Lafeu's jibes at Paroles'
notorious failure to recover the drum
in Florence (see 5.2.42 and below

5.3.321).
258-9 **I did . . . her** i.e. I carried messages
between them of the nature I've
described (manoeuvres of a gentleman
trying to seduce a woman of inferior
class), but his feelings were stronger
than those of a mere philanderer
263 **motions** proposals
268 **fine** subtle, artful

KING
  Where did you find it then?
DIANA   I found it not.
KING
  If it were yours by none of all these ways,   275
  How could you give it him?
DIANA   I never gave it him.
LAFEU This woman's an easy glove, my lord, she goes
  off and on at pleasure.
KING
  This ring was mine. I gave it his first wife.
DIANA
  It might be yours or hers for aught I know.   280
KING (*to Attendants*)
  Take her away. I do not like her now.
  To prison with her. And away with him.
  —Unless thou tell'st me where thou hadst this ring,
  Thou diest within this hour.
DIANA   I'll never tell you.
KING
  Take her away.
DIANA   I'll put in bail, my liege.   285
KING
  I think thee now some common customer.
DIANA
  By Jove, if ever I knew man 'twas you.
KING
  Wherefore hast thou accused him all this while?
DIANA
  Because he's guilty and he is not guilty.
  He knows I am no maid, and he'll swear to't.   290
  I'll swear I am a maid, and he knows not.
  Great King, I am no strumpet, by my life.
  I am either maid or else this old man's wife.
KING
  She does abuse our ears. To prison with her.

---

278 **off and on** The phrase completes the
  glove metaphor while conveying inter-
  mittent motion.

285 **put in bail** offer another person as
  guarantor
286 **customer** prostitute

DIANA

Good mother, fetch my bail.   *Exit the Widow*
                                        —Stay, royal sir.   295
The jeweller that owes the ring is sent for,
And he shall surety me. But, for this lord
Who hath abused me as he knows himself,
Though yet he never harmed me, here I quit him.
He knows himself my bed he hath defiled,   300
And at that time he got his wife with child.
Dead though she be, she feels her young one kick.
So there's my riddle: one that's dead is quick.
And now behold the meaning.
            Enter Helen and the Widow

KING   Is there no exorcist
Beguiles the truer office of mine eyes?   305
Is't real that I see?

HELEN   No, my good lord.
'Tis but the shadow of a wife you see,
The name and not the thing.

BERTRAM   Both, both. O pardon!

HELEN

O my good lord, when I was like this maid,
I found you wondrous kind. There is your ring,   310
And look you, here's your letter. This it says:
'When from my finger you can get this ring
And are by me with child, etc.' This is done.
Will you be mine, now you are doubly won?

295 *Exit the Widow*] *not in* F   304 *the*] *not in* F   313 are] ROWE; is F

296 **jeweller** Presumably the point of designating Helen a *jeweller*, beyond suggesting enough wealth to *surety* Diana, is to underline her dealings in rings that this scene unravels.
299 **quit him** (a) acquit him (b) give up my claim to him
303 **quick** (a) alive (b) pregnant
304 *Enter . . . Widow* Moshinsky's BBC production made effective use of the medium to bring across the impact of this entrance, focusing the camera not on the familiar figure of Helen whom we have recently seen but on the wonderstruck faces of the other characters.
exorcist raiser of spirits (compare

Caesar 2.1.322–3, 'Thou like an exorcist hast conjured up | My mortifièd spirit')
305 **Beguiles . . . eyes** plays tricks with the accurate operation of my sight
307–8 **'Tis but . . . thing** Helen's *shadow* plays on the spirit or shade an *exorcist* might call up, but principally denies her own reality by the opposition of shadow and substance, the title of wife but not the full acceptance. Bertram's *Both, both* affirms that acceptance by recognizing their sexual union.
313 **are** Taylor speculates that F's *is* might have come about through Shakespeare's forgetting whether the

BERTRAM

If she, my liege, can make me know this clearly,   315
I'll love her dearly, ever, ever dearly.

HELEN

If it appear not plain, and prove untrue,
Deadly divorce step between me and you.
—O my dear mother, do I see you living?

LAFEU (*to Paroles*)

Mine eyes smell onions, I shall weep anon.   320
Good Tom Drum, lend me a handkerchief.
So, I thank thee. Wait on me home, I'll make sport
with thee. Let thy curtsies alone, they are scurvy
ones.

KING (*to Helen*)

Let us from point to point this story know,   325
To make the even truth in pleasure flow.
(*To Diana*) If thou be'st yet a fresh uncroppèd flower,
Choose thou thy husband and I'll pay thy dower.
For I can guess that by thy honest aid
Thou kept'st a wife herself, thyself a maid.   330
Of that and all the progress, more and less,
Resolvedly more leisure shall express.
All yet seems well, and if it end so meet,
The bitter past, more welcome is the sweet.
          Flourish

Epilogue

The King's a beggar, now the play is done.
All is well ended if this suit be won,

Epilogue] ROWE; *not in* F

original challenge appeared in Helen's
letter or the Countess's, so that the
second person quotation slips into the
third person, and that the following
&c. suggests his intention, not carried
out, to check the wording.

321 **Tom Drum** The drum joke again, and
probably an allusion to *John* (*Tom*)
Drum's entertainment (3.6.38–9 and
note)—though the 'entertainment'
Lafeu offers Paroles in the next line is
more humane.

326 **even** exact

331 **progress, more and less** course of

events, major and minor

332 **Resolvedly** so as to resolve all questions

333 **so meet** accordingly

Epilogue 1 For a parallel emphasis on the
actor made potent by his role who is
suddenly returned to his unpowerful
ordinary state when the play is over,
compare Prospero in the *Tempest* epilogue: 'Now my charms are all o'er-
thrown, | And what strength I have's
mine own'. Within this general sense
there is probably, as Malone thought,
a more specific reference to the ballad
of King Cophetua and the Beggar-Maid.

That you express content; which we will pay
With strife to please you, day exceeding day.
Ours be your patience, then, and yours our parts: 5
Your gentle hands lend us, and take our hearts.

Exeunt

6.1 *Exeunt*] F (Exeunt omn.)

4 **strife . . . day** Compare the closing line
of *Twelfth Night*, 'And we'll strive to
please you every day'.
day exceeding day more and more
every day
5–6 The final couplet is a double
exchange. First actors and audience
change roles, the first becoming
passive hearers and the second cre-
ators of expressive sound, i.e. applause.
Second, as this applause is given the
actors will repay with their gratitude.

1.1.60, 'HOW UNDERSTAND WE THAT?'

LAFEU's question has struck many editors as more probably responding to a problematic statement, either Helen's (l. 54) or the Countess's (ll. 57–8), than to Bertram's straightforward one. If lines 59 and 60 have been transposed, as Kittredge supposes, compositor memory error is possible. Wilson, working on the theory that a transcript lies between Shakespeare's foul papers and the F text, thought the transcriber 'first omitted the question and then added it in the margin with insufficient direction as to its insertion'. Hypothesizing that the heading *La.* led the compositor to confuse *Lady* with *Lafeu*, he first reassigned it to the Countess as a preface to her response to Lafeu (l. 57); later both he, following a suggestion by A. W. Ayling, and Sisson independently replaced the question before Lafeu's preceding speech to address Helen's cryptic assertion. One might accept either resolution without assuming the transcriber, attributing the marginal addition to a revising Shakespeare. The Schlegel–Tieck arrangement, keeping F's order of lines but giving the Countess's speech to Helen, deserves consideration, even though it must presuppose a kind of authorial or compositorial error not typical of this text, in which lines are misassigned by being wrongly attached to what precedes or follows (e.g. 4.3.119, 140), rather than full speeches being attributed to a clearly wrong speaker. It implies a change in stage grouping from ensemble to two pairs: the Countess crosses on the dash ending l. 53 to stand apart with her son while Helen and Lafeu talk to each other, and Bertram's request for her blessing does not interrupt but belongs to a separate conversation.

On the other hand, interruption is as likely from the callow and doubtless impatient Bertram as it was unlikely earlier from Helen, and Lafeu's question may be understood as a veiled rebuke: 'What do we make of this rudeness?' As the original text offers an acceptable reading in this sense, and none of the emendations is clearly preferable to the others, I retain the F text.

2.1.168–72: HELEN'S GAMBLE

ASKED what she dares venture on the King's cure, Helen's response in the F text is

> Taxe of impudence,
> A strumpets boldnesse, a divulged shame
> Traduc'd by odious ballads: my maidens name
> Seard otherwise, ne worse of worst extended
> With vildest torture, let my life be ended.

Editors have debated the meaning of *ne worse of worst, extended, otherwise,* and *traduced,* and the attendant larger issues: what goes with what in Helen's list of phrases, which participles stand independently and which modify another phrase, and what meaning should be attached to the latter part—is death the climactic sacrifice or is the 'worst' already realized in the loss of her maiden reputation? Taylor defends his repointing (supplying a stop after *shame,* as Theobald suggested, and removing the heavy stop after *ballads*) as more powerful rhetorically: Helen's speech 'begins with three phrases, each of three words, then follows with three more phrases, each with a past participle' (*Textual Companion,* p. 495). The opening phrases are not grammatically parallel, since *tax* (accusation) *of* governs both *impudence* (immodesty) and *a strumpet's boldness,* but if *shame* has the meaning of (female) sexual dishonour as frequently in Shakespeare (especially *Measure,* a play closely related to *All's Well*) all three phrases have the same import. Creating a break after *shame* also avoids the linkage suggested by the F punctuation between *divulgèd shame* and *Traduced by odious ballads,* which produces a verbal attack, not on her reputation but on its loss. (*Traduced* could conceivably mean 'put in another mode of expression' or 'transmitted', but in Shakespeare's other uses it always means 'calumniated'). *Otherwise* may mean 'as other than maiden', or 'in ways other than ballads'; *extended* may refer to being tortured on the rack or to drawing out still more suffering, impossible after the *worst* (loss of her maiden name). The archaic *ne* appears only once in Shakespeare, in the consciously antique language of Gower in *Pericles* (5.36). Here it is probably an error, either for *no,* supplied in F2, or for *nay.* If the original word was *no,* the error presumably came about through foul case, since it is unlikely that the compositor would substitute for this familar word the uncommon *ne.* Taylor's arguments for *nay* distorted by aural or memory error are persuasive, but his initial assumption that 'Helen surely wants her willingness to die after torture to be the climax of this speech' (p. 495) is far from obvious. *Nay, worse of worst* accords death the status of 'beyond the worst'; *no worse of worst* asserts rather that death by torture cannot be worse than being publicly shamed as a strumpet. Thiselton finds the latter meaning reinforced by F punctuation, reading what precedes the disputed phrase as a dependent clause: 'since my maiden's name will thus be otherwise seared, not even death will add to my misery'.

SPEECH PREFIXES: VARIATIONS

Countess:

    1.1 *Mother* and afterwards *Mo.*

    1.3 *Coun.* first four times, then *Cou.*; *Old.Cou.* or *Ol.Cou.*
        128–85

    2.2 *Lady.* seven times (page set by Compositor C), then *La.* in
        remainder (set by Compositor B)

    3.2 *Count.* first two times, then *Lad.* or *La.*; at 64 *Old La.*

    3.4 *La.*

    4.5 *La.*, *Lad.*, *Lady.*

    5.3 *Old La.*; at 195 *Coun.*

Bertram:

    1.1 *Ros.* or *Ro.*

    1.2 *Ber.*

    2.1 *Rossill.*, *Ross.*, *Ros.*

    2.3 *Ros.* at opening, then *Ber.* starting at 107, then *Ros.* or
        Rossill. on re-entry

    2.5, 3.3, 3.6, 4.2 *Ber.*

    4.3 *Ber.*; at 317, *Count.*

    5.3 *Ber.* until 204, then *Ros.*

Lafeu:

    1.1 *Laf.*

    2.1 *L.Laf.*, then *Laf.*

    2.3 *Ol.* or *Old Laf.*; at 100, *Ol.Lord*; in final exchanges with
        Paroles, *Laf.*

    2.5, 4.5, 5.2, 5.3 *Laf.*

Helen:

    Hel. or *Hell.*, except at 2.3.97, *La.*

First Soldier:

    4.1 *1.Sol.* until 69, then *Inter.* or *Int.*

    4.3 *Int.* and *Inter.* continue

French Lords:

1.2 1.*Lo.* (*Lor.*) *G.*, 2.*Lo.E.*, once *L.2.E.*
2.1 *Lord.* (*L.*, *Lo.*) *G.*, 1 *Lo.G.*, 2.*Lo.E.*
3.1 1.*Lord*, *Fren.G.*, *French E.*
3.2 *French* (*Fren.*) *G.*, 1.*G.*, *Fren.E.*, *French E.*
3.6 *Cap.G.*, *Cap.* (*C.*) *E.*
4.1 1.*Lord E.*, *Lor.* (*Lo.*) *E.*
4.3 *Cap.G.*, *Cap.E.*, *Lo.E.*

The following analysis is based primarily on the work of Fredson Bowers, 'Speech-Prefixes'.

The considerable variation in speech-prefix designations in the Folio text of *All's Well that Ends Well* suggests strongly that the printers' copy was not a transcript made for playhouse purposes, which would require regularized speech headings. But are the printers themselves responsible for differing speech prefixes? Bowers, after a close examination of the variants with an eye to the order in which the pages were set and the identities of the different compositors, concludes that compositors may occasionally follow the form given in the entrance direction rather than the authorial prefix. This influence may account for *Count.* twice in 3.2, after an entrance direction for *Countesse*, before reverting to *La.*, presumably the form in the copy; Bowers suspects as well a preference for *Ber.*, influenced by stage directions, over copy's mixture of *Ber.* and *Ross.* Compositors may sometimes—though not consistently—be responsible for moving to shorter forms (*Laf.* for *L.Laf.*, *Ross.* or *Ros.* for *Rossil.*). In one case, a variant seems to have resulted from Compositor B's misinterpreting at 2.3.100 something like *Ol.L.* in copy, being unaware of Lafeu's presence in this scene because he had not yet set the opening of it and presumably influenced by the prefix for 4.*Lord* immediately preceding. In general, however, Bowers concludes that the principal compositor, B, as well as C and D in their two pages, 'were completely conservative in the treatment of names and titles in the stage-directions and that copy was followed in these respects with fidelity' (p. 79).

The variations are mainly the author's, then, jotted down as he was writing with no compulsion to be consistent. What, if anything, do the variations tell us? Sometimes the speech prefix seems to indicate how Shakespeare was thinking of the character in a given scene, the function or relationship that was most prominent. Most obviously, the First Soldier becomes *Interpreter* when he assumes that role in 4.1. The Countess when bidding farewell to her son in 1.1 is *Mother*. More problematically she is *Countess* in 1.3 because she is dealing with Helen's desire to be her daughter-in-law, a family matter that involves rank (although one could make a good case for *Mother* here too). Otherwise (if Bowers is right in attributing to the compositor rather than the author the two *Countess* prefixes in 3.2), the Countess is viewed more generally as lady of the house. Shakespeare may have added *Old* to *La.* for one speech in 3.2 automatically, to keep her distinct from Helen whom she addresses in that speech as 'Lady'. When on stage with all the young people in the final scene, she is, more consistently, *Old La.*

Changes in speech prefix within a scene that do not mark a change in function or salient relation and do not reflect compositorial habits probably came about through a lapse of time in the writing process: Shakespeare broke off work and came back later to resume it, possibly with a plan different from the original one, or he returned after some time to revise what he had written. For the switch to *Ol.Cou.* at 1.3.128–85 as a sign of revision, see Introduction, pp. 54–5. Bowers connects the introduction of new prefixes in the course of 5.3 (*Ol.La.* to *Coun.* at 195, *Ber.* to *Ros.* at 204) with the premature entrance for Paroles at 157 as mutually reinforcing evidence for a hiatus in the writing and a change of plan. The full change shows up only after 191, the beginning of page Y1, which was set after a considerable interruption; in the lines between Diana's entrance and 191, Compositor B had gone on with *Ber.* as the prefix he was accustomed to, but after the delay he would have to follow copy, where he would find *Ros.*

For the French Lords, see Introduction, pp. 58–64.

ALTERATIONS TO LINEATION

CHANGES of verse to prose and prose to verse, and of line arrangement within verse, are recorded below. In both the lemma and any rejected line arrangement, spelling is modernized and punctuation at the end of the line is ignored. Attribution to an editor or text after the lemma refers only to the arrangement of lines and does not imply that all the words in the passage are those printed in this edition.

Eccentricities in F's lineation, as opposed to passages that could be either prose or verse, can usually be traced to spacing problems. With an excess of space to fill, Compositor B several times prints some prose lines as verse to fill out a column, sometimes helping his endeavour by surrounding an entrance direction with generous spacing (see Commentary on 1.1.189, 3.5.1–15, and 4.5.100–4). Compositor D turns some of the Clown's ballad-snatches to prose in 1.3 to crowd more into the first column of his sheet. Here the rationale is not clear, though, as there seems ample enough space in the second column; but since some of this following material shows signs of having been added on (see Text section of Introduction), his calculations may have been thrown off.

1.1.189	Monsieur . . . you] CAPELL; *as verse* (Paroles /) F
204–5	So . . . safety] POPE; *as verse* (away /) F
1.3.16	No . . . poor] POPE; F *divides after* 'madam'
60–3	**For** . . . kind] ROWE 1714; *as prose* F
72–3	**Fond** . . . joy] THEOBALD; *as one line* F
74–5	With . . . **stood,** | With . . . stood] With . . . **stood,** *bis* F
76–9	And . . . ten] **ROWE** 1714; *as prose* F
137–8	You . . . you] CAPELL; *as one line* F
139–40	Nay . . . 'a mother'] POPE; *as one line* F
193–4	That . . . son] POPE; *as one line* F
2.1.29	An . . . bravely] POPE; *as verse* (boy /) F
65–70	And . . . medicine] CAPELL; F *divides after* 'for't', 'thus', 'infirmity', 'No', 'fox', *and* 'if'
2.3.64–5	Gentlemen . . . health] CAPELL; *as prose* F
79–80	I . . . life] POPE; *as verse* (throw /) F
109–12	Know'st . . . bed] POPE; *as prose* F
271–2	Although . . . her] ROWE 1714; *as prose* F
277–8	There's . . . yet] CAPELL; *as prose* F

2.5.78–9	Let . . . home] POPE ; *as prose* F
86–7	I . . . yes] DYCE 1864 ; *as one line* F
3.2.62–3	Ay . . . pains] CAPELL ; *as prose* F
76–7	'Tis . . . to] RIVERSIDE ; *as prose* F
83–4	A servant . . . known] POPE ; *as prose* F
89–96	Indeed . . . affairs] CAPELL ; *as prose* F
3.5.1–15	Nay . . . companion] POPE ; *as verse* (come /, city /, sight /, done /, service /, reported /, commander /, slew /, labour /, hark /, trumpets /, again /, it /, earl /, name /, rich /, honesty /, neighbour /, gentleman /) F
33	God . . . bound] CAPELL ; *as prose* F
80–81a	*as one line* F
89–90	The troop . . . penitents] ROWE (bring /); *as prose* F
3.6.6	Do . . . him] POPE; *as verse* (far /) F
82–3	I know . . . Farewell] POPE ; *as verse* (valiant /, soldiership /) F
108–9	I must . . . caught] POPE ; *as verse* (twigs /) F
3.7.28–9	Now . . . purpose] CAPELL ; *as one line* F
4.1.68	O . . . eyes] POPE ; *as verse* (ransom ! /) F
79–80	O . . . *dulche*] STAUNTON ; *as verse* (pray /) F
4.5.100–1	A scar . . . that] POPE ; *as verse* (got /, honour /) F
103–4	Let us . . . soldier] POPE ; *as verse* (see /, talk /) F
5.1.36–8	And you . . . provide] POPE ; *as prose* F
5.3.28	What . . . spoke] THEOBALD ; F *divides after* 'daughter'
30–1	Then . . . fame] POPE ; *as prose* F
225–6	Sir . . . finger] CAPELL ; *as one line* F
270	*as prose* F

GILETTA OF NARBONNE

SHAKESPEARE'S major source, the story of Giletta of Narbonne, appears as Novel 38 in William Painter's *The Palace of Pleasure* (see p. 1). The complete text is reprinted below, modernized from the 1575 edition.

Giletta, a physician's daughter of Narbonne, healed the French king of a fistula, for reward whereof she demanded Beltramo, Count of Roussillon, to husband. The Count, being married against his will, for despite fled to Florence, and loved another. Giletta, his wife, by policy found means to lie with her husband in place of his lover, and was begotten with child of two sons; which known to her husband, he received her again, and afterwards he lived in great honour and felicity.

In France there was a gentleman called Isnardo, the Count of Roussillon, who because he was sickly and diseased kept always in his house a physician named Master Gérard of Narbonne. This count had one only son, called Beltramo: a very young child, amiable and fair. With whom there was nourished and brought up many other children of his age: amongst whom one of the daughters of the said physician, named Giletta, who fervently fell in love with Beltramo, more than was meet for a maiden of her age. This Beltramo, when his father was dead, and left under the royal custody of the king, was sent to Paris, for whose departure the maiden was very pensive. A little while after, her father being likewise dead, she was desirous to go to Paris, only to see the young Count, if for that purpose she could get any good occasion. But being diligently looked unto by her kinsfolk, because she was rich and fatherless, she could see no convenient way for her intended journey; and being now marriageable, the love she bare to the Count was never out of her remembrance, and [she] refused many husbands with whom her kinsfolk would have matched her, without making them privy to the cause of her refusal.

Now it chanced that she burned more in love with Beltramo than ever she did before, because she heard tell that he was grown to the state of a goodly young gentleman. She heard by report that the French king had a swelling upon his breast, which by reason of ill cure was grown to be a fistula, which did put him to marvellous pain and grief, and that there was no physician to be found, although many were proved [tried], that could heal it, but rather did impair the grief and made it worse and worse. Wherefore the King, like one in despair, would take no more counsel or help. Whereof the young maiden was wonderful glad, thinking to have by this means not only a lawful occasion to go to Paris but, if the disease were such as she supposed, easily to bring to pass that she might have the Count Beltramo to her husband.

Whereupon, with such knowledge as she had learned at her father's hands beforetime, she made a powder of certain herbs which she thought meet for that disease and rode to Paris. And the first thing she went about when she came thither was to see the Count Beltramo. And then she repaired to the King, praying his grace to vouchsafe to show her his grief. The King, perceiving her to be a fair young maiden and a comely, would not hide it but opened the same unto her. So soon as she saw it, she put him in comfort that she was able to heal him, saying, 'Sir, if it may please your grace, I trust in God without any great pain unto your highness within eight days to make you whole of this disease.' The King, hearing her say so, began to mock her, saying, 'How is it possible for thee, being a young woman, to do that which the best renowned physicians in the world can not?' He thanked her for her good will, and made her a direct answer that he was determined no more to follow the counsel of any physician. Whereunto the maiden answered, 'Sir, you despise my knowledge because I am young and a woman. But I assure you that I do not minister physic by profession but by the aid and help of God, and with the cunning of master Gérard of Narbonne, who was my father and a physician of great fame so long as he lived.'

The King, hearing these words, said to himself, 'This woman peradventure is sent unto me of God, and therefore why should I disdain to prove her cunning?—forsomuch as she promiseth to heal me within a little space, without any offence or grief unto me.' And, being determined to prove her, he said, 'Damsel, if thou dost not heal me but make me to break my determination, what wilt thou shall follow thereof?' 'Sir,' said the maiden, 'let me be kept in what guard and keeping you list, and if I do not heal you within these eight days let me be burnt; but if I do heal your grace, what recompense shall I have then?' To whom the King answered, 'Because thou art a maiden and unmarried, if thou heal me according to thy promise I will bestow thee upon some gentleman that shall be of right good worship and estimation.' To whom she answered, 'Sir, I am very well content that you bestow me in marriage. But I beseech your grace, let me have such a husband as I myself shall demand, without presumption to any of your children or other of your blood.' Which request the King incontinently granted.

The young maiden began to minister her physic, and in short space before her appointed time she had thoroughly cured the King. And when the King perceived himself whole [he] said unto her, 'Thou hast well deserved a husband, Giletta, even such a one as thyself shalt choose.' 'I have then, my lord,' quoth she, 'deserved the County Beltramo of Roussillon, whom I have loved from my youth.' The King was very loath to grant him unto her. But for that he had made a promise, which he was loath to break, he caused him to be called forth and said unto him, 'Sir County, knowing full well that you are a gentleman of great honour, our pleasure is that you return home to your own house to order your estate according to your degree; and that you take with you a damsel which I have appointed to be your wife.' To whom the County gave his humble thanks, and demanded what she was. 'It is she', quoth the King, 'that with her medicines hath healed me.' The Count knew her well and had already seen her. Although she was fair, yet knowing her not to be of a stock convenable to his nobility, [he] scornfully said unto the King, 'Will you then, sir, give me a physician to wife? It is not the pleasure of God that ever I should in that wise bestow myself.' To whom the King said, 'Wilt thou then that we should break our faith, which we to recover health have given to the damsel, who for a reward asked thee to husband?' 'Sir,' quoth Beltramo, 'you may take from me all that I have, and give my person to whom you please, because I am your subject; but I assure you, I shall never be contented with that marriage.' 'Well, you shall have her,' said the King, 'for the maiden is fair and wise and loveth you most entirely—thinking verily you shall lead a more joyful life with her than with a lady of a greater house.'

The County therewithal held his peace, and the King made great preparation for the marriage. And when the appointed day was come, the Count in the presence of the King, although it were against his will, married the maiden, who loved him better than her own self. Which done, the Count, determining before what he would do, prayed licence to return to his country to consummate the marriage. And when he was on horseback he went not thither, but took his journey for Tuscany where, understanding that the Florentines and Senois were at wars, he determined to take the Florentines' part, and was willingly received and honourably entertained and was made captain of a certain number of men, continuing in their service a long time.

The new-married gentlewoman, scarce contented with his unkindness, hoping by her well doing to cause him to return into his country, went to Roussillon, where she was received of all his subjects for their lady. And, perceiving that through the Count's absence all things were spoiled and out of order, she like a sage lady, with great diligence and care, disposed his things in order again; whereof the subjects rejoiced very much, bearing to her their hearty love and affection, greatly blaming the Count because he could not content himself with her. This notable gentlewoman, having restored all the country again to their ancient liberties, sent word to the Count her husband by two knights, to signify unto him that if it were for her sake that he had abandoned his country, upon return of answer she, to do him pleasure, would depart from thence. To whom he churlishly replied, 'Let her do what she list; for I do purpose to dwell with her when she shall have this ring (meaning a ring which he wore) upon her finger, and a son in her arms begotten by me.' He greatly loved that ring and kept it very carefully, and never took it from his finger, for a certain virtue that he knew it had.

The knights, hearing the hard condition of two things impossible and seeing that by them he could not be removed from his determination, returned again to the lady, telling her his answer; who, very sorrowful, after she had a good while bethought her, purposed to find means to attain the two things, that thereby she might recover her husband. And, having advised herself what to do, she assembled the noblest and chiefest of her country, declaring unto them in lamentable wise what she had already done to win the love of the Count, showing them also what followed thereof. And in the end said unto them that she was loath the Count for her sake should dwell in perpetual exile; therefore she determined to spend the rest of her time in pilgrimages and devotion for preservation of her soul, praying them to take the charge and government of the country, and that they would let the Count understand that she had forsaken his house and was removed far from thence, with purpose never to return to Roussillon again.

Many tears were shed by the people as she was speaking those words, and divers supplications were made unto [her] to alter [her] opinion, but all in vain. Wherefore, commending them all unto God, she took her way with her maid and one of her kinsmen, in the habit of a pilgrim, well furnished with silver and precious jewels, telling no man whither she went, and never rested till she came to Florence; where, arriving by fortune at a poor widow's house, she contented herself with the state of a poor pilgrim, desirous to hear news of her lord, whom by fortune she saw the next day passing by the house where she lay, on horseback with his company. And although she knew him well enough, yet she demanded of the goodwife of the house what he was; who answered that he was a strange [foreign] gentleman called the Count Beltramo of Roussillon, a courteous knight and well beloved in the city, and that he was marvellously in love with a neighbour of hers that was a gentlewoman, very poor and of small substance, nevertheless of right honest life and good report, and by reason of her poverty was yet unmarried and dwelt with her mother that was a wise and honest lady.

The Countess, well noting these words and by little and little debating every particular point thereof, comprehending the effect of those news, concluded what to do; and when she had well understanded which was the house, and the name of the lady, and of her daughter that was beloved of the Count, upon a day repaired to the house secretly in the habit of a pilgrim; where, finding the mother and daughter in poor estate amongst their family, after she had saluted them, [she] told the mother that she had to say unto her. The gentlewoman, rising up, courteously entertained her; and being entered alone in a chamber, they sat down, and the Countess began to speak unto her in this wise. 'Madam, methinks that ye be one upon whom fortune doth frown, so well as upon me. But if you please, you may both comfort me and yourself.' The lady answered that there was nothing in the world whereof she was more desirous than of honest comfort. The Countess, proceeding in her talk, said unto her, 'I have need now of your fidelity and trust, whereupon if I do stay and you deceive me you shall both undo me and yourself.' 'Tell me, then, what it is hardly [boldly],' said the gentlewoman, 'for you shall never be deceived of me.'

Then the Countess began to recite her whole estate of love, telling her what she was and what had chanced to that present day in such perfect order as the gentlewoman, believing her because she had partly heard report before, began to have compassion upon her. And after that the Countess had rehearsed the whole circumstance, she continued her purpose, saying, 'Now you have heard amongst other my troubles what two things they be which behoveth me to have if I do recover my husband, which I know none can help me to obtain but only you, if it be true that I hear, which is that the Count my husband is far in love with your daughter.' To whom the gentlewoman said, 'Madam, if the Count love my daughter I know not, albeit the likelihood is great; but what am I able to do in that which you desire?' 'Madam,' answered the Countess, 'I will tell you. But first I will declare what I mean to do for you if my purpose be brought to effect. I see your fair daughter of good age, ready to marry but, as I understand, the cause why she is unmarried is the lack of substance to bestow her. Wherefore I purpose, for recompense of the pleasure which you shall do for me, to give so much ready money to marry her honourably as you shall think sufficient.'

The Countess's offer was very well liked of the lady, because she was poor. Yet, having a noble heart, she said unto her, 'Madam, tell me wherein I may do you service, and if it be a thing honest I will gladly perform it; and, the same being brought to pass, do as it shall please you.' Then said the Countess, 'I think it requisite that by someone you trust you give knowledge to the Count my husband that your daughter is, and shall be, at his commandment. And to the intent she may be well assured that he loveth her indeed above any other, she must pray him to send her a ring that he weareth upon his finger, which ring as she knoweth he loveth very dearly. And when he sendeth the ring, you shall give it unto me, and afterwards send him word that your daughter is ready to accomplish his pleasure; and then you shall cause him secretly to come hither and place me by him instead of your daughter. Peradventure God will give me the grace that I may be with child; and so, having this ring on my finger and the child in my arms begotten by him, I may recover him, and by your means continue with him as a wife ought to do with her husband.'

This thing seemed difficult unto the gentlewoman, fearing that there would follow reproach unto her daughter. Notwithstanding, considering what an honest part it were to be a mean that the good lady might recover her husband, and that she might do it for a good purpose, having affiance in her honest affection, [she] not only promised the Countess to bring this to pass but in few days, with great subtlety, following the order wherein she was instructed, she had gotten the ring, although it was with the Count's ill will, and took order that the Countess instead of her daughter did lie with him. And at the first meeting so effectuously desired by the Count, God so disposed the matter that the Countess was begotten with child of two goodly sons; and her delivery chanced at the due time. Whereupon the gentlewoman not only contented the Countess at that time with the company of her husband but at many other times, so secretly as it was never known: the Count not thinking that he had lyen with his wife but with her whom he loved. To whom at his uprising in the morning he used many courteous and amiable words, and gave divers fair and precious jewels which the Countess kept most carefully. And when she perceived herself with child, she determined no more to trouble the gentlewoman, but said unto her, 'Madam, thanks be to God and you, I have the thing that I desire, and even so it is time to recompense your desert, that afterwards I may depart.'

The gentlewoman said unto her that if she had done any pleasure agreeable to her mind she was right glad thereof, which she did not for hope of reward but because it appertained to her by well doing so to do. Whereunto the Countess said, 'Your saying pleaseth me well, and for my part I do not purpose to give unto you the thing you shall demand in reward, but for consideration of your well doing, which duty forceth me to do.' The gentlewoman then, constrained with necessity, demanded of her with great bashfulness an hundred pounds to marry her daughter. The Countess, perceiving the shamefastness of the gentlewoman and her courteous demand, gave her five hundred pounds, and so many fair and costly jewels as almost amounted to like valour. For which the gentlewoman, more than contented, gave most hearty thanks to the Countess, who departed from the gentlewoman and returned to her lodging. The gentlewoman, to take occasion from the Count of any farther repair or sending to her house, took her daughter with her and went into the country to her friends. The Count Beltramo, within few days after, being revoked home to his own house by his subjects, hearing that the Countess was departed from thence, returned.

The Countess, knowing that her husband was gone from Florence and returned home, was very glad, continuing in Florence till the time of her childbed, being brought abed of two sons which were very like unto their father; and caused them carefully to be nursed and brought up, and when she saw time she took her journey, unknown to any, and arrived at Montpellier; and resting herself there for certain days, hearing news of the Count and where he was, and that upon the day of All Saints he purposed to make a great feast and assembly of ladies and knights, in her pilgrim's weed she repaired thither. And knowing that they were all assembled at the palace of the Count, ready to sit down at the table, she passed through the people without change of apparel, with her two sons in her arms. And when she was come up into the hall, even to the place where the Count sat, falling down prostrate at his feet, weeping, saying unto him, 'My lord, I am thy poor infortunate wife who, to th'intent thou mightest return and dwell in thine own house, have been a great while begging about the world. Therefore I now beseech thee, for the honour of God, that thou wilt observe the conditions which the two knights that I sent unto thee did command me to do: for behold, here in mine arms, not only one son begotten by thee but twain, and likewise thy ring. It is now time then, if thou keep promise, that I should be received as thy wife.'

The Count, hearing this, was greatly astunned and knew the ring, and the children also, they were so like him. 'But tell me,' quod he, 'how is this come to pass?' The Countess, to the great admiration of the Count and of all those that were in presence, rehearsed unto them in order all that which had been done and the whole discourse thereof. For which cause the Count, knowing the things she had spoken to be true and perceiving her constant mind and good wit and the two fair young boys, to keep his promise made and to please his subjects and the ladies that made suit unto him to accept her from that time forth as his lawful wife and to honour her, abjected his obstinate rigour, causing her to rise up, and embraced and kissed her, acknowledging her again for his lawful wife. And after he had apparelled her according to her estate, to the great pleasure and contentation of those that were there and of all his other friends, not only that day but many others he kept great cheer, and from that time forth he loved and honoured her as his dear spouse and wife.

ERASMUS' *COLLOQUIES*

As mentioned in the Introduction (pp. 6–8), there are verbal and conceptual reminiscences in *All's Well* of a dialogue on marriage from Erasmus' *Colloquies*. The extracts given here are modernized from *A Modest Mean to Marriage, pleasantly set forth by that Famous Clerk Erasmus Roterodamus, and translated into English by N[icholas] L[eigh]* (1568). The speakers are Pamphilus, the lover, and Maria, the woman he loves.

In the early pages, Pamphilus tries to demonstrate that he is dead from unrequited love and the unresponsive Maria is his murderer, in arguments that Maria wittily refutes.

Pam. . . . In case you set light by the crime of homicide, I will aguilt you also of sorcery and enchanting me.

Mar. Marry, gods forbid, man! What, will you make of me a Circe's imp, a witch?

Pam. Yea, and somewhat more cruel yet than ever was Circe. For I had rather be a grovelling hog or bear than as I am, without life or soul.

Mar. And with what kind of sorcery, I pray ye, do I destroy men?

Pam. By evil aspect.

Mar. Will you then that I hurt you no more with looking upon you?

Pam. Not so, for God's sake, but rather look more upon me.

Mar. If mine eyes be witches, how happeneth it then that other[s] also do not consume away whom I look upon as oft as' you? Therefore, I fear me much the bewitching is in your own eyes, not in mine.

Pam. Why, think you it not enough to slay Pamphilus except you triumph over him being dead?

Mar. O quaint, handsome, nice dead body: when shall your funerals be provided for?

Pam. Sooner than you think, ywis, except you remedy in time.

Mar. I remedy? Good Lord! Am I able to do such a cure?

Pam. Yea, surely. All were I dead, it lieth in you to raise me up again to life, and that with a light thing.

Mar. As you say. Peradventure I might do it if somebody would help me to the herb *Panaces*, whereunto they ascribe so great a virtue.

Pam. There needeth none herbs to do it, only vouchsafe to love again. What is more easy to be performed? Nay, rather, what is more due and just? Otherwise you shall never acquit yourself of manspilling.

Mar. And before what judgement seat shall I be arraigned? Before the severe Areopagites if God wills?

Pam. Not so, but before the tribunal seat of Venus.

Mar. Best of all, for they say she is a patient and pitiful goddess.

Pam. Say you so? There is not one amongst them all whose wrath is more to be feared.

Mar. Why, hath she a thunderbolt?

Pam. No.

Mar. Hath she a threeforked mace like Neptune?

Pam. Not so.

Mar. Hath she a spear, as Pallas?

Pam. Neither. But she is a goddess of the sea.

Mar. I come not within her kingdom.

Pam. But she hath a boy.

Mar. I fear no boys.

Pam. He is ready to revenge, and will pay home when he striketh.

Mar. And what shall he do to me?

Pam. What shall he do! The gods forlet him! I will prognosticate none evil unto one whom I bear good will.

Mar. Yet tell me, I pray you. I will take no conceit of it.

Pam. Then will I tell you. If you shall disdain this lover, who doubtless is not unworthy of your love, verily I believe that same boy (peradventure at the commandment of his mother) will thirl into your heart a lance imbrued with so bad a poison, whereby you shall set your affection miserably upon some hob-lout who shall not love you any whit again.

Mar. Marry, that were a plague indeed, of all other most to be detested. Certes I had rather to die than to be entangled in the love of one which is deformed and could not find in his heart to love me likewise again.

Pam. But it is not long time since there was a right noble example of this evil which I now speak of, showed in a certain young damsel.

After relating the wretched fate of this damsel, also named Maria, Pamphilus woos more directly. He points to their compatibility in age, temperament, and station in life as 'augural signs' of a happy married life, and argues that though they will grow older they will renew their youth in their children.

Mar. But in the meantime virginity is lost.

Pam. Truth, in good faith. Tell me, if you had a goodly orchard plot, whether would you wish nothing should therein grow but blossoms, or else had you rather—the blossoms fallen away—behold your trees fraught and laden with pleasant fruit?

Mar. How slyly he reasoneth!

Pam. At the least, answer me to this: whether it is a better sight for a vine to lie upon the ground and rot, or the same to embrace a pole or an elm and load it full with purple grapes?

Mar. Now, sir, answer me to this again: whether is it a more pleasant sight, a rose trim and milkwhite, yet growing on his stalk, or the same plucked with the hand and by little and little withering away?

Pam. Certes, in mine opinion the rose is the happiest and cometh to the better end which withereth and dyeth in the hand of man, delighting in the meanwhile both the eyes and nostrils, than th'other which withereth on the bush, for there must it needs wither also at length—even as that wine hath better luck which is drunken, than that which standeth still and is turned into vinegar. And yet the flowering beauty of a woman doth not decay forthwith as soon as she is married, for I know some myself who before they were married were pale-coloured, faint, and as it were pined away, who by the friendly fellowship of an husband have waxed so fair and well-favoured that you would think they never came to the flower of their beauty till then.

Mar. But for all your saying, virginity is a thing much beloved and liked with all men.

Pam. I grant you, a young woman, a virgin, is a fair, a goodly thing; but what by course of kind is more unseemly than an old wrinkled maid? Had not your mother been contented to lose the flower of her virginity, surely we had not had this flower of your beauty. So that in case, as I hope, our marriage be not barren, for the loss of one virgin we shall pay God many.

Mar. But they say chastity is a thing wherein God is much delighted.

Pam. And therefore do I desire to couple myself in marriage with a chaste maiden, that with her I may lead a chaste life. As for our marriage, it shall rather be a marriage of our minds than of our bodies. We shall increase unto Christ, we shall increase unto the commonwealth. How little shall this marriage differ from virginity! And peradventure hereafter we shall so live together as blessed Mary lived with Joseph. No man cometh at the first to perfection.

Mar. What is that I heard you say even now? Must virginity be violated and lost, thereby to learn chastity?

Pam. Why not, even as by drinking of wine moderately we learn by little and little to forbear wine utterly? Which of these two seemeth unto thee to be more temperate, he that sitting in the midst of many dainty dishes abstaineth from them all, or he which forbeareth intemperance having none occasion to move him unto the same?

Mar. I suppose him to have the more confirmed habit of temperance whom plenty always prest [at hand] cannot corrupt.

Pam. Whether deserveth more the praise of chastity, he that geldeth himself or he which keeping his members all and sound abstaineth from all woman's company?

Mar. Verily, by my consent the latter shall have the praise of chastity, that other of mad folly.

Pam. Why? Those which by vow have abjured matrimony, do they not after a sort geld themselves?

Mar. Verily, it seemeth so.

Pam. Thus you see it is no virtue to forbear woman's company.

Mar. Is it no virtue?

Pam. Mark me this: if it were simply a virtue to forbear the company of a woman then should it also be a vice to use the company of a woman; but sometime it befalleth that it is sin to refuse the act, and a virtue to use it.

Mar. In what case is it so?

Pam. In case the husband requireth of his wife the debt of marriage, even so often as he shall do it, especially if he requireth it for the desire of generation.

Mar. But what if he be flesh-fond and wanton, may she not lawfully deny it him?

Pam. She may admonish him of his fault and, rather, gently persuade him to bridle his affections. To give him a flat nay when he frayneth upon [requests of] her, she may not. Albeit I hear very few men complain of their wives' uncourtesy this way.

Mar. Yet methinks liberty is sweet.

Pam. Nay, rather virginity is a heavy burden. I shall be to you a king, and you shall be to me a queen. And either of us shall rule the family, as we think good. Take you this to be a bondage?

Mar. The common sort calleth marriage an halter.

Pam. Now, on my faith, they are well worthy an halter that so termeth it. Tell me, I pray you, is not your soul bound unto your body?

Mar. I think so.

Pam. Yea, surely, even as a bird unto her cage; and yet if ye should ask him the question whether he would be loosed or no, I suppose he would say nay. And why so? Because he is willingly and gladly bound thereunto.

Mar. We have little [fortune] to take to neither of us both.

Pam. So much the less endangered to fortune are we. That little you shall increase at home with saving, which as they [say] countervaileth a great revenue, and I abroad with diligence.

Mar. An household of children bringeth innumerable cares.

Pam. On the other side again, the same children bringeth infinite pleasures, and oftentimes requiteth the parents' natural pains to the uttermost, with great overplus.

Mar. Then to lead a barren life in marriage is a great misery.

Pam. Why, are you not now barren? Tell me whether had ye rather never be born, or born to die?

Mar. Certes I had rather be born to die.

Pam. So that barrenness is yet more miserable which never had nor ever shall have child, even as they be more happy which have already lived than they which never have nor shall hereafter be born to live.

Mar. And what be those, I pray you, which neither are nor shall be?

Pam. For he that cannot find in his heart to suffer and abide the changes and chances whereunto all we indifferently be subject—as well men of poor estate as kings and emperors—he is not to dwell here; let him get him out of this world. And yet, whatsoever shall mischance unto us two, yours should be but the one half thereof: the greater part I will always take unto mine own self. So that if any good thing do happen unto us our pleasure shall be double; if any evil betide us you shall have but the one half of the grief and I the other. As for myself, if God so would, it were unto me a pleasure even to end my life in your arms.

Mar. Men can better sustain and bear with that which chanceth according to the common course and rule of nature. For I see that some parents are more troubled with their children's evil manners than with their natural deaths.

Pam. To prevent such misfortune, that it happen not unto us, it resteth for the most part in our power.

Mar. How so?

Pam. For commonly parents which be good and virtuous have good and virtuous children—I mean as concerning their natural disposition, for doves do not hatch puttocks. Wherefore we will first endeavour to be good ourselves, and our next care shall be that our children may even from the mother's breast be seasoned with virtuous counsels and right opinions; for it skilleth not a little what liquor you pour into a new vessel at the first. Finally, we shall provide that they may have even at home in our house a good example of life to follow.

Mar. Hard it is to bring that to pass that you say.

Pam. No marvel, for commendable and good it is. And for that also are you hard to be entreated and won. The more difficile and hard it is, the more good will and endeavour shall we put thereunto.

Mar. You shall have me a matter soft and pliant. See you that you do your part in forming and shaping me as you ought.

Pam. But in the meanwhile, say those three words which I require of you.

Mar. Nothing were more easy for me to do. But words be winged, and when they be flown out once do not retire. I will tell you what were a better way for us both: you shall treat with your parents and mine, and with their will and consent let the matter be concluded.

Pam. Ah, you set me to woo again. It is in you with three words to dispatch the whole matter.

Mar. Whether it lieth in me so to do, as you say, I know not, for I am not at liberty. And in old time marriages were not concluded without the will and consent of their parents or elders. But howsoever the case be, I suppose our marriage shall be the more lucky if it be made by the authority of our parents. And your part is to seek and crave the good will; for us to do it, it were unseemly. Virginity would seem always to be taken with violence—yea, though sometime we love the party most earnestly.

Pam. I will not let to seek their good will, so that I may always be in an assurance of your consent.

Mar. You need not doubt thereof. Be of good cheer, my Pamphilus.

Pam. You are herein more scrupulous yet than I would wish you to be.

Mar. Nay, marry, weigh and consider well with yourself before, whereto you have set your mind and will. And do not take into your counsel this blind affection borne towards my person, but rather reason, for that which affection discerneth is liked for a season, but that which reason adviseth is never misliked.

Pam. Certes thou speakest like a witty wench; wherefore I intend to follow thy counsel.

Mar. You shall not repent you thereof. But howbe (ho!), sirrah, there is now fallen into my mind a doubt which beareth me sore.

Pam. Away with all such doubts, for God's sake.

Mar. Why, will you have me marry myself to a dead man?

Pam. Not so, for I will revive again.

Mar. Now, lo, you have voided this doubt. Fare ye well, my Pamphilus.

Pam. See you, I pray, that I may so do.

Mar. I pray God give you a good night. Why fetch you such a sigh, man?

Pam. A good night, say you? I would to God you would vouchsafe to give me that which you wish me.

Mar. Soft and fair, I pray you. Your harvest is as yet but in the green blade.

Pam. Shall I have nothing of yours with me at my departure?

Mar. Take this pomander to cheer your heart with.

Pam. Yet give me a kiss withal, I pray thee.

Mar. I would keep my virginity whole and undefiled for you.

Pam. Why doth a kiss take aught away from your virginity?

Mar. Would you think it well done that I should be free of kisses unto other men?

Pam. Nay, marry, I would have [thy] kisses spared for myself.

Mar. I keep them for you, then. And yet there is another thing in the way which maketh me that I dare not at this time give you a kiss.

Pam. What is that?

Mar. You say that your soul is already gone well near altogether into my body and a very small part thereof tarrieth behind in your own, so that I fear in time of a kiss that which remaineth might happen to start out after it, and then were you altogether without a soul. Have you therefore my right hand in token of mutual love, and so fare you well. Go you earnestly about your matters. And I for my part in the meanwhile shall pray unto Christ that the thing which you do may be unto the joy and felicity of us both. Amen.

INDEX

LISTED below are words of more than routine interest defined in the Commentary; topics considered in the Introduction (except where these are indicated in the Introduction's headings); names and works cited in both Introduction and Commentary from the period before 1700; biblical allusions and proverbial phrases, grouped together. Citations of Shakespeare's plays are not listed. An asterisk indicates that the entry supplements information in the *OED*. Page numbers indicate Introduction, while act, scene, and line identifications indicate Commentary.

abstract of success, 4.3.86
across, 2.1.65
addition, 2.3.128; 4.2.3
advice, 3.4.19
Aesop, fable of the fox and the grapes, 2.1.67–70
*affect, 1.1.53, 54
alarum, 4.1.65.1
alone, 1.1.187
ambs-ace, 2.3.80
and (for emphatic agreement), 2.1.56
armipotent, 4.3.239
artists, 2.3.10

backward, goers, 1.2.45–8
Bacon, Francis, *Natural History*, 1.1.206
bail, put in, 5.3.285
Bajazet's mule/mute, 4.1.42–3
balls bound, 2.3.298
bare (*v.*), 4.1.50
Beaumont, Francis, and John Fletcher, *The Maid's Tragedy*, 2.2.57–8
bed-trick, pp. 10–11, 26, 41
Benthall, Michael, pp. 41, 46 fig. 8
Bentii, 4.3.163–8
Bertram, critical dissatisfaction with, pp. 26–30
Biblical allusions, p. 10, n.3
   1.3.46–50; 2.1.12–16; 2.1.77;
   2.1.134–5; 2.1.136–7;

   2.1.137–9; 4.4.23–4;
   4.5.21–2; 4.5.50; 4.5.51–3
blade, i'th', 5.3.6
blame, to/too, 5.3.129
blow up . . . blow down, 1.1.121–7
Boccaccio, Giovanni, tale of Giletta di Nerbona, (*Decameron* iii. 9), tr. Painter, pp. 1–3, 32; Shakespeare's alterations and additions in *All's Well*, pp. 3–5
bold, 5.1.5
bottom, 3.6.36
box, 2.3.280–2
braid, 4.2.73
brains and stomach, 3.2.14–16
breath, 2.1.146
brief (*sb.*), 2.3.179–80; 5.3.137
broke (*v.*), 3.5.71
Brome, Richard, *The Northern Lass*, 2.3.22
brought up, 4.4.19
bubble, 3.6.5
bunting, take a lark for a, 2.5.6–7
Burton, Robert, *The Anatomy of Melancholy*, 3.2.3–7
business, 2.2.60
butter-woman, 4.1.42–3
by, 3.7.11; 4.5.5–7; 5.3.85, 237

cap'cious and intenible sieve, 1.3.202
capriccio, 2.3.294
care for, 1.3.164
case (*sb.*), 1.3.23

cat, 4.3.241
catastrophe and heel, 1.2.57
Chapman, George, *Bussy D'Ambois*, 2.3.193
charter . . . privilege, 4.5.91–3
chill (*adj.*), 4.5.54
class difference, pp. 11–13
Cleveland, John, 'How the Commencement Grows New', 2.2.41
clew, wound a goodly, 1.3.182
cold, 1.1.105
collateral light, 1.1.90–1
colour, hold, 2.5.61–3
come, 5.3.76
commission, 2.3.263–4
commoner, 5.3.194
companion, 2.3.193
composition, 1.1.205; 4.3.18
convoy, 4.3.89–90
Corambis, 4.3.163–8
corrupt (*v.*), 2.1.118; 2.3.116–17
counsel/council and act, 4.3.46
*cry, 2.1.17
curiously, 4.3.33–4
custard, jumping into, 2.5.37–8

dark house, 2.3.293
date, 1.1.161
debauched, 2.3.139; 5.3.206
default, in the, 2.3.230
delay (*v.*), 4.3.19
delivering, deliverance, 1.1.1; 2.1.80
Diana, 4.2.0.1, 1–2
diet (*v.*), 4.3.29–30; 5.3.221
dilemmas, 3.6.75–6
distance, knew her, 5.3.212
distempered, 1.3.151
do, 2.3.234–5; do as we may, 1.3.19
Donne, John, *The First Anniversary*, 5.3.50–1
drum, as attribute of Mars, 3.3.11; as regimental symbol, 3.5.86; as announcing players, 4.3.269–70; as drummer, 5.3.253–4; John/Jack/Tom Drum's entertainment, 3.6.38–9
Dumaine, Persons of the Play, note

egg, 4.3.253
egregious, 2.3.217

Eliot, John, *Ortho-epia Gallica*, 4.3.281
Elizabeth I, p. 23; 2.1.30
encounter (*sb.*), 3.7.32; (*v.*), 1.3.208
ending, problematic, pp. 49–52
engaged, 5.3.96
Erasmus, Desiderius, 'Proci et puellae', trans. Nicholas Leigh as *A Modest Mean to Marriage*, pp. 6–8, Appendix F
Escalus, p. 24; 1.3.19
esteem, 5.3.1
estimate, estimation, 2.1.178; 5.3.1
Ettmueller, Michael, *Etmullerus Abridg'd*, 2.3.72
even (*adj.*), 2.1.189; 5.3.326
even (*v.*) your content, 1.3.3–4
exorcist, 5.3.304
expedient on, 2.3.179–80
extended, Appendix B

*fetch off, 3.6.19
fistula, 1.1.34
*fit you, 2.1.88
fleshes his will, 4.3.16
Fontybel, 4.2.1–2
fool (*sb.*), 4.3.257
for my life, 2.3.80
Ford, John, *'Tis Pity She's a Whore*, 4.5.27–32
fore-horse to a smock, 2.1.30–3
forward top, 5.3.39

gamester, 5.3.188
Garrick, David, p. 25
gender roles, reversal of, pp. 31–40, 48
gifts, 1.1.40
go to the world, 1.3.18, 20
go under, 3.5.20
good lord, 2.3.247
Grange, John, *The Golden Aphroditis*, 1.3.62–3
Gratii, 4.3.163–8
great, 4.3.333
Greene, Robert, *Greene's Never Too Late*, 4.2.73
Guiltian, 4.3.163–8
Guthrie, Tyrone, pp. 26, 27; fig. 2, p. 4; fig. 5, p. 28; fig. 6, p. 29; 1.2.0.1

hand, in any, 3.6.43

hawking, 1.1.96
heels usurping spurs, 4.3.103–4
Helen, form of name, Persons of
  the Play, note
heraldry, 2.3.263–4
(salad-)herbs, 4.5.19
Hesperus, female gender for,
  2.1.162
Heywood, Thomas, *I Fair Maid of
  the West*, 4.3.227; *The Silver
  Age*, p. 10, n. 3; *A Woman
  Killed with Kindness* 4.1.41
Hic Mulier, 2.3.164
higher (*adv.*), 4.3.42
higher Italy, 2.1.12–16
his love (= love of him), 1.1.73;
  2.3.74
hit, 'tis, 5.3.195
holding, has no, 4.2.23–30
honour, pp. 14–15; 2.1.109;
  2.3.81–2, 280–2; 4.2.42, *45
honoured, 2.3.142
hope, 1.3.201
housewife, 2.2.57–8

idle, 2.5.51; 3.7.26; 4.3.217
image, 2.1.196
impostor, 2.1.153
Indian (as sun-worshipper),
  1.3.204–6
ingaged/ungaged/engaged, 5.3.96
ingenious/ingenuous, 5.2.24
inhibited, 1.1.147–8
instance, 4.1.41
Isbel, p. 24, 1.3.19

Jacques, Saint, 3.4.4
Jones, David, fig. 7, p. 37
Jonson, Ben, *The Alchemist*, 5.2.9;
  5.3.212; *Catiline*, 3.2.110;
  Cynthia's Revels, 2.2.41; *The
  Devil is an Ass*, 2.5.37–8; *Every
  Man Out of His Humour*,
  1.1.206; 2.2.41; *Poetaster*,
  4.1.20; 'To Captain Hungry',
  2.3.203

Kemble, John Philip, pp. 32–3
kicky-wicky, 2.3.280–2
know straight, 4.1.16–19
Kyd, Thomas, *The Spanish Tragedy*,
  2.1.88

lackey, outruns any, 4.3.293

last monarchy, 2.1.12–16
lattice, 2.3.214
Lavatch, Persons of the Play, note;
  5.2.1
lead on, 4.1.83
ling, 3.2.13–14
Lodowick, p. 24; 1.3.19, 4.3.163–8
lordship, 5.3.156
lost/found, 1.1.133; 2.3.206–7
Lover's Complaint, A, p. 46
Love's Labour's Won, pp. 21–2
lustig, 2.3.42

man, 2.3.195, 199; 2.4.24
manifest, 1.3.223
Mariana, p. 00; 1.3.19
Marlowe, Christopher, *Doctor
  Faustus*, 2.1.100; *Edward II*,
  2.5.28–31
marrow, 2.3.280–2
Marston, John, *Antonio's Revenge*,
  2.3.228; *The Malcontent*, 4.1.20
Massinger, Philip, *The City Madam*,
  2.1.115; *The Picture*,
  2.3.280–2; *The Renegado*,
  3.6.19
match (*sb.* and *v.*), 4.3.228
medicine, 2.1.70
medieval religious drama, pp. 41–3
meet, 5.3.72
melancholy and music, 3.2.3–9
Meres, Francis, *Palladis Tamia*,
  pp. 21–2
metal/mettle, 1.1.131; 2.1.39
Middleton, Thomas, *The Spanish
  Gypsy*, 2.2.21–7; *Your Five
  Gallants*, 4.2.45
Mile End, 4.3.273
militarist, 4.3.143
Milton, John, 'On the New Forcers
  of Conscience', 2.3.22; *Paradise
  Lost*, 2.1.6
*mistaken, 2.5.42–3
modest, 2.1.126
monumental ring, 4.3.17
Mort du vinaigre, 2.3.45
mortal, 1.1.57–8; mortal
  preparation, 3.6.76
Moshinsky, Elijah, p. 26;
  1.1.62–4; 2.1.39; 2.3.46;
  5.3.304
motion, 3.1.11–13; 5.3.263
motive, 4.4.20, 5.3.215

M^r, 5.2.1
musics, 3.7.40

Nashe, Thomas, *Pierce Penniless*
    and *Christ's Tears Over*
    Jerusalem, 2.3.45; *A Wonderful*
    Strange . . . Prognostication
    4.5.59–60
native things, 1.1.225
naturalize, 1.1.209–14
ne, Appendix B
Nessus, 4.3.253–4
next, 1.3.59
noble, 2.2.57–8
Nunn, Trevor, pp. 26, 27; fig. 1,
    p. 4; fig. 4, p. 28; 1.2.0.1

O Lord, sir, 2.2.41
officer, 3.5.17
outward, 3.1.11–13

pass (*sb.*), 2.5.55
passage, 1.1.19
passed, 3.7.36
passport, 3.2.56
pile (*sb.*), 4.5.95–9
*pity, 1.1.43
plausive, 1.2.53; 4.1.27
Plutarch, *Life of Pyrrhus*, 4.3.191–2
Plutus, associated with alchemy,
    5.3.101–2
point to point, from, 3.1.1
policy, 1.1.123
presumptuous, 1.3.197–200
prince of the world, 4.5.50
proud, 2.3.228
proverbs and proverbial phrases, p.
    49; 1.3.19; 1.3.23–4; 1.3.26;
    1.3.29–30; 1.3.37; 1.3.44;
    1.3.52–5; 1.3.62–3; 1.3.88;
    1.3.182; 2.2.3; 2.2.17;
    2.2.21–7; 2.2.38; 2.3.43;
    2.3.100–1; 2.3.119–22;
    2.3.206–7; 2.3.293; 2.3.299;
    2.5.6–7; 2.5.28–31; 2.5.55;
    3.6.38–9; 4.1.20; 4.1.42–3;
    4.3.107–8; 4.3.253; 4.4.35
pull at, 2.3.225–6
pur, 5.2.20

quality, 1.3.113–14; 4.2.4
quart d'écu, 4.3.281
quatch, 2.2.18

*rational, 1.1.129–30
rebellion, 4.3.19
relics, 1.1.99, 5.3.25
remorseful, 5.3.58–9
remove (*sb.*), 5.3.131
reports, 2.1.43; 4.1.32
resolvedly, 5.3.332
Revenger's Tragedy, The, 2.3.230
right/rite, 2.4.42; 4.2.17
Rinaldo, Persons of the Play, note
roses, 4.2.18
ruff, 3.2.7
rush-ring, 2.2.21–7

saffron, 4.5.1–4
salad-herbs, 4.5.19
score (*sb.* and *v.*), 4.3.227
season, of, 5.3.32
seem, 1.2.8; 2.3.179–80
send for, 5.3.223
Senois, 1.2.1
sense, 1.1.227; 1.3.110;
    2.1.120–2, 175–6; common
    sense, 2.1.175–6
senseless, 2.1.120–2
sentence, 3.2.61
set down before, 1.1.120
set up your rest, 2.1.133
sexuality, pp. 10–11, 35
shame, Appendix B
shameful, 5.3.65–6
showing, in, 2.3.21
sick, 4.2.35; sick for, 1.2.16–17
simple, simply, simpleness, 1.1.44;
    2.1.73; 2.3.68
single, 4.2.22
smiles/similes, 5.2.25
Sonnets, pp. 22, 23–4, 44–8;
    1.1.147–8; 2.1.164; 2.3.6;
    4.5.91–3
sovereignty, 1.3.224
space, 1.1.225–6
Spenser, Edmund, *The Faerie*
    Queene, 1.1.168–77; 5.3.39;
    The Shepheardes Calender,
    2.2.21–7
spoil (*sb.*), 4.3.16
staggers, 2.3.164
stain (*sb.*), 1.1.113
stand for, 1.1.135
stand off, 2.3.119–22
stand to't, 3.2.41–2
stay, 2.1.46–7

still-peering/piecing, 3.2.110
superfluous, 1.1.105
suspected, 1.3.181
sweet heart, 2.3.270, 272
swine-drunk, associated with sleep, 4.3.258–9

taffeta, 2.2.21–7; snipped taffeta, 4.5.1–4
take up, 2.3.208
Taylor, John, the Water Poet, *Jack a' Lent*, 4.3.293
tender, 4.5.54
thou, in addressing king, 2.1.191
tile, death by falling, 4.3.191–2
time, 5.3.36
title, 2.4.26
to, 2.4.44
toll for, 5.3.148–9
too much, 3.2.90–1
tooth, 2.3.43
toothpick, 1.1.160
touch, 1.3.117
traduced, Appendix B
traitor, 4.3.21, 21–5
traveller, 2.3.261–2
traveller's tales, 2.5.28–31
tricks, 5.3.239
trust, 4.4.15
twigs, 3.5.24–5; 3.6.108

understand, 1.1.209–14; 2.2.66
ungaged, 5.3.96
unsealed, 4.2.23–30

use, 4.4.22

velvet, patch of, 4.5.95–9
Vergil, *Aeneid*, 1.3.212–13
Violenta, 3.5.0.1–2
virtues, virtuous qualities, 1.1.42

waiting on, 1.1.105
war, between Florence and Siena, pp. 14–15
wardship, p. 12
wear (v.), 1.1.160; 2.3.280–2
wear themselves in the cap of the time, 2.1.51
well, 2.4.2–5
well fed, 2.4.39
well found, 2.1.100
what-do-ye-call, 2.3.22
white death, 2.3.72
Whitney, Geoffrey, *A Choice of Emblems*, figs. 9–12, pp. 66–7; 4.3.191–2
Willman, Noël, fig. 3, p. 25
wing, good, 1.1.206
Wither, George, *A Collection of Emblems*, 4.3.191–2
woman (v.), 3.2.51
woodcock, 4.1.92
word, 4.4.31
world, the, 1.3.34
worthy, worthiest, 3.2.96; 4.3.6
write, writ, 2.3.62, 199; 3.5.66

ye, 2.1.46–7
yet, 4.4.27, 30

The Oxford World's Classics Website

www.worldsclassics.co.uk

- Information about new titles
- Explore the full range of Oxford World's Classics
- Links to other literary sites and the main OUP webpage
- Imaginative competitions, with bookish prizes
- Peruse the Oxford World's Classics Magazine
- Articles by editors
- Extracts from Introductions
- A forum for discussion and feedback on the series
- Special information for teachers and lecturers

www.worldsclassics.co.uk